MATTER, MATERIALITY AND MODERN CULTURE

The modern world around us is more mysterious than we think. This book looks beneath the surface of modern material culture to ask how the very stuff of our world has shaped our societies, and how and why it is that we have made the material culture that surrounds us.

Matter, Materiality and Modern Culture offers a new approach to the study of contemporary objects, from academics prominent in disciplines ranging from archaeology to philosophy and psychology. All have diverse perspectives on what material culture is, but all are equally concerned with how the very material nature of artefacts comes to form human life. The questions they address include:

- Why did the electric car fail?
- Why do Berliners have such strange door keys?
- Should the site of the Isle of Wight pop festival be preserved?
- Why do autistic children have problems with objects?
- Could aliens tell a snail shell from a waste-paper basket?
- Why did Victorian England make so much of death and burial?

Taken together, the eight contributions in this book lead the reader to a new understanding of the relationship between people and their material world. They will be of great interest to everyone studying modern material culture.

P.M. Graves-Brown studied Archaeology and Prehistory at Sheffield University and gained his Ph.D. in Archaeology at Southampton University. He currently works as an archaeological curator in South Wales. He has published a wide variety of work, mainly on human origins and modern material culture.

MATTER, MATERIALITY AND MODERN CULTURE

Edited by
P.M. Graves-Brown

London and New York

First published 2000
by Routledge
11 New Fetter Lane, London EC4P 4EE

Simultaneously published in the USA and Canada
by Routledge
29 West 35th Street, New York, NY 10001

Routledge is an imprint of the Taylor & Francis Group

© 2000 Selection and editorial matter, P. M. Graves-Brown;
individual chapters, the contributors

Typeset in Bembo by Taylor & Francis Books Ltd
Printed and bound in Great Britain by Biddles Ltd, Guildford and King's Lynn

British Library Cataloguing in Publication Data
A catalogue record for this book is available from the British Library

Library of Congress Cataloging in Publication Data
Matter, materiality, and modern culture/edited by P.M. Graves-Brown.
Includes bibliographical references and index.
1. Material culture. 2. Civilization, Modern. I. Title.
GN406.G73 2000
306 – dc21   99–056410

ISBN 0–415–16704–3 (hbk)
ISBN 0–415–16705–1 (pbk)

CONTENTS

List of illustrations   ix
Notes on contributors   xi
Acknowledgements   xii

Introduction   **1**
PAUL GRAVES-BROWN
Background   2
Embodiment   3
Mutuality   4
Functionality and power   5
Indigenous theory and illusion   6

1 **The Berlin key or how to do words with things**   **10**
BRUNO LATOUR

2 **The functions of things: a philosophical perspective on
   material culture**   **22**
BETH PRESTON
Introduction   22
Two philosophical conceptions of function   24
Function in material culture   29
Implications for archaeology   34
Conclusion   46

3 **Making culture and weaving the world**   **50**
TIM INGOLD
Artefacts and organisms   50
Making and growing   51
On encountering a basket   53
Surface, force and the generation of form   55

v

CONTENTS

Spirals in nature and art   57
The limits of design   59
On the growth of artefacts   60
Baskets and textiles   62
Making as a way of weaving   64
Weaving by birds and humans   65
Conclusion   68

4 Indigenous theories, scientific theories and product
   histories   72
   MICHAEL BRIAN SCHIFFER
   Introduction   72
   Indigenous theories and the demise of the early electric car   73
   Indigenous theory: the dark side   78
   Behavioural theories and scientific product histories   80
   Discussion and conclusion   92

5 Taking things more seriously: psychological theories of
   autism and the material-social divide   97
   EMMA WILLIAMS AND ALAN COSTALL
   The social context of object use   98
   How children with autism relate to objects   99
   Current theoretical models of autism and the material-social divide 101
   The material-social divide   105
   'Socialising' affordances   106
   Conclusion   107

6 Pomp and circumstance: archaeology, modernity and the
   corporatisation of death: early social and political Victorian
   attitudes towards burial practice   112
   GEORGE NASH
   Introduction: the growth of secularised society   112
   Good mourning: respectability of death   113
   Time for change   115
   Health and social security   116
   Ascending Highgate Hill   117
   Termination at the London Necropolis Company Terminus   119
   To summarise …   126

7 **Never mind the relevance? popular culture for archaeologists**   **131**

A.J. SCHOFIELD

Snapshots   131
Introducing popular culture   133
Heritage and anti-heritage: definitions, contradictions   135
Exploring youth culture: 1962–75   140
Conclusion   150

8 **Always crashing in the same car**   **155**

PAUL GRAVES-BROWN

Habitat or skin?   156
The secret life of things   159
Symbolic wounds   159
Pornography   160
Risk and control   162
In conclusion: who, or what, is to blame?   163

Index   166

ILLUSTRATIONS

Figures

1.1 Ceci est une clef
1.2 Berliner key symmetry
1.3 Berliner key reversibility
1.4 Berliner keyhole
1.5 Key operation – street side
1.6 Key operation – courtyard side
1.7 Berliner master key
1.8 Lock mechanism
1.9 Key holder
3.1 The surface of the artefact as a physical interface between solid substance and gaseous medium (left), and as an instance of the metaphysical interface between culture and the material world (right)
3.2 My waste-paper basket and crumpled bed-linen
3.3 Patterns of wrapping in coiled basketry; (1) plain; (2) figure of eight ('Navajo'); (3) long and short ('lazy squaw'); (4) Peruvian coil; (5) sewn coil. From Hodges (1964: 131)
3.4a Coiled basketry. From Boas (1955 [1927]: 20)
3.4b Gastropod shell. The angle is known as the 'spiral angle', which in this case is large. From Thompson (1961 [1917]: 192)
3.5 Common stitches and fastenings used by weaverbirds in the construction of their nests. From Collias and Collias (1984: 207)
4.1 The number of companies producing electric passenger automobiles during the years 1894 to 1942. From Schiffer (1995a)
4.2 The number of companies producing their first electric automobile in a given year. From Schiffer (1995a)
4.3 The number of companies producing electric automobiles for a given number of years. From Schiffer (1995a)
4.4 Ad for a Detroit Electric, 'Society's Town Car'. From *Literary Digest* (20 July 1912)
4.5 Ad for a Baker Electric Automobile. From *Life* (18 April 1912)

4.6   A paradigmatic classification, displayed as a tree diagram, representing the target and actual markets of the electric passenger automobile during its Classic Age

6.1   Highgate Cemetery – entrance to the 'Circle of Lebanon' (English Heritage Photo Library)

6.2   Within the 'Circle of Lebanon' – a self-contained city of the dead (English Heritage Photo Library)

6.3   Termination at the London Necropolis Company Terminus (from the J.M. Clarke Collection)

6.4   Plan and section of the S.W.R. Hearse Carriage (drawn by G.R. Weddell)

6.5   The Non-Conformist Chapel at Brookwood Cemetery (from the Barry Devonshire Collection)

6.6   Plan of the London Necropolis Brookwood Cemetery. (Courtesy of the Brookwood Cemetery Society)

6.7   The Last Stop (for the dead). Brookwood Cemetery Station (*c.* 1900) (from the Barry Devonshire Collection)

6.8   Main entrance to the Garden of Eden – Brookwood Cemetery (Postcard *c.* 1920) (from the Barry Devonshire Collection)

7.1   Crowd scene at 'The Last Great Event', Afton Down, 26–30 August 1970

7.2   The construction of the perimeter fence (top), and its breaching (bottom), an event representing the death-cry of the pure hippy dream, or the radiant dawn of hip capitalism? (After Williams 1995).

7.3   Cleaning-up after the second Isle of Wight festival, Wootton, 1969

Table

4.1   A Threshold Performance Matrix for Gasoline and Electric Automobiles, *c.*1912.

CONTRIBUTORS

Alan Costall Department of Psychology, University of Portsmouth, PO1 2DY, UK.

Paul Graves-Brown Brynffynnon, 88 Trallwm Rd, Llwynhendy, Llanelli, Carmarthenshire, SA14 9ES, UK.

Tim Ingold Department of Sociology, University of Aberdeen, AB24 3QY, UK.

Bruno Latour Centre de Sociologie de l'Innovation. École Nationale Supérieure des Mines de Paris. 60 boulevard Saint Michel 75272 Paris, France.

George Nash Centre for the Historic Environment, University of Bristol, Woodland Road, Clifton, Bristol, BS8 1HH, UK.

Beth Preston Philosophy Department and Artificial Intelligence Center, University of Georgia Athens, GA 30602–1627, USA.

Michael Brian Schiffer Department of Anthropology, University of Arizona Tucson, Arizona 85721, USA.

A.J. Schofield English Heritage, 23 Savile Row, London W1X 1AB, UK.

Emma Williams Department of Psychology, King Alfred's College, Sparkford Rd, Winchester, UK.

ACKNOWLEDGEMENTS

I would like to thank all the contributors to this volume for their patience – somehow production of edited books always takes longer than you expect. I would particularly like to thank George Nash for getting involved in the project very late in the day and thereby helping in no small degree to bring things to fruition. Alan Costall, as ever, has been an invaluable support and gave some good advice on the introduction. I would like to thank Vicky Peters at Routledge for commissioning the project and for her patience. Finally I would like to thank Carolyn Graves-Brown, both for comments on the introduction and for her unending moral support which somehow preserves (what's left of) my sanity.

INTRODUCTION

Paul Graves-Brown

The material world around us, the cultural world we have fashioned over thousands of years, is both a product of and a constraint upon all aspects of our societies, our individual psychologies, our beliefs, our understanding of our past and our goals for the future. By its very nature, our material culture is something with which we are all, at first glance, familiar. Yet this very familiar world is also one which we, as both quotidian individuals, and as scholars, are inclined to overlook. The very familiarity, mundanity of the material world around us leads us to leave it unquestioned.[1] The purpose of this enterprise, then, is to make the familiar unfamiliar, to lead the reader to take their day-to-day experience and re-examine how the things around them shape practice, and are used to shape practice.

The core theme of the book is materiality. Of how the very material character of the world around us is appropriated by humanity. This is an issue which has been largely bypassed by recent accounts of modern (material) culture (e.g. Featherstone 1991; Miller 1987, 1995) where the emphasis has been on post-modern word play and the culture of consumption.[2] Miller himself (1995: 1) has complained of social science's 'romantic antipathy to the world of goods' yet the very notion of 'goods' implies a concern with 'commodities' or 'style' rather than artefacts in themselves – essentially the triumph of surfaces of things over what they can do (see Ingold Chapter 3). Indeed there is a strong tendency to treat culture as something that exists either in the heads of people or in their social relations with one another and to disregard the role that *material* culture plays in shaping our lives. However materiality *has* had considerable currency in recent debates about the body (Butler 1993, esp. chapter 1) where material characteristics of sexuality have been seen as grounding the arguments of feminism. Butler and others have argued that reference to such material conditions actually imprisons the feminist project. In this work we address similar issues with respect to the material world around us (if this is indeed distinct from our embodied selves) but come to different conclusions. Indeed, the authors in this volume contend that material conditions radically shape human actions, but this is not to say that we adopt a simply determinist or 'functionalist' stance. Rather, the

1

relationship is seen as one of mutuality, both between people and things and, as Williams and Costall (Chapter 5) clearly show, the triangular relationship between people as social beings and the things which they use.

Background

The topic of modern material culture could represent a research domain in its own right. Since the second world war, but particularly since the 1960s (e.g. Leroi-Gourhan 1964, 1993; Mcluhan 1964; Pye 1968; Ucko 1969), the study of the artefacts of our own era has been taken up by a wide variety of disciplines. Beginning perhaps in history (Mumford 1948; Needham 1954), anthropology (Ucko 1969 and later Lemmonier 1989; Pfaffenberger 1988) and art and design (Pye 1968), modern material culture has become the concern of archaeologists (Hodder 1983; Rathje 1979; Schiffer 1991), cognitive scientists (Joerges 1988), technologists and engineers (Bijker and Law 1992; Winner 1986), sociologists (Hall 1973; Hebdige 1988; Latour 1992), philosophers (Millikan 1984, Salmon 1982) and has to some extent spawned the new discipline of cultural studies (see e.g. Miller 1987, 1995).

At the same time, and particularly in the 1990s, critical studies of the body, which perhaps share their roots with the study of material culture (particularly in the work of Marcel Mauss 1979), have come to the fore, bringing with them many of the issues, debates and contradictions that also haunt the study of material culture (see Ingold Chapter 3 for the relationship between 'culture' and 'material culture'). This 'discovery' of the body by sociologists in the 1990s might be seen as a reaction to the abstractions spawned by French post-structuralism and by post-modernism.[3] The recent history of other disciplines shows a similar disquiet with the rationalist disposition to ignore the material world (Bloch 1990; Still and Costall 1991; Joerges 1988)

The current volume cannot and does not claim to be definitive. The contributions share a common perspective and hence promote a particular account of the topic of modern material culture. Nevertheless the purpose here is to be inclusive and the contributions bring together perspectives from sociology, philosophy, anthropology and archaeology, whilst drawing on concepts from all the disciplines mentioned above. What this book *does* do is to explore what we see as key questions in understanding modern culture through its material aspect; the relationship between embodied individuals and the physical world around them; the relationship between material culture and society; functionality; the exercise of power through material culture/technology and in a related sense, the ways in which modern material culture can be misrepresented or misunderstood both in popular/indigenous accounts and in the academic world.

Embodiment

In his article 'Technology in everyday life' Bernhard Joerges accused the human sciences, and particularly psychology, of delineating 'a world of actors devoid of things' (1988: 220), an approach which Marshall McLuhan (1964) once christened 'techno somnambulism' (see also Pfaffenberger 1988). In such an account it is as if the material world were merely a stage set in which the props could be made to assume any value chosen by the actors. Yet as McLuhan (1964: 11) says, nothing could be further from the truth:

> Suppose we were to say, 'Apple pie is in itself neither good nor bad; it is the way it is used that determines its value.' Or, 'The smallpox virus is in itself neither good nor bad; it is the way it is used that determines its value.'

Conversely, many accounts of technological culture err in the opposite direction of a determinism where human agents seem irrelevant either to the development or functioning of artefacts. Such 'technological determinism' is rooted in a very Victorian notion of inexorable scientific 'Progress' and has been variously used to justify the development of nuclear power, industrial automation and most recently the growth of biotechnology and genetic modification.[4] Ironically, the most radical position lies somewhere between these poles – it is, as Ingold (Chapter 3) says, the proposition that 'we work from within the world, not upon it'.

As such, it is worth remembering, as Mauss (1979) pointed out, that the first human artefact is the human body itself, and that action by and upon the body is the core to understanding our culture. In my own contribution (Chapter 8) and in that by Nash (Chapter 6), the nature of the body in life and death is confronted with the material process of enculturation. The same might also be said of Williams and Costall's account of autism (Chapter 5). In each case, as in the work of Butler (1993), we encounter the tension between concepts of matter as natural and its transformed state in the artefactual (see Ingold Chapter 3). In Nash's account of nineteenth-century burial practices, the process of entombment is inextricable from the natural process of bodily decay, but at the same time in the denial of that process. Williams and Costall, on the other hand, examine how a 'natural' developmental defect of the human brain is shaped through material and social actions. In my own chapter, I consider how one archetypal artefact of modernity, the car, is incorporated in the bodily self and at the same time becomes its habitat.

Contrary to the tendency represented by Butler's feminist account of embodiment, the authors in this book do not see matter as something which is transcended by cultural practice. Here I believe it is the false equation of the material with nature, in the sense of something given and immutable (raw nature: raw material), that has led post-structuralist thinkers to argue that

3

culture acts upon material givens from outside. Rather, the limited freedom we have derives from the possibility, both socially and individually, to change the material world from within. This is by no means a new idea (see, e.g. Heidegger 1971; Merleau-Ponty 1964) but it is an approach which has been ignored in the seemingly unending struggle between rationalist advocacy of the power of the mind and empiricist insistence on deterministic 'Science'.

Post-modern, and in archaeology, post-processual accounts of culture are set in opposition to the individualism of cognitive and cognitivist approaches of 'Science' (see, for example, Thomas 1998 versus the other chapters in Renfrew and Scarre 1998). Yet curiously such accounts (like that of Butler) seem to reject the possibility of grounding a social/collective understanding of humanity in the material world. Baudrillard, for example, in his (1988) critique of Marx suggests that use value is as much an abstraction as exchange value. Thomas (1998: 153), whilst rejecting the individualism of the other contributors to Renfrew and Scarre's *Cognition and Material Culture*, goes on to say that 'we never read meaning out of a signifier, we read meaning into it'. In such an account material culture is merely something upon which meaning is inscribed − a world of surfaces on to which we project significance. Yet if meaning is only ever 'read into' things, there can be no common basis for understanding. In fact, then, whilst acknowledging the importance of embodiment, post-modernists and post-processualists still talk in terms of abstract symbols, signs and signifiers rather than the materiality of human culture.

Mutuality

The sense of humanity acting within the world[5] has recently been termed 'mutualism' and current work in this area derives in large part from the work of George Herbert Mead (1934) and James J. Gibson (1979). Gibson, in particular, saw the potentials of material conditions in terms of an ambience within which action took place. This contrasts with the neo-Platonism of representations, symbolism and signification described above. Gibson talked of perception in terms of 'affordances' − characteristics of the world which emerge in the relationship between the actor and matter. Thus, for example, both a chair and the stump of a tree 'afford' sitting as a product of the relationship between the form and scale of the human body and that of the material object. Similarly, stairs afford climbing to adult humans but do not do so to young children or mice!

From this mutualist perspective, as Ingold (Chapter 3) explains, a new explanation of culture emerges which challenges the prevailing view in anthropology and, I suggest, in other disciplines such as sociology and cultural studies. Culture exists neither in our minds, nor does it exist independently in the world around us, but rather is an emergent property of the relationship between persons and things. This point is forcefully underlined in Preston's account (Chapter 2) of functionality which challenges the notions that function is either intrinsic to things in themselves or simply a product of the social, systematic milieu within which they exist.

Functionality and power

Any attempt at an account of material culture which stresses the material is invariably accused of being functionalist. The closer one gets to giving an account of how things 'work' the more one is likely to be accused of ignoring social forces, symbolic meanings and representations. As Preston points out (Chapter 2) this situation has been particularly pressing for archaeologists attempting to explain the past where many aspects of socio-cultural context are unknown.[6] However, despite the fact that we know, or think we know (see Schiffer Chapter 4), the socio-cultural context of modern material culture, the same accusation may also be levelled at forays into contemporary experience.

Writers in this volume, particularly Preston, Latour, Schofield and Schiffer, make it clear that functionality is not just an infrastructural 'given' which is subsumed by social and cultural values. Rather, they demonstrate that functionality is itself an integral of social process.

Things are often said to have life histories (see Appadurai 1986), technologies have phases of invention, commercialisation and adoption (Schiffer), artefacts are manufactured (Ingold, Schiffer), used (Preston, Nash, Latour, Williams and Costall) and ultimately either discarded, preserved or reused (Preston, Schofield, Schiffer). Through all these phases, functionality changes. As Preston demonstrates, functions that are 'proper' or seemingly intrinsic can mutate. For functions are also defined by systems, which include other artefacts, actions, social contexts. Mead (1934) described artefacts as 'collapsed acts' in that they embody all that has been enacted upon them (often by many actors). Perhaps this explains the rather anthropomorphic way in which we describe artefacts as having *lives* – they are in a sense animated by their passage through the lives of people.

The fact that the function of material artefacts can change should be evidence enough that functionality is not simply a mundane given, a part of the 'raw nature' of any artefact, but is in itself part of society and culture. Indeed, the contested nature of functionality is one (perhaps the) nexus of change in social values and practices (Latour, Preston, Schofield). This fact is particularly evident in the growing domain of popular culture as it has emerged in opposition to the elite definitions of high culture inherited from art history. Here, and contrary to Adorno and Horkheimer (1972), the importance of popular values in contesting power is indicative of the fact that the function of artefacts can change and hence change society itself[7] (see particularly Schofield Chapter 7)

One important point here is how materiality itself is a nexus through which power relations operate. The novelist William Gibson (1993) says of technology that 'the street will always find a use for things'. These uses may not be those intended by their inventors or makers, but they must potentially exist, must be immanent, as affordances of those artefacts. The folk originators of the guitar, or those who electrified it could not have foreseen how it would be used, both practically and symbolically, in late twentieth-century youth culture (Preston, Schofield), yet as affordances the potentials of the electric guitar (and for that matter other electronic instruments) to generate new kinds of sound, to reach large live audiences and to symbolise the power of the performer existed at its inception. In a slightly different way, the material ephemerality of some cultural icons makes them immune to preservation as mainstream 'heritage' (Schofield) despite their social importance at a particular time – whilst the conquest of Everest was an important event, little exists on site to record who conquered it, when or why. Humans draw out the affordances of the material world, be they topographic (Highgate Hill – Nash), physical/chemical (electric versus internal combustion power – Schiffer) or mechanical (the filed Berliner key – Latour) but the ways in which such affordances are systematised and ultimately made proper to things derives from the relationship between people, things and other people (Williams and Costall). The conventions that emerge and evolve around material things inevitably depend upon shared understanding.

Indigenous theory and illusion

The impetus of this book is to render the familiar unfamiliar. For the very fact that most (at least Western) readers should find the substantive topics herein familiar is itself part of the problematic. Archaeologists are constantly warned not to take assumptions from the present and apply them to the past, but by the same token such assumptions ought not be applied to the present either! This again has been an issue in ethnographic approaches to the 'Other' for many years, but in considering our own culture and recent history, we assume that we know (Schiffer Chapter 4).

Of course we must accept that as beings in the world we cannot objectify it and, moreover, in studying the cultures of the present we are always dealing with unfinished business. This is the thrust of Schofield's account of popular culture (Chapter 7) – how do we decide what is of value from the plethora of artefacts and remains created and discarded by our own culture? How do we decide *a priori* whether the reputation of Jimi Hendrix will be as lasting as that of George Fredrick Handel? Similarly, as Schiffer points out, ad hoc/indigenous theories, even if they are misconceived, actually help people cope with the world around them. Thus, for example, I suggest in Chapter 8 that popular understanding of the car culture is based upon beliefs that are in some sense illusory. The belief of car drivers in their 'freedom', not to say invulnerability, is belied by their dependence upon other road users and on the authorities that build, maintain and police the roads. Yet if road users were to become too clearly aware of their dependence upon others, and the risks inherent in car use, they would lose their sense of invulnerability and feel impelled to travel by train instead!

The methodological problems of understanding material culture also lie in the mutuality between people and things. As Schiffer argues, we can try to rely simply on the material traces of culture, but it is all too tempting and probably reasonable that we measure these against the accounts given by participants in the creation and use of artefacts. In some cases, as documented by Williams and Costall, the evidence of action in relation to the material world actually undermines prevailing theories, demonstrating (in this case) that theories of autism that relate only to social interaction cannot account for the autistic child's idiosyncratic relationship with the material world.

Perhaps then, the key is to accept that we are ourselves part of the world we seek to understand and, rather than seeking to stand aside from society and pontificate upon it, we need to be within the process and, albeit critically, allow experience to guide our understanding. At the same time we must accept that the culture we study is part of a politics of power, either at a small scale (Latour's Berliner key as a means of domestic social control) or at the larger scale – in the car culture; in changing practices of disposal of the dead; or in who or what we decide to be an 'important' part of our cultural heritage. Just how one deals with this politics of power is (thankfully) beyond the scope of this introduction, but one might hope that a sense of the way in which materiality grounds our understanding of the human world can act as a firm basis for informed opinion.

NOTES

1   For a similar view see West 1998.
2   Although this topic is taken up much earlier by Packhard 1957.
3   Sociology had also belatedly discovered culture – as Featherstone (1991: 29) points out, the American Sociological Association did not have a 'culture' section until 1987.
4   Interestingly, the idea of Progress has also been resurrected as a political creed by the UK Labour party, no doubt as part of the enthusiasm surrounding the Millenium.
5   Something I think Marx had in mind when he spoke of Man (sic.) as 'one of nature's forces'.
6   It is perhaps significant here that archaeologists have habitually assumed that mundane, subsistence 'function' is easier to infer from archaeological remains than are other aspects of past society such as social organisation, beliefs, etc. (see Graves-Brown 1994).
7   Adorno and Horkheimer believed that popular culture and mass production were, unlike high culture, a threat to enlightened values – a mass deception. Although this is perhaps understandable given their experience of Nazi propaganda it sits uneasily with their Marxist agenda!

References

Adorno, T. and Horkheimer M. 1972 *Dialectics of Enlightenment*. New York: Herder and Herder.

Appadurai, A. 1986 *The Social Life of Things: Commodities in Cultural Perspective*. Cambridge: Cambridge University Press.

Baudrillard, J. 1988 *Selected Writings* (edited by M. Poster). London: Polity Press.

Bijker W.E. and Law, J. (eds) 1992 *Shaping Technology/Building Society*. Cambridge Massachusetts: MIT Press.

Bloch, M. 1990 'Language, anthropology and cognitive science'. *Man* 26: 183–198.

Butler, J. 1993 *Bodies that Matter. On the Discursive Limits of 'Sex'*. London: Routledge.

Featherstone, M. 1991 *Consumer Culture and Postmodernism*. London: Sage.

Gibson, J.J. 1979 *The Ecological Approach to Visual Perception*. Boston: Houghton Mifflin.

Gibson, W. 1993 *Neuromancer* London: HarperCollins.

Graves-Brown, P.M. 1994 'Flakes and ladders: what the archaeological record does not tell us about the origins of language'. *World Archaeology* 26(2): 158–171.

Hall, S. 1973 'Encoding and decoding in the TV discourse'. Reprinted in S. Hall, I. Connell and L. Curti (1981) (eds) *Culture, Media, Language*. London: Hutchinson.

Hebdige, D. 1988 *Subculture: The Meaning of Style*. London: Routledge.

Heidegger, M. 1971 *Poetry, Language, Thought*, trans. A. Hofstadter. New York: Harper and Row.

Hodder, Ian 1983 *The Present Past: An Introduction to Anthropology for Archaeologists*. New York: Pica Press.

Joerges, B. 1988 'Technology in everyday life: conceptual queries'. *Journal for the Theory of Social Behaviour* 18(2): 219–237.

Latour, B. 1992 'Where are the missing masses? The sociology of a few mundane objects.' W.E. Bijker and J. Law (eds) *Shaping Technology/Building Society*. Cambridge Massachusetts: MIT Press, pp. 225–258.

Lemmonier, P. 1989 'Bark capes, arrowheads and Concorde: on social representations of technology'. In I. Hodder (ed.) *The Meaning of Things*. London: Unwin Hyman, pp. 156–171.

Leroi-Gourhan, A. 1964 *Le Geste et la parole*. Paris: Albin Michel.

——— 1993 *Gesture and Speech*. Cambridge Mass. MIT Press.

McLuhan, M. 1964 *Understanding Media: The Extensions of Man*. McGraw Hill, New York.

Mauss, M. 1979 'Body techniques'. In *Sociology and Psychology: Essays* by Marcel Mauss, Part IV, trans. B. Brewster, London: Routledge and Kegan Paul, pp. 97–123.

Mead, G.H. 1934 *Mind, Self and Society*. Chicago: Chicago University Press.

Merleau-Ponty, M. 1964 *The Primacy of Perception* (trans. Carleton Dallery). Seattle: Northwestern University Press.

Miller, D. 1995 'Consumption as the vanguard of history. A polemic by way of introduction'. In D. Miller (ed.) *Acknowledging Consumption*. London: Routledge.

——— 1987 *Material Culture and Mass Consumption*. Oxford: Basil Blackwell.

Millikan, Ruth Garrett 1984 *Language, Thought, and Other Biological Categories*. London and Cambridge, MA: The MIT Press.

Mumford, L. 1948 *Technics and Civilisation*. London: Routledge.

Needham, J. 1954 *Science and Civilisation in China*. Cambridge: Cambridge University Press.

Packhard, V. 1957 *The Hidden Persuaders*. New York: Pocket Books.

Pfaffenberger, B. 1988 'Fetishised objects and human nature. Towards an anthropology of technology.' *Man* 23: 236–252.

Pye, D. 1968 *The Nature and Art of Workmanship*. Cambridge: Cambridge University Press.

Rathje, W.L. 1979 *Modern Material Culture Studies. Advances in Archaeological Method and Theory* 2: 1–37.

Salmon, Merrilee 1982 *Philosophy and Archaeology*. New York and London: Academic Press.

Schiffer, M.B. 1991 *The Portable Radio in American Life*. Tucson: University of Arizona Press.

Still, A. and Costall, A.P. 1991 *Against Cognitivism*. Brighton: Harvester.

Thomas, J. 1998 'Some problems with the notion of external symbolic storage. and the case of neolithic material culture in Britain'. In C. Renfrew and C. Scarre (1998) *Cognition and Material Culture: the Archaeology of Symbolic Storage*. Cambridge: McDonald Institute Monographs, pp. 149–156.

Ucko, P.J. 1969 'Penis sheaths: a comparative study'. *Proceedings of the Royal Anthropological Institute* pp. 24–66.

West, S. 1998 'Introduction.' In S. Tarlow and S. West (eds) *The Familiar Past*. London: Routledge.

Winner, L. 1986 *The Whale and the Reactor: A Search for Limits in the Age of High Technology*. Chicago: Chicago University Press.

1

THE BERLIN KEY OR HOW TO DO WORDS WITH THINGS[1]

Bruno Latour

A social dimension to technology? That's not saying much. Let us rather admit that no one has ever observed a human society that has not been built with things. A material aspect to societies? That is still not saying enough; things do not exist without being full of people, and the more modern and complicated they are, the more people swarm through them. A mixture of social determinations and material constraints? That is a euphemism, for it is no longer a matter of mixing pure forms chosen from two great reservoirs, one in which would lie the social aspects of meaning or subject, the other where one would stockpile material components belonging to physics, biology and the science of materials. A dialectic, then? If you like, but only on condition that we abandon the mad idea that the subject is posed in its opposition to the object, for there are neither subjects nor objects, neither in the beginning – mythical – nor in the end – equally mythical. Circulations, sequences, transfers, translations, displacements, crystallisations – there are many motions, certainly, but not a single one of them, perhaps, that resembles a contradiction.

In Carelman's *Catalogue des objets introuvables* (Carelman 1995) one does not find the surrealistic key that appears below – and for good reason. This key does exists, but only in Berlin and its suburbs.[2]

Here is the sort of object which, though it may gladden the hearts of technologists, causes nightmares for archaeologists. They are in effect the only ones in the world to study artefacts that somewhat resemble what modern philosophers believe to be an object. Ethnologists, anthropologists, folklorists, economists, engineers, consumers and users never see objects. They see only plans, actions, behaviours, arrangements, habits, heuristics, abilities, collections of practices of which certain portions seem a little more durable and others a little more transient, though one can never say which one, steel or memory, things or words, stones or laws, guarantees the longer duration. Even in our grandmothers' attics, in the flea market, in town dumps, in scrap heaps, in rusted factories, in the Smithsonian Institution, objects still appear quite full of use, of memories, of instructions. A few steps away there is always someone who can take possession of them to pad those whitened bones with new flesh. This resurrection of the flesh may be forbidden to archaeologists, since

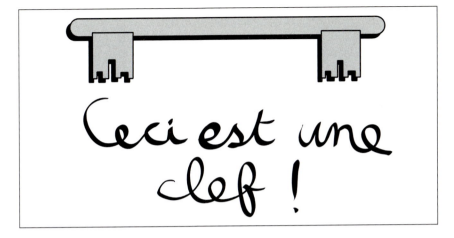

Figure 1.1 Ceci est une clef

the society that made and was made by these artefacts has disappeared, body and goods. Yet even if they must infer, through an operation of retro-engineering, the chains of associations of which the artefacts are only one link, as soon as they grasp in their hands these poor fossilised or dusty objects, these relics immediately cease to be objects and rejoin the world of people, circulating from hand to hand right at the site of the excavations, in the class-room, in the scientific literature. The slightly more resistant part of a chain of practices cannot be called an 'object', except at the time it is still under the ground, unknown, thrown away, subjected, covered, ignored, invisible, in itself. In other words, there are no visible objects and there never have been. The only objects are invisible and fossilised ones. Too bad for the modern philoso-phers who have talked to us so much about our relations with objects, about the dangers of objectification, of auto-positioning of the subject and other somersaults.

As for us, who are not modern philosophers (and still less post-modern ones), we consider chains of associations and we say that they alone exist. Associations of what? Let us say, as a first approximation, of humans (H) and non-humans (NH). Of course, one could still make a distinction, on any given chain, between the old divisions and the modern. H-H-H-H-H would resemble 'social relations'; NH-NH-NH-NH-NH a 'machine'; H-NH a 'person-machine interface'; NH-NH-NH-NH-NH-H 'the impact of a tech-nology on a person'; H-H-H-H-NH 'the influence of society on technology'; H-H-H-NH-H-H-H the tool shaped by the human, while NH-NH-NH-H-NH-NH-NH would resemble those wretched humans crushed by the weight of automatisms. But why endeavour to recognise the old divisions if they are artificial and prevent us from following the only thing that matters to us and that exists: the transformation of these chains of associations? We no longer know just how to characterise the elements that make up these chains once one has isolated them. To speak of 'humans' and 'non-humans' allows only a rough approximation that still borrows from modern philosophy the stupefying idea that there exist humans and non-humans, whereas there are only trajectories and dispatches, paths and trails. But we know that the elements, whatever they may be, are substituted and transformed. Association – AND – substitution – OR: this is what will give us the precision that could never be given us by the distinction between social and technological, between humans and things, between the 'symbolic dimension' and 'material constraints.' Let us allow the provisional form of humans and the provisional essence of matter to emerge from this exploration through associations and substitutions, instead of corrupting our taste by deciding in advance what is social and what is technological.

'What is this thing? What's it used for? Why a key with two bits? And two symmetrical bits? Who are they trying to kid?' The archaeologist turns the Berlin key over and over in her hands. Because she has been told, she now knows that this key is not a joke, that it is indeed being used by Germans and that it is even used – the detail is important – on the outer doors of apartment buildings. She had certainly spotted the side-travel allowed by the fact that the two bits were identical, and the lack of asymmetry in the teeth had struck her. Of course she was aware, because she had been using keys for a long time, of their usual axis of rotation and felt clearly that one of the bits, either one, could serve as a head in order to exert enough leverage to disengage the bolt.

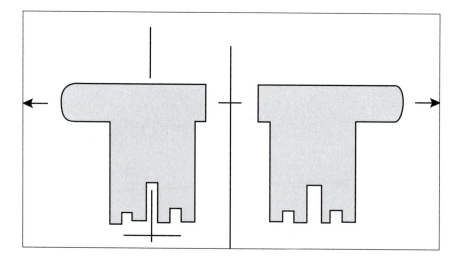

Figure 1.2 Berliner key symmetry

It was only afterwards that she noticed the groove. The latter did not break the side-travel but re-established an asymmetry when she considered the key in profile. However, by turning the key 180° on its vertical axis, one found the same groove at the same place. Translation, 360° rotation on the horizontal axis, 180° on the vertical axis – all this probably meant something, but what?

There had to be a lock for this key, she felt sure. It was the lock that would provide the key to this little mystery. However, when she looked at the hole into which it was to be engaged, the mystery only increased.

She had never before seen a keyhole shaped like this, but it was clear to her that the whole business, the whole affair, was based on the arrangement of the notch of the horizontal hole that would or would not allow the hole to receive the groove in the key.

Our archaeologist's surprise was still greater when she was unable to withdraw the key after having introduced it vertically and having turned it 270° counterclockwise. The lock was certainly open, the bolt had certainly retracted into the black box as in the case of any honest lock, the outer door was certainly opening, but try as she might, to pull, push, twist her key, our friend could not extract it again. The only way out, she found, was to lock the door again by a 270° clockwise rotation. And so she found herself locked out again, back where she started. 'What foolishness!' she says to herself. 'In order to get my key back, I have to lock the door again. Yet I can't stay behind the door, on the courtyard side, while I bolt it again on the street side. A door has to be either open or closed. And yet I cannot lose a key each time I use it, unless the door in question is an asymmetrical one that has to remain unbolted while one is inside. If it were a key to a mailbox, well, then I could

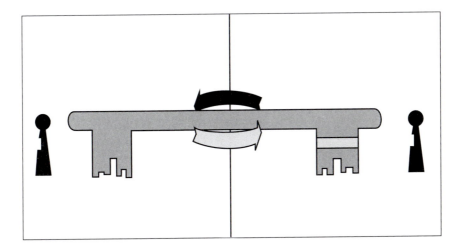

Figure 1.3 Berliner key reversibility

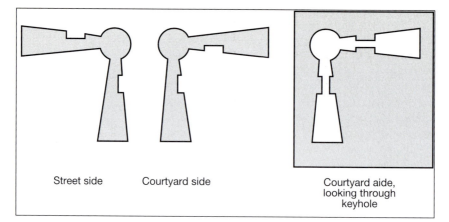

Street side   Courtyard side   Courtyard aide,
                                                  looking through
                                                  keyhole

Figure 1.4   Berliner keyhole

understand it. But this is absurd, anyone could lock me in with a turn of the key, and anyway, we're talking about the door to an apartment house. And on the other hand, if I bolt the lock without the door being closed, the bolt will stop it from closing. What protection can a door offer if it is carefully bolted but wide open?'

Good archaeologist that she is, now she sets about exploring the specifications of her miraculous key. What action would permit her to preserve all the elements of common sense at once? A key serves to open and close and/or to bolt and unbolt a lock; one cannot lose one's key each time, nor leave it inside, nor bolt an open door, nor believe there would be a key to which a locksmith had, just for fun, added a bit. What gesture would allow one to do justice to the particularity of this key – two bits symmetrical through 180° rotation around the axis and identical through side-travel ? There must be a solution. There is only one weak link in this little socio-logical network. 'Damn, of course!' A reader avid for topology, an inhabitant of Berlin, the astute archaeologist, have probably already understood the gesture that must be made. If our archaeologist cannot withdraw her key after having bolted the door by a 270° rotation as is her habit with every key in the world, she must be able to make the key, now horizontal, slip from the other side through the lock.

She tries this absurd move, and actually succeeds. Without underestimating our archaeologist's mathematical aptitudes, we can bet that she might remain standing at the door of her building the whole night through before learning how to get in. Without a human being, without a demonstration, without directions, she would certainly have an attack of hysterics. These keys that pass through walls are too reminiscent of ghosts not to frighten us. This gesture is so unhabitual that one can only learn it from someone else, a Berliner, who

14

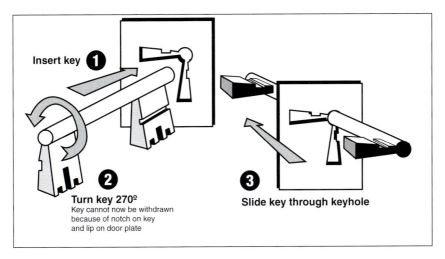

Figure 1.5   Key operation – street side

has in turn learned it from another Berliner, who in turn … and so on and so forth by degrees all the way back to the inspired inventor, whom I will call, since I don't know him, the Prussian Locksmith.

If our friend were fond of symbolic anthropology, she could have consoled herself for not being able to get in by endowing this key with a 'symbolic dimension': in West Berlin, before the Wall fell, the people supposedly felt so locked in that they doubled the number of bits on their keys. 'There, that's it, a repetition compulsion, a mass psychosis of the besieged, a Berlin–Vienna axis; hm, hm. I can already see myself writing a nice article on the hidden meaning of German technological objects. That is certainly worth spending a cold night in Berlin.' But our friend, thank God, is only a good archaeologist devoted to the harsh constrains and exigencies of objects.

She finds herself on the other side of the door again, the key still hori-zontal, and feels that she will at last be able to recover it. 'That's the Germans all over', she says to herself. 'Why make something simple when you can make it complicated!'

However, just when she thought she was out of the woods, our archaeolo-gist once again comes close to a fit of hysteria. Once she and her key – one in a human manner, the other in a ghostly manner – have passed to the other side, she still cannot recover her sesame. In vain she pulls, pushes, there is nothing to be done, the key is no more inclined to come out than it was when one engaged it on the other side. Our friend can find no other solution than to go back to where she started, on the street side, by pushing the wall-penetrating key back through in a horizontal position, then once again bolting the door, finding herself back outside, in the cold … with her key!

15

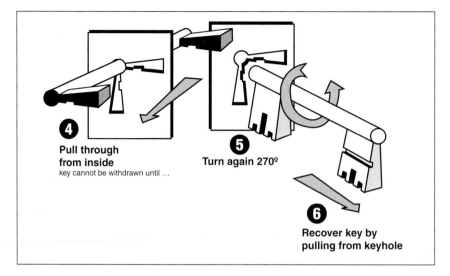

Figure 1.6   Key operation – courtyard side

She starts everything over again from the beginning, and finally sees (someone has shown her; she has read some sort of directions; she has groped around for a long enough time) that *by bolting the door again behind her*, on the courtyard side, she is at last authorised to recover her key. Oh joy, oh delight, she understands how it works !

These shouts of joy were premature. When, in the morning at around ten o'clock, she wanted to show her friend what a good Berliner, as well as a good archaeologist, she had become, she covered herself with shame. Instead of demonstrating her brand new attainments, she could not turn the key more than five degrees. This time, the door remained open permanently without her being able to bolt it. It was only at ten o'clock at night, when she came back from the movies, that she could exercise her know-how, for the door, as it had been the night before, was hermetically sealed. She was forced, then, to participate voluntarily in this hermeticism by bolting it behind her in order to recover her precious key.

It was only at eight o'clock in the morning the next day that she met the concierge; as he withdrew his key from the door he gave her the key to the mystery. The caretaker's passkey had no groove, was thinner, and in quite the classical manner had only one bit. The concierge, and he alone, could bolt or unbolt the door as he pleased, by inserting his key in a horizontal position but then withdrawing his key as one does in Paris, remaining snug on the side where his lodge was. After that action, however, the inhabitants of the building found they either could not bolt the door (during the day), or were obliged to bolt it from eight o'clock at night until eight o'clock in the

16

morning). In Berlin, this steel key performs mechanically the same function as is performed electronically in Paris by the door codes.

Our archaeologist, somewhat versed in sociology, was quite delighted by the way in which the Prussian Locksmith obliged all the inhabitants of Berlin to conform to a strict collective discipline, and was already preparing to write an article rather in the style of Foucault on the subject, when her colleague from the *Wissenshaft Zentrum* took from his pocket a Berlin key from which he had carefully filed away the grooves! His key had become a passkey similar in every aspect to that of the concierge. Instead of being obliged to lock the door behind him, he could either leave the door open for his nightwalking visitors, or bolt it during the day in the face of intruders, thus annulling the concierge's unlocking. ... Master of his destiny, he escaped the Prussian Locksmith once again. Berlin was decidedly the ambivalent city symbolised by the doubling of the bits and then their preclusion ...

If we call the 'script' of a device its 'program of action' (Akrich 1992), what is the programme of action of such a key? 'Please bolt the door behind you during the night and never during the day.' Into what material is this

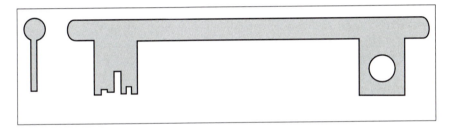

Figure 1.7   Berliner master key

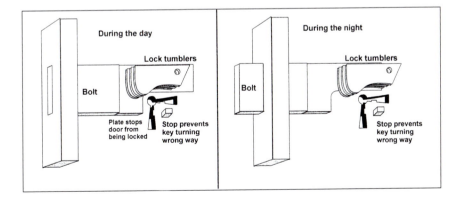

Figure 1.8   Lock mechanism

programme translated? Into words, of course. All large cities, all groups of co-owners, all union newspapers, all concierge's lodges, are full of complaints, notices, recriminations and groans about the doors, the fact that they are impossible to lock and impossible to open. But if it was a question of words, or notices, or howls of 'Lock the door!' or placards, we would merely be in the world of signs. If we were still living in the blessed days in which concierges kept watch night and day so as to pull the door-cord only for those they had carefully examined, we would be immersed in social relations – except for the door-pull, we forgot that, which allowed the slave in the lodge not to reveal her undies by getting up. The denunciations, palm-greasing permitted by these relations fed the plots of more than one novel. But now with this Berlin key we find we are neither altogether in the world of signs nor altogether in the realm of social relations. Are we in the world of technology? Of course we are, since here we are confronting keyholes and a handsome steel key with teeth, grooves and lips. And of course we are not, since we are encountering know-how, punctual concierges, and obstinate cheats, not to speak of our Prussian Locksmith.

All devices that seek to annul, destroy, subvert, circumvent a programme of action are called anti-programmes. The thief who wishes to get through the door, representatives of the opposite sex, are pursuing their anti-programmes, from the point of view, of course, of our dedicated concierge. No one has acknowledged their competence to go through the front entrance, but they insist on going through. Delivery people, tradespeople, mail carriers, doctors, legitimate spouses, also wish to go through during the day and believe they have the necessary authorisation. The Berlin key, the door and the concierge are engaged in a bitter struggle for control and access. Shall we say that the social relations between tenants and owners, or inhabitants and thieves, or inhabitants and delivery people, or co-owners and concierges, are mediated by the key, the lock and the Prussian Locksmith? The word mediation, quite useful, can also become an asylum for ignorance depending on the meaning one gives it. One person will take mediation to mean *intermediary*, another to mean *mediator*.

If the key is an intermediary, it does nothing in itself except carry, transport, shift, incarnate, express, reify, objectify, reflect, the meaning of the phrase: 'Lock the door behind you during the night, and never during the day', or, more politically: 'Let us settle the class struggle between owners and tenants, rich people and thieves, right-wing Berliners and left-wing Berliners.' Give me the society of Berlin, and I will tell you how the key is shaped! Technology is nothing more than discourse, totally expressible in other media. But then, why this key, these grooves, these surrealistic keyholes and this subtle inversion of the horizontal slot? If the transition to steel, to brass, to wood changes nothing, all technological mediators count for nothing. They are there for show; to give the idle something to chatter about. The material world confronts us only to serve as a mirror for social relations and a source of entertainment for sociologists. Of course, it carries meaning, it can receive it, but it does not fabricate it. The social is made elsewhere, always elsewhere.

Everything changes if the word mediation fills out a little in order to designate the action of mediators. Then the meaning is no longer simply transported by the medium but in part constituted, moved, recreated, modified, in short expressed and betrayed. No, the asymmetrical slot of the keyhole and the key with two bits do not 'express', 'symbolise', 'reflect', 'reify', 'objectify', 'incarnate' disciplinary relations, they make them, they form them. The very notion of discipline is impracticable without steel, without the wood of the door, without the bolt of the locks. The proof? Owners did not succeed in constructing a social relation solidly established on discipline, on verbal coercion, on printed notices, on warnings or the gentleness of customs. The doors remained wide open during the night or locked during the day. This is why they had to extend the network of their relations, forge other alliances, recruit the Prussian Locksmith, and mobilise mathematics and its principles of symmetry. It is because the social cannot be constructed with the social that it needs keys and locks. And it is because classical locks still allow too much freedom that keys with double bits are needed. Meaning does not antecede technological devices. The intermediary was not a means to an end, whereas the mediator becomes at once means and end. From being a simple tool, the steel key assumes all the dignity of a mediator, a social actor, an agent, an active being.

As for the symmetry and the little break in symmetry that one sees when looking through the keyhole, are they or are they not social relations? This would be endowing them with, at once, too much and not enough. Not enough, since all of Berlin must pass this way: it is impossible to withdraw the key because of the stagger of the horizontal slot. Are these, then, social relations, relations of power? No, because nothing allowed Berlin to foresee that a break in symmetry, a key with two bits, and an obsessed concierge had to unite to transform into an obligatory point of passage a programme of action that, until now, was composed only of words and customs. If I take my key with two bits that authorises me to re-enter my house and obliges me to bolt the door at night and forbids me to bolt it during the day, am I not dealing with social relations, with morality, with laws? Of course, but made of steel. To define them as social relations continued by other means would not be too bad, if we were capable, indeed, of recognising in means, media, mediators, the eminent alterity, the eminent dignity that modern philosophy has for so long refused them.

Along with their alterity, one must also recognise their fragility, that eminent weakness that the technologists, this time, refuse to grant them. A cunning little person equipped with a file is enough to rob the concierge of his role as alternative caretaker. And this concierge, in his turn, must also be disciplined. There is no point in holding the key in one's hand, for the human concierge must be kept in hand also so that he will trigger the mechanism morning and night punctually. And the solidity of this chain consisting of good-social-behaviour-practical-know-how-concierge-key-lock-door is no less provisional, for a poser of an electronic code can now transform the vigilance of the concierge into an electric signal regulated by the clock and turn the steel key into a code I will have to memorise. Which is more fragile, '45–68E' (my door code) or the handsome steel key? Which is more technological, the steel or the little counting-rhyme 'end of the war, May 68, Europe' which I say over to myself at the end of the day in order to remember the thing that authorises me to re-enter my house? Which of the two, this solid key or that mnemotechnological counting-rhyme wired into my neurons, is more durable?

Consider things, and you will have humans. Consider humans, and you are by that very act interested in things. Bring your attention to bear on hard things, and see them become gentle, soft or human. Turn your attention to humans, and see them become electric circuits, automatic gears or softwares. We cannot even define precisely what makes some human and others technical, whereas we are able to document precisely their modifications and replacements, their rearrangements and their alliances, their delegations and representations. Do technology, and you are now a sociologist. Do sociology, and now you are obliged to be a technologist. It is no more possible for you to avoid this obligation, this connection, this consequence, this pursuit, than it is permitted for you to enter your building at night in Berlin without taking out your key and locking the door again behind you. It is now (and has been for two or three million years) inscribed in the nature of things.

Readers must have been wondering from the outset how people in Berlin contrive to hook this surrealistic key onto their keychains. Not to mention the fact that two bits instead of one gives that much more chance of tearing one's pockets. I do not wish to leave them in suspense. The Prussian Locksmith has applied himself to inventing a Berlin keychain, a little case endowed with claws that holds the bit, to which is attached a ring, which, in its turn, allows one to hook it onto a keychain, which can be attached to one's belt.

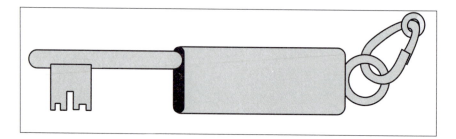

Figure 1.9 Key holder

With mediators, in fact, there always begin chains of mediators, otherwise known as networks. One is never done with them. But sociologists, like technologists, enemy brothers, believe they can come to an end, the former with the social, the latter with objects. The only thing they do not manage to end is their fratricidal war, a war that prevents us from understanding the world in which we live.

NOTES

1   This chapter originally appeared as : 'La clef de Berlin et autres leçons d'un amateur de sciences', La Découverte 1993 pp. 25–46. This English-language version was translated by Lydia Davis with additional editing by PMGB. Illustrations redrawn by PMGB.
2   My warmest thanks to Bernard Joerges for having presented me with this key and to Wanfred Schweizer of the Kerfin Company for having sold me a sample of his lock, real enough to guarantee him his livelihood. It should be pointed out that this article was written before the Berlin Wall came down, in West Berlin, which was at the time besieged by real socialism.

References

Akrich, M. 1992 'The De-scription of technical objects.' In W.E. Bijker and J. Law (eds) *Shaping Technology/Building Society*. Cambridge Massachusetts: MIT Press, pp. 203–224.
Carelman, J. 1995 *Catalogues des Objets Introuvables*. Paris: Livre de Poche.

2

THE FUNCTIONS OF THINGS
A philosophical perspective on material culture

Beth Preston

Introduction

A common conceptual framework for studying material culture considers artefacts under two main aspects. First, there is the form of the thing – the material out of which it is made and the shape that material has been induced to take. Second, there is the function of the thing – the specific use for which it is designed, or the uses to which it is put. Other characteristics of interest can be classified under one or the other of these headings: for example, quantitative measurements or counts under form, and relationships to other artefacts (the relationship between pens and paper, for instance) under function. Although form is more easily ascertainable, function is of particular interest to archaeologists because it is a central point of articulation between the form of the thing and the behaviour of the people who made and used it (Salmon 1982; Schiffer 1976, 1995). For the archaeologist, then, one of the first steps towards deciphering the lifeways and forms of thought of vanished cultures is to decipher the functions of the more durable things they left behind them.[1]

However, this step is notoriously difficult, and one of the major reasons for the difficulty is not far to seek. The relationship between form and function is many to many. For any function, abstractly specified, there are a multitude of ways to carry it out. For example, interior lighting may be accomplished by means of torches, candles, oil lamps or electric light bulbs; and each of these, in turn, can take a multitude of different forms. On the other hand, a particular form may serve equally well for the carrying out of more than one function. For example, Hodder (1983: 68) discusses Iron Age artefacts with a toothed, comb-like form. The functions these items reasonably could have served include combing human hair, grooming the manes of horses, tattooing, making decorations on pots, dressing skins and weaving. This many to many relationship means that inferences in either direction are fraught with peril; you cannot count on inferring the function reliably from the form alone, or the form from the function. Of course there are other kinds of evidence which can aid these inferences, such as use wear analysis or the observable contemporary functions of similar artefacts. But these are not necessarily available in all cases, and all have their own sources of unreliability. On the other hand, if you have an artefact at all, it necessarily has some form or other. Thus form ends up being the most consistently available evidence for function. And its unreliability for that purpose is thus a consistently encountered difficulty.

This inherent difficulty with the form–function relationship is admitted on all hands, but opinions differ as to its implication for archaeological theory and practice. First, there is disagreement over the extent to which the study of sheer form without reference to function ought to be encouraged as a more cautiously realistic way of doing archaeology (Chippindale 1992). And then there are disagreements over how function attributions are to be made reliably, assuming they are to be made at all. An important example is the longstanding debate as to whether analogies to the functions of artefacts in modern material cultures can be employed to establish the functions of artefacts from previous ones, and if so, to what extent and with what limitations (Gould 1980; Salmon 1982; Binford 1989).

Rather than entering into these debates about whether and how function attribution can be made in archaeology, I will instead concentrate on what might be regarded as a more basic set of questions, namely: What is a function? How do functions get established in the first place, and how do they change? Are there different kinds of function, and if so, what are the basic classifications into which they fall? These are philosophical questions about the nature of function in general. The motivation for recurring to this level of inquiry is twofold. First, it has not received as much attention from archaeologists, taken up as they naturally have been with the more pressing methodological questions about function attribution. But the answers to the philosophical questions may have important implications for the methodological questions – the nature of function constrains how functions can or should be attributed to items of material culture, past or present. Second, the discussion of function in philosophy has been very lively over the last decade, but it has not been couched in terms of material culture, nor have its results been applied to this domain of functionality explicitly and in detail. The most recent writer to do this was Merrilee Salmon in her *Philosophy and Archaeology* (1982). But since her excellent discussion was published, a considerable further body of philosophical literature on function has been generated. So the time is ripe for renewed efforts at interdisciplinary incorporation.

I will first describe two conceptions of function current in the philosophical literature. These have been regarded as rival conceptions, since they propose quite different understandings of what it is for something to have a function. But I will show that they are in fact complementary conceptions. Specifically, both of them are needed in order to understand the range of functions attributable to items of material culture.[2] The second section of the chapter will substantiate this claim, drawing on commonplace examples of the modern material culture of the US for evidence and illustration. In the final section I will outline some implications of this dual conception of function for the study of material culture.

Two philosophical conceptions of function

Interest in function first arose among philosophers of biology trying to conceptualise the function of biological organs. Subsequently, it began to interest philosophers of mind, motivated by the idea that to ascribe meaning to a mental representation is to say what its function is in the mental economy of the organism. However, the claim is routinely made – although not substantiated – that the resulting conceptions of function apply to items of material culture as well. So the philosophical aim is a very general conception of function. In developing this, one of the main problems has been to distinguish those performances which constitute a thing's function from those performances which are accidental or adventitious. The classic example is the heart, which in addition to circulating blood also makes a characteristic noise. An example from material culture is spoons, which are for stirring and picking up food, but which also make a characteristic noise when dropped or struck against one another. A viable conception of function ought to distinguish the circulating function from the noise, which is an accidental by-product in both cases – or so it was thought.

Larry Wright (1973) proposed an account of function designed to do just that. This account has since been superseded by the two conceptions of function which are the subject matter of this section. However, they will be better understood against the background of Wright's account. The central idea is that the performance which constitutes a thing's function must be linked to the causes or reasons why the thing is there in the first place; that is, why it is in existence or why it is where it is. Specifically, Wright proposed that a given performance X is the function of a thing Y if and only if (1) Y is there because it does X, and (2) the performance X is a result of Y's being there. Because things are not always actually carrying out their functions, he added the qualification that the performance should be understood as something the thing has the capacity or the disposition to do. Wright's account thus ties together the current capacity or disposition of a thing to produce certain performances and the history of causes or reasons which explains why the thing is there at all. Returning to our examples, it is clear that this does solve the problem of picking out the function, while relegating other performances to limbo. From the point of view of selection history, hearts are there because they circulate blood, not because they go pit-a-pat. Similarly, spoons are there because they are good for handling food, not because of the noise they make when struck or dropped. However, Wright's account raises some other problems, and it was in the process of resolving them that two distinct conceptions of function have been generated out of Wright's single one.

The first problem was diagnosed by Robert Cummins (1975). He pointed out that the current capacity or disposition of a thing is often unrelated to – or at odds with – the reasons for its being there. Specifically, there are many cases of biological structures which evolved under selective pressure for one use but which now are used for something else entirely. A good example is the panda's 'thumb' made famous by Stephen Jay Gould (1980). Originally a wristbone, this 'thumb' is used by pandas to grip things, much as ours is. Similarly, both the feathers of birds and the wings of insects are thought to have evolved for thermal regulation, and only much later to have been pressed into service for flight. There are many such cases in material culture as well. Cummins mentions the hypothetical case of a large depression made by glacial activity in a boulder, but now functioning in some hypothetical culture as a container for holy water. Actual cases would include common things such as a treadless old tyre used as a swing; the handle of a spoon used to open a cocoa tin, soft drink bottles with the bottoms removed functioning as cloches in the vegetable garden, and so on. In these last cases, current capacity or disposition might in fact help explain why the thing is where it is, provided that is construed narrowly enough. (In the case of the spoon, for instance, it might not even help explain why it is in the cook's hand at the moment, although it would explain why it is being applied to the lid of the cocoa tin.) But in none of these cases does present function explain why the thing is in existence.[3]

So Wright's account is too restrictive. It insists that only those performances which do account for things being there are really their functions. Cummins' criticism, in effect, is that this rules out a whole host of common performances which we do intuitively think of as the current function of something. In response, Cummins proposes a very different conception of what it is to have a function; a conception I shall call system function. The central idea here is that function is to be understood solely in terms of the capacity or disposition to perform a specific role in the context of a specific system. A system, in turn, is understood as a configuration of components interacting in an orderly way, such that the overall performance of the system can be understood and explained in terms of the performances of the components.[4] So on this view, in order to ascribe a function to something you look not at its history, but rather at its current performance (or disposition to perform) within the embedding system. The system function account agrees with Wright that the heart has the function of pumping blood, because this is its role in the circulatory system. But it might equally well be said to have the function of making noise, because that is its role in the system used by the doctor or veterinarian to detect and diagnose heart problems. Similarly, the two accounts agree that spoons have the function of stirring and picking up food; but the system function account also ascribes to them a noisemaking function in the context of some folk music traditions in which pairs of spoons are used as clappers, a very basic sort of musical rhythm instrument.[5] On the other hand, both accounts would reject the noise the spoon makes when accidentally dropped as a function – Wright because the spoon is not there (in either sense) because of this noise, and Cummins because there is no plausible embedding system in which the noise plays a functional role.

So Cummins offers a much more liberal account of what counts as a function and what does not. This liberalism allows him to capture our intuitions about some functions of both biological structures and items of material culture. It also deals effectively with the disparity between current utility and evolutionary or manufacturing history by eliminating one of the conflicting elements. On the system function view, historical considerations simply do not enter into the analysis of function at all.

However, there is still a problem remaining, and it is a problem Wright and Cummins share. Intuition also indicates that function is a normative concept. We often talk about things malfunctioning, and have very definite ideas about what they are supposed to have the capacity or disposition to do even in cases where they clearly are not so capable or so disposed. But neither Wright's account nor Cummins' gives us a good basis for an analysis of malfunction, since there is no mechanism in either case to separate what a thing is supposed to do from what it in fact does. It is perfectly possible on these accounts to say a thing has *no* function, or that it has a function different from the one it used to have; but not that it has a function it is incapable of performing or never performs. So, for example, a heart so badly deformed that it is from the first incapable of circulating blood just does not have that function, since it does not have either the capacity or the disposition in question. Similarly, some types of spoons (plastic ones, for instance) do not have the capacity or disposition to produce the noise required of a decent rhythm instrument, and so do not have that function. But these two cases are intuitively different. In the case of the plastic spoons we might very well be satisfied with an analysis under which they simply do not have a musical function. But in the case of the non-circulating heart, we want to say it ought to circulate blood, that it is malfunctioning if it does not or cannot do so; in short, that it has a function it is just not able to perform. But neither Wright nor Cummins can capture this intuition. A capacity or disposition is either there or it is not. But the strong normativity involved in the notion of malfunction implies a justified expectation of a capacity or disposition. If the new telephone does not ring when someone calls in, I can expect to get my money back from the manufacturer – not because the telephone does not have a function I thought it had, but because it does have a function it is not currently able or disposed to perform.

Ruth Millikan (1984, 1993) proposes a conception of function she calls *proper function* which deals handily with this second problem.[6] The central idea here is closely related to Wright's insistence that function must be specified in terms of a performance which explains why the thing is there. On Millikan's view, this explanation must be a causal-historical account modelled on the biological notion of a selection history. In the case of biological organs like the heart, this will be an evolutionary history mediated by natural selection. In the case of equipment like spoons, it will be a history of conscious (or at least intentional) selection by a user or community of users. So something has a given performance as its proper function when it has been reproduced or copied from ancestors which *did* engage in that performance, and which survived and proliferated precisely in virtue of performing it. So the proper function of a heart is to circulate blood, not to make noise, because it is in virtue of successfully circulating blood that ancestral hearts helped their owners survive and engender similarly equipped offspring down to the present day. Likewise, the proper function of spoons is to be used for stirring and picking up food, not to make noise; since it is in virtue of successful stirring that spoons have historically been kept and copied into new exemplars.

The most important difference between Millikan's account and those of both Wright and Cummins is that she rejects current capacity or disposition as unnecessary for the specification of function at all. It is only past capacity or disposition of some (perhaps very few) ancestors which is required. But this feature allows Millikan to advance a full-blooded notion of malfunction. The proper function of a thing is what it is supposed to do, given what the ancestors it has been copied from in fact *did* just often enough to survive and proliferate. This means that if the thing is unable to undertake this performance – a heart might be deformed or a spoon broken, for instance – it is malfunctioning. It ought to perform in the relevant way because it has in effect inherited a proper function from its ancestors even if it is never able to perform it, or as a matter of fact never does perform it.

Thus Millikanian proper function is normative in a strong sense. It expresses standards of performance which all members of a group or class of similar things are supposed to meet in virtue of their belonging to that group. Any other performances in which such a thing engages are either irrelevant (because idiosyncratic) or outright malfunctions (if they take the place of, or interfere with, the performance of the proper function). Proper function is thus oriented towards understanding the normative structure of groups of things – the norms which govern their performances – and consequently ignores the particular characteristics and idiosyncratic performances of individual things. Cummins' notion of system function, on the other hand, is non-normative. It focuses on what a thing in fact does, or is disposed to do, in its current system context. If a thing has no such functional role in its current context, then it simply has no system function with regard to it – it is just not part of that system. But if it does have a role in a system, then it has a system function, no matter how transient this role may be, and regardless of whether anything of that type has ever filled such a role before. System function is thus oriented towards understanding the particular capacities and actual performances of individual things, and ignores their historical group affiliations, if any. This contrast between a normative, group-centred conception of function

27

and a non-normative individual-centred conception will be taken up again in the last section of this chapter, with specific reference to archaeological theory.

But Millikan's conception of function also differs from both Wright's and Cummins' in another significant respect. It restricts what performances count as functions to those which, when performed by ancestors, were causally responsible for the existence of the exemplar under consideration. Thus Millikan rejects the ambiguity inherent in the term 'there' which is tolerated by both Wright and Cummins. A proper function is a performance which accounts for the existence of something, but not necessarily for its location. This is more consistent with the idea that the history involved in establishing a function is a history of natural selection. Things whose existence is accounted for by selective forces may be displaced from the environment in which those forces operated by completely different forces, so the selection history cannot account for why a thing is where it is. Selection history accounts for why the various parts of an orchid flower exist and have the proper functions they have, but not for why it is growing in a greenhouse in Alaska.

To summarise, then: Wright's conception of function turns out to be unstable because it assumes the history explaining how a thing got there and that the current capacity or disposition of that thing will correspond. But they do not always do so. In the case of malfunction, the thing does not have the capacity or disposition expected on the basis of the history of things of that type. In the cases noticed by Cummins, the thing has a *different* capacity or disposition than what would be expected on the basis of such a history. So it seems a consistent conception of function must either drop the historical considerations and depend entirely on current capacity or disposition (system function); or it must drop considerations of current capacity or disposition and depend entirely on the selection history (proper function). But as we have seen, each of these solutions violates some intuition we have about function. System function does not allow for any robust notion of malfunction, even though function does intuitively seem like a normative matter. Proper function does not allow for novel uses of things to count as functions, even though intuitively it does seem that there are lots of such permanent or transient changes of function. So what is a poor function theorist to do?

The usual way of understanding this situation is to take these two conceptions of function as outright competitors. This interpretation is encouraged by the fact that in most cases, proper function and system function coincide. A spoon in use in the kitchen or a beating heart is carrying out its proper function and simultaneously filling a functional role in the culinary or circulatory system, respectively. So it appears system function and proper function are competing conceptions of the same, unitary phenomenon. In that case, the project is to find out which one of them is on the right track, and adjust it (or, possibly, adjust our intuitions) until all the remaining difficulties are resolved. On the other hand, there is a significant number of cases where they do not coincide – the badly deformed heart, the spoon co-opted as a musical instrument, and so on – and this suggests a different understanding of the situation. Perhaps these two conceptions of function indicate that there are really two distinct but overlapping domains of functional phenomena. Under this interpretation, which I am advocating, the two conceptions are regarded as complementary, and the project is to develop both of them in tandem. This pluralist interpretation has also been advocated by Ruth Millikan (1989), who notes that the arguments for these two conceptions of function are quite different arguments; and perhaps even more importantly, that each of these conceptions is appropriate to a different mode of explanation.[7] System function lends itself to explanation by functional decomposition, whereas proper function lends itself to explanation in terms of selection history. In the next section I will support this pluralist interpretation on the grounds that these two distinct conceptions of function do, in fact, correspond to two distinct ranges of phenomena in material culture. Consequently, we need both conceptions in complementary roles in order to understand the nature of function in material culture.

Function in material culture

The idea that there are several different types of function is, of course, not new. Michael Schiffer (1992: 9–12) distinguishes three types, for instance, which he calls technofunction, sociofunction and ideofunction.[8] The technofunction is the utilitarian function of a thing. Schiffer gives the example of a chair, which has the technofunction of supporting seated humans. The sociofunction of a thing involves the manifestation of social facts. So an expensive luxury chair may have the sociofunction of manifesting the economic status of its owner. The ideofunction of a thing involves symbolising more abstract ideas, values or beliefs. Schiffer's example here is the pope's throne, which in addition to indicating the occupant's social status also symbolises authority in general, which is why we sometimes speak metonymously of the power or authority of the throne.

Schiffer's proposal classifies functions in terms of a concrete aspect of their content, namely, what kind of purpose they embody. The classification of functions in terms of the distinction between proper function and system function is not intended to replace Schiffer's classification, or indeed any other content-based classification. Rather it cross classifies the same functions at a more basic, abstract level having to do with what might be called the ontological form of functions. Functions are distinguishable in terms of the structural conditions which establish them. In the case of system function, these structural conditions consist of the current systemic interrelations of a thing with other things. In the case of proper function, they consist of the historical relations of a thing with other things similar to it. And these structural conditions are independent of the specific content of the function.

A direct comparison between these two classification schemes may make

29

this point clearer. A technofunction, sociofunction or ideofunction may be either a proper function or a system function. For example, although chairs have the *proper* technofunction of supporting seated humans, they routinely have the *system* technofunction of supporting standing humans who need to change a light bulb or get something off a high shelf. Chairs are not reproduced for this purpose, but they regularly serve it. Similarly, an expensive luxury chair with the *proper* sociofunction of manifesting its owner's economic status may subsequently be acquired by a collector. It thereby acquires the *system* sociofunction of manifesting its new owner's social status as a connoisseur – someone who is not merely wealthy, but who understands which things have historical or artistic worth. And ideofunctions, too, may be either proper or system functions. For example, thrones are usually a special kind of chair, reproduced in order to represent authority, which is thus one of their proper functions. But it might easily happen in some culture that a perfectly ordinary chair reproduced only in order to serve its basic techno-function might, as a matter of sheer historical fact, come to be the hereditary throne of the rulers. In that case it would have representing authority as a system ideofunction. Conversely (and perhaps obviously, at this point), a proper function or system function may be either a technofunction or a sociofunction or an ideofunction, as the examples just rehearsed demonstrate. So the distinction between proper function and system function is orthogonal to classifications of function in terms of content, represented here by Schiffer's scheme.

The task of this section, then, is not to defend classification in terms of ontological form as a rival to classification in terms of the content of a function. Rather it is to defend the importance of a separate and complementary classification scheme consisting of the ontological distinction between the proper and system forms of function. I will begin by making some general observations. As many readers already will have remarked, it is clearly the exception rather than the rule for a thing to have only one function. This is obvious in the case of Schiffer's classification, where a throne has a techno-function, a sociofunction and an ideofunction all at the same time. On the other hand, all of a thing's functions might fall into only one of these categories. For instance, jewellery normally has only sociofunctions, tools like screwdrivers normally have only technofunctions, and symbols like the Christian cross normally have only ideofunctions. It is also possible for a thing to have several functions in any or all of these categories simultaneously. A carpenter's hammer has two technofunctions: you pound nails in with one side of it and pull them out with the other. An engagement ring usually has two sociofunctions: manifesting the economic status of the groom and manifesting the social status of the wearer as a woman engaged to be married. In short, a thing can have any number of functions in any combination of the types Schiffer distinguishes. But since any one of Schiffer's types of function may be either a system function or a proper function, it is also the case that a thing may have any number and any combination of functions in this cross-classification as well.

A second general point is that this multiplicity of functions is dynamic in the sense that things are constantly losing or acquiring functions. It is particularly important to understand this process with regard to proper and system functions, because it is a different process in each case. Individual existing things acquire or lose *system* functions by being brought into or displaced from the relevant system contexts. A pair of spoons removed from the kitchen, used in a folk music band, and kept henceforth among the band's equipment, has acquired a musical system technofunction. If the irate cook seeks them out and brings them back to the kitchen, they lose that system technofunction.[9] *Proper* functions are acquired or lost not by individual existing things but by lineages of things. The key question to ask here is: Is this *sort* of thing now being reproduced because previous things of that sort successfully performed the function in question? If the answer is 'yes', then this function is a proper function, regardless of what the original proper function of the thing may have been (or may still be, since it may be retained alongside the new proper function). Take pipecleaners, for instance. Originally reproduced for the cleaning of tobacco pipes, they were later adopted by craft hobbyists for making stick figures and animal shapes. You can now buy them in craft stores in a whole range of colours for this purpose. It is reasonable to believe that even if pipe smoking died out entirely, pipecleaners would continue to be made for the craft market. So they currently have two proper technofunctions, but might in the future lose the original one and retain the second. Similarly, the swastika as reproduced on clothing, jewellery, and so on, originally had the proper ideofunction of representing well-being. As adopted and reproduced in similar media in Nazi Germany, it acquired the proper ideofunction of symbolising anti-semitism. In this case the original proper ideofunction has been completely eclipsed, at least in Europe and the US.

This lability of material culture functions leads to an observation which at first might seem to threaten the integrity of the distinction between proper function and system function. In many cases a system function of an individual thing *becomes* a proper function of a lineage of things as they gradually come to be reproduced for that function. For example, the first use of the swastika by the Nazis had representing anti-semitism at best as a *system* ideofunction. But when it was found to fulfil this function successfully and was reproduced more and more widely in consequence, it clearly came to have this ideofunction as a *proper* function. This transition from system to proper function is typical of sociofunctions and ideofunctions, since styles of dress, jewellery, insignia, styles of home furnishing, and so on, when adopted by a few influential individuals tend to spread through the whole social group. But this transition from system to proper function occurs with technofunctions, too. For example, the pipecleaners mentioned above when first used for craft projects had this function only as a system technofunction; that is, it was a purpose for which they were co-opted rather than one for which they had been made. But since they are now made specifically for the craft market to some extent, this system technofunction has accomplished the transition to a proper technofunction. Indeed, the first use of an exemplar of a given type of thing for any function must be a system function by definition. The function in question is established as a proper function only on the basis of successful performance and consequent reproduction of more of that type of thing for that purpose. And this holds even for things which are explicitly invented, designed and manufactured for a specific function. Suppose you invent a new kind of vegetable peeler, for instance. If the prototype you produce works as you hoped it would, it has a system technofunction of removing peels from vegetables. If it works well enough that you produce more of them, these 'descendants' of the prototype now have that technofunction as a proper function.

But if every proper function starts off as a system function you might wonder whether system functions really are a distinct phenomenon. Might it not be better to regard them simply as nascent proper functions? In that case, they would not be a distinct type of function, but merely the first, transient phase in the establishment of a proper function with exactly the same content. This is a reasonable objection. And the observation that proper functions inevitably are born out of pre-existing system functions of things is important. However, there is an equally important countervailing observation which will show that this objection is ultimately not viable.

While it is true that many system functions eventually metamorphose into proper functions, it is equally true that many of them do not. We have already seen some examples. People regularly stand on chairs to reach high shelves, co-opt spoons as rhythm instruments, and co-opt old tyres to make into swings. But none of these items is reproduced for these purposes, and it is unlikely they ever would be. If we stopped making chairs for their proper function, we would find something else to stand on to reach high shelves rather than continuing to make chairs for this purpose alone. Indeed, in this case there already exist artefacts like step stools and step ladders which have this function as a proper function, and which would no doubt proliferate in the absence of chairs. Cases in which a thing is permanently available and frequently used for a system function, but is never reproduced for that function, are cases of *ongoing system functions*.

This phenomenon is exceedingly common in material culture, and occurs in a number of variations. There are some ongoing system functions which correspond to widespread practices in the culture, and may be termed standardised ongoing system functions. In Western culture, everybody stands on chairs from time to time, and most cooks open cocoa tins with the handles of spoons and remove the skins from garlic cloves by hitting them sharply with the flat of a knife. On the other hand, many ongoing system functions are highly idiosyncratic. Here are a few from my own kitchen. An antique doorstop is the bookend for the cookbooks; clothes-pins hold half-used bags of potato chips and dry catfood shut; in a double co-optation, the radio cord has been induced to function as an antenna by fastening a loop of it up to the handle of an overhanging cabinet with a twist-tie;[10] several more twist-ties litter the floor – they are favoured cat toys;[11] an antique canning jar holds wooden spoons and wire whisks. I could go on, but instead I will just recommend that you check your own home or office for more examples of such co-optations of common items for ongoing system functions.

Some ongoing system functions are prompted by the non-existence of any type of thing having the requisite function as a proper function. There is no special utensil for opening cocoa tins, for example, so the co-optation of a spoon handle is practically forced. But it is more often the case that items with the requisite proper function do exist, and the co-optation is prompted instead by local unavailability or a disinclination to do what would be necessary to make the thing available. Why buy a step stool when you have sturdy chairs all over the house, for instance? Or even supposing you have a step stool, why bother fetching it from another room when you have a sturdy chair in this one? In short, co-optation as a pattern of behaviour and the ongoing system functions it engenders persist even in the face of directly competing items with the relevant proper functions.[12]

One important feature of these examples is that they show clearly that not all system functions are on their way to becoming proper functions. It is not only possible but common for a system function to persist indefinitely. Moreover, we can now understand that system function is in one sense the more fundamental type, because unless you have a successful system functional thing to begin with, the process of establishing a lineage of proper functional things cannot get off the ground. On the other hand, once a proper function has been established, it can persist in the face of repeated or frequent co-optation of an item for other purposes. No matter how many people stand on how many chairs, the proper function of those chairs remains the support of *seated* humans. So system function and proper function are in principle distinct and independent forms of function in material culture.

An equally important feature of the contrast between system function and proper function which can be glimpsed from the point we have now reached is that proper function emphasises the *stability* of function over time and across groups of things; whereas system function emphasises its *lability* – the tendency of functions to change and fluctuate over time as one function replaces another, additional functions are layered over an original one, or things are transiently co-opted for different system functions. In particular, the concept of system function is central to any analysis of change of function, because a proper function can only be acquired or changed on the basis of an already existing system function, as we noted above.

BETH PRESTON

Implications for archaeology

Since the distinction between proper function and system function is a philosophical one in the first instance, the archaeologist may well ask what importance it has for the theory and practice of archaeology. In this section I will first make some general points, and then discuss its specific application to the concerns of some working archaeologists.

This essay began with a rehearsal of the reasons for the problematic status of function in archaeological practice. The chief difficulty mentioned, you will remember, was the many–many relationship between form and function. Specifically, since the archaeologist often has only the material form of the artefact to work from, narrowing down the possibilities for a determination of the function is a dicey business at best. Considerations which are of aid in this task include the associational context in which the artefact is found at the site, analysis of use wear patterns on the artefact itself, and clues provided by the known functions of similar artefacts in contemporary cultures. It is, of course, understood that any of these sources of evidence may be misleading. The object may have been deposited in the association context by accident rather than because of some inherent connection with the other objects found there. Similarly, accidental abrasion or damage may be mistaken for use wear, or apparent correspondence with the function of current use objects may be merely apparent. But the recognition of the distinction between proper function and system function adds a new and uncomfortable wrinkle to these difficulties.

Clearly it is the proper function of unearthed artefacts which is the primary object of the archaeologist's inquiry. But if items of material culture often have system functions in addition to their proper functions, and if proper functions can and do change over time by going through a system functional phase of gradual establishment, then the erstwhile evidence for the proper function must be recognised as possibly equivocal or misleading for this reason as well. The association context may be misleading because it may reflect a systematic use of the object for something other than its proper function. For example, spoons found in conjunction with the remains of a guitar and a drum set might mislead you as to the proper function of spoons in US culture. This misleading impression might even be reinforced by a use wear analysis indicating they had been struck repeatedly against each other. And if spoons were not in use in any contemporary culture, or were in use there exclusively as rhythm instruments in bands, there might not be any countervailing evidence to correct the mistaken impression gathered from the first two sources.

The obvious objection to this example is that since spoons are both widespread in US culture and usually made of durable materials, the musical association context and wear pattern would quickly be identified as anomalous in the face of the much more prevalent culinary association contexts and use wear patterns. This is exactly the right objection to make. But it merely serves to highlight the moral of the story, which is that isolated association contexts or use wear patterns are always potentially misleading. Good evidence for a thing's proper function thus requires careful attention to the patterns indicating typical contexts and wear. And this is exactly what we should expect, since proper functions are established for lineages rather than individual objects. But with items less common or less durable than spoons, the archaeologist might well find herself working with only isolated finds. And in such cases it is of course impossible to know for sure whether you are dealing with an anomalous case or a typical one.

So the use of artefacts for functions other than their proper ones is another important factor responsible for the difficulties in deciphering proper function. It is not always sheer accidental deposition which accounts for anomalous association contexts, or accidental abrasion which accounts for anomalous wear. So archaeological analysis may find it useful to take system function into account as an explanatory resource. Specifically, a worked out theory of system function in material culture (which admittedly I have only begun here) would provide a useful technical terminology and conceptual framework for describing situations where the associations or condition of the object in question do not seem accidental, but do not reflect a plausible proper function either.

But this also raises the possibility of taking system functions as one of the subjects of archaeological research alongside proper function. It is surely an important fact about US musical culture (parts of it, anyway) that items with non-musical proper functions are routinely pressed into service as musical instruments. Besides the spoons I have used as an ongoing example in this paper, a list of such co-optations would include the jugband's eponymous jug which functions as a wind instrument; the old fashioned corrugated washboard, also used as a rhythm instrument, and played with a fork, a nail, or sewing thimbles worn on the fingers; and the musical saw, which is a carpenter's saw played with a bow. (In case you are wondering what the latter sounds like, it produces unearthly tones, somewhat reminiscent of the theremin.) There is also the tradition of slide guitar playing, in which the flat of a knife or a glass bottleneck was originally used to slide along the strings over the fretboard. (This not only changes the quality of the sound produced in aesthetically interesting ways, but also turns the guitar into a fretless instrument, thus making possible the production of microtones, among other things.) Nowadays you can buy specially made cylinders of glass or steel for this purpose. Here we have cultural phenomena and cultural processes (e.g., the transition from system functional co-optations to artefacts with that same function as a proper function) which certainly call for investigation by the anthropologist or archaeologist studying modern material culture. And although it would be even more difficult than deciphering proper function, there is no reason why similar studies should not be conducted with regard to past material cultures as well. Here again, the distinction between proper function and system function is central to a theoretical framework for such research projects.

One research project which has already made a contribution in this regard is the Reuse Project reported by Schiffer *et al.* (1981). It will give us an opportunity to explore in a specific instance some implications of the philosophical distinction between proper and system function. The Reuse Project focused on understanding two kinds of reuse. First, there is reuse in the form of second-hand furniture and appliances, usually acquired from more affluent friends and relatives, or at yard sales, flea markets, and so on. Second, there is reuse in the form of collecting for purposes of preservation and display. These items are also usually acquired at yard sales, flea markets, swap meets, antique stores, and the like. Schiffer *et al.* report that despite the popular perception of US culture as wasteful and consumerish, there is in fact an enormous amount of reuse of these types going on. More importantly for our purposes, though, they put forward a provisional classification of reuse processes in general.

> *Recycling* … occurs when a used item is remanufactured into a new item. … For example, after cutting and filing, a leaf from an automobile spring becomes a machete. *Secondary use* takes place when an unmodified item is employed in a different activity. … A common example is the use of a peanut butter jar for storing nuts and bolts. Recycling and secondary use may or may not involve a change in the user. *Lateral cycling* occurs when an object is transferred, without change in form or use, from one user to another. … For example, a sofa is sold to a new owner who uses it as a sofa. *Conservatory processes* or collecting behaviour bring about a change in the use (but not the form) of an object such that preservation is intended. … (In effect, it is a specialised variety of secondary use.) American individuals as well as public and private institutions collect everything from Mickey Mouse memorabilia to light bulbs.
>
> (Schiffer *et al.* 1981: 68)

There are three distinct categories of reuse here (conservation being only a special case of secondary use), and clearly one of the most important factors marking off one from another is the fate of the function of the reused item. In summary, *recycling* is where both the form and the function are new; *secondary use* is where only the function (but not the form) is new; and *lateral cycling* is when neither the form nor the function is new, but the item changes hands.[13] The Reuse Project studied only lateral cycling and one special kind of secondary use (collecting). This clearly suggests that further work on reuse might profitably concentrate on recycling and secondary use.[14] And since secondary use is paradigmatically a matter of system function – the reuse of something for a function other than its proper one – this suggestion echoes the more general one I made above, that system function is a neglected but significant subject of research for students of material culture.

But not only is secondary use paradigmatically a matter of system function; lateral cycling is paradigmatically a matter of proper function. This is clearest in the examples given. In the case of secondary use, the peanut butter jar now functioning as a storage container for nuts and bolts is performing a system function; in the case of lateral cycling, both the original and the new user use the sofa as a sofa, and thus manifestly for its proper function. So it seems that the reuse classification scheme implicitly recognises the distinction between system function and proper function, and classifies reuse strategies straightforwardly according to it. However, if we bring our previous discussion of system and proper functions to bear on this classification scheme, some hidden complexities will be revealed.

Rather than accepting the implicit picture of a simple alignment between types of function and types of reuse, then, we will ask about each type of reuse whether and how it might involve each type of function. Let us start with the definition of secondary use as the use of an unmodified object for a new function. Clearly this new function can be, and usually is, a system function, as the peanut butter jar example illustrates. But could this new function be a proper function? In principle, yes; providing 'new' is understood as a function not hitherto performed by this particular object. For things can have proper functions which they have never yet performed, and indeed which they may have been hitherto incapable of performing. And in fact there are some instances of things with more than one proper function, where one of these is a planned secondary use, as it were. For example, in any airport gift shop in the US you can buy souvenir bells imprinted with the name of the local state or city. These have the usual proper technofunction of all bells, but are also specifically intended for sale to bell collectors, who often try to complete sets of all fifty states, for instance. (Usually by insisting their friends and relatives bring back bells from wherever they go, as I happen to know because my sister is just such a collector of bells.) In some even more compelling cases of planned reuse, the idea is that when the thing is no longer usable for one proper function it will become usable for another. For example, the Vermont Country Store (a well-known US mail order company) sells maple syrup in tins, including one in the shape of a log cabin which is advertised as convertible into a child's bank when the syrup is gone. In this case the second proper function (repository for coins) cannot be performed until the first one (containing syrup) has been exhausted.

So contrary to our initial impression, there are some instances of secondary uses which are proper functions. These do seem to be less prevalent than the paradigm cases involving system functions. Nevertheless, what we have discovered is that the category of secondary use, rather than being aligned neatly with only one type of function, has two sub-categories, corresponding to the two types of function. Is this also true of the category of lateral cycling, which at first blush seemed to involve only proper functions? The definition of this category is that a thing is transferred to another user, but undergoes no change in function. The paradigm cases are ones where something is sold or given to someone else for continued use in accordance with its proper function. But there are also cases of lateral cycling where the continuity of use is a matter of a system function. For example, a spoon player might sell, give or bequeath a pair of spoons to another spoon player. So here too we have generated two sub-categories by application of the distinction between system function and proper function. As a result, we have a more complex reuse classification scheme to work with.

Even more sub-categories can be generated by considering different types of system function or proper function. For instance, we noted in the previous section that many system functions are transient rather than involving permanent assignment of an object to a new function. The peanut butter jar now holding nuts and bolts is – one would hope, at least, for reasons of hygiene – permanently reassigned. But a drinking glass might well be transiently reused as a vase for cut flowers or as a measuring cup when cooking, and then returned to its proper functional primary use in the interim. So the secondary use category now has some internal structure. First it is divided into system functional secondary use and proper functional secondary use; and then system functional secondary use is in turn divided into transient system functional uses on the one hand and permanent ones on the other. More such sub-categories could no doubt be distinguished, but I will stop here since I think I have demonstrated the general principle that the distinction between proper function and system function can be used to generate refinements to Schiffer *et al.*'s original classificatory scheme.

In addition to helping develop the internal structure of reuse categories, the distinction between proper and system functions can also be of use in understanding the external relationship between categories. The important point to be made here is that more than one of these categories may apply simultaneously to many reused objects. This is a direct implication of the discussion in the previous section, which indicated that there is normally no such thing as *the* function of an object. If things have multiple functions simultaneously, corresponding multiple reuse categories may apply simultaneously. We have already mentioned one example of this – the lateral cycling of objects for continued system functional use, e.g. the gift of a pair of spoons from one player to another. Here an event of secondary use (co-opting the spoons for musical purposes) is followed by an event of lateral cycling (transferring the spoons from one user to another). So in the end the spoons are being used by a new user for what was already a secondary use. Another important group of cases arises from the fact that things often have system functions – even multiple system functions – in addition to their proper functions. And especially when these system functions are transient, ongoing co-optations, they do not interfere with the proper uses of the thing at all. For example, standing on a chair, even if done regularly, does not give it new proper functions or change any of its existing ones; nor does it normally hinder the chair in the performance of any of its proper functions, except very briefly. This means that something can undergo no change of use with regard to its proper functions, while at the same time acquiring new system functional uses. (Alternatively, it might undergo no change of use with regard to a system function it *already* has, while at the same time acquiring new system functional uses.) And this in turn means that lateral cycling can occur in conjunction with secondary use. For example, the sofa which is laterally cycled to a new user may continue to be used for its proper technofunction by day, while now also serving its new user as a bed by night. In other words, the requirement of lateral cycling that there be no change of use after transfer can be satisfied with regard to one function, while at the same time satisfying the conflicting requirement of secondary use that there be such a change of use with regard to some other function. The general point we have uncovered here is that reuse categories are not mutually exclusive in their application to any particular case of reuse. And this is just what we would expect, based on a prior understanding of system function and proper function as themselves not mutually exclusive in their application to individual items of material culture.

The application of the distinction between system function and proper function to Schiffer *et al.*'s reuse classification scheme shows that this distinction can be employed to generate a more complex and refined understanding of concrete phenomena of interest to archaeologists and other students of material culture. But it can also be put to good use at the level of more abstract theoretical endeavours. I will briefly describe one such case in order to round out the discussion.

Ian Hodder criticises functionalist currents in archaeology for failing to theorise adequately the relationship between individuals and social structures, and for failing in particular to theorise the causes of social change, especially as they relate to the activities of individuals.

> The functional view gives little emphasis to individual creativity and intentionality. Individual human beings become little more than the means to achieve the needs of society. The social system is organised into subsystems and roles which people fill. The roles and social categories function in relation to each other to allow the efficient equilibrium of the whole system. In fact, however, individuals are not simply instruments in some orchestrated game. ... Adequate explanations of social systems and social change must involve the individual's assessments and aims. This is not a question of identifying individuals ... but of introducing the individual into social theory.
>
> (Hodder 1992: 98–99)

Hodder advances essentially the same criticisms against structuralism (1992: 105–106). The general problem in both cases is that individuals are not just passive placeholders, as functionalism and structuralism often seem to assume. Individuals do indeed fill prescribed roles, but they do so rebelliously, sloppily, imaginatively, reflectively, and so on. And on Hodder's view, this has not been taken into account in the right sort of way in recent social theory, and in its application to archaeology.

In social philosophy, similar concerns have surfaced in some quarters. For example, Jürgen Habermas criticises Michel Foucault (whose structuralist affiliations are well known) in a similar vein.

> In place of socialisation as individuating (which remains unconceptualised), he [Foucault] puts the concept of a fragmenting empowerment, a concept that is not up to the ambiguous phenomena of modernity. From his perspective, socialised individuals can only be perceived as exemplars, as standardised products of some discourse formation – as individual copies that are mechanically punched out.
>
> (Habermas 1987: 293)

Now this is not really fair to Foucault, since it was precisely at this period (the last few years of his life, as it turned out) that he was making his most explicit attempts to theorise the socialised individual as in part the result of processes of self-creation, and the role of the individual vis-à-vis the social order as inherently iconoclastic and revolutionary. Foucault (1982: 208) states that although his work has often been characterised as a theory of power relations, his real interest has always been a theory of how human beings are turned into subjects. Moreover, he says that although his early work centred around the ways in which social institutions (which for Foucault are constituted mainly by systematic relations or configurations of power) turn human beings into subjects of various prespecified sorts by the application of external control and pressure, his most recent work deals with the ways human beings turn *themselves* into subjects; for example, by taking advantage of socially instituted opportunities for becoming reflective about their sexuality. Similarly, Foucault (1982: 220–222) points out that his conception of power is not a conception of it as violent oppression, but rather as governmental. Thus power is exercised in principle only with regard to individuals who are free – that is, who are faced with an array of alternative possible courses of action – and who are thus capable of resisting or circumventing attempts to govern their behaviour. In short, individual creativity and intransigence are actually built into Foucault's understanding of how power operates, even though in other respects his characterisation of the institutions within which this power is exercised does often make them seem like vast machines which process individuals willy-nilly. All of this promises well for a response to Hodder's concerns. But Foucault himself did not live to continue his project. And in any case, it is a vast project, the success of which is by no means assured, and the details of which can by no means be read straight off the foundations he proposed. So I join Hodder in his appeal for renewed efforts to understand the role of the individual in social institutions.

But where to begin? What sort of research projects would shed new light on this large and difficult problem? One possibility is to start with artefacts. The human world is pervasively artefactual. And as Schiffer (1992: 12–13) remarks, social roles and cultural distinctions are universally mediated by artefacts. Foucault concurs (1982: 217–219). He distinguishes three aspects of human activity: objective capacities, which concern our dealings with objects; power relations, which concern our active governing of, or being governed by, the actions of other humans; and communicative relationships, which concern the linguistic transmission of meaning and information. But while conceptually distinguishable, these aspects are never operationally distinct.

> It is a question of three types of relationships which in fact always overlap one another, support one another reciprocally, and use each other mutually as means to an end. The application of objective capacities in their most elementary forms implies relationships of communication (whether in the form of previously acquired information or of shared work); it is tied also to power relations (whether they consist of obligatory tasks, of gestures imposed by tradition or apprenticeship, of subdivisions and the more or less obligatory distribution of labour).
>
> (Foucault 1982: 218)

If power relations regularly pass through objective capacities, then the relationship between the individual and the social order is articulated already in our dealings with material culture. And I want to suggest that the distinction between system function and proper function is an important analytical tool for understanding that articulation. Moreover, this distinction supports Foucault's conception of power as inherently involving a permanent possibility of resistance on the part of the individuals over whom it is exercised, which in turn sheds some light on the role of the individual in causing social change. I will take up these two topics in order.

Social structures are defined in large part by the prescribed material culture they involve. More specifically, it is the *proper* functions of the objects making up the material culture which define these structures at the most basic level. For example, eating behaviour is organised systematically with regard to the proper functions of the tableware available. Take cutlery in Western culture. Forks, spoons and knives each have a specific set of eating functions which are proper to them, and these functions govern the behaviour we call table manners. A knife is for cutting up large pieces of food on the plate, and for helping to slide food (e.g., peas) from the plate onto the fork. But it is not for lifting food to the mouth, and it is bad manners to use it that way. Similarly, a soup spoon is specifically for eating soup, and it is bad form to eat your dessert with it, let alone your peas or your fish. Now there is quite a bit of leeway here with regard to the details. For example, in the US the fork is properly held in the right hand when raising food to the mouth; whereas in Europe it is held in the left hand for this purpose. Similarly, elaborate sets of cutlery may have distinct salad, dinner and dessert forks, thus generating more elaborate distinctions in appropriate behaviour at table; whereas less elaborate sets of cutlery get by with a single type of fork to be used for all of these purposes, and appropriate fork use is correspondingly less nuanced. Nevertheless, the most basic tenets of appropriate behaviour at table are keyed to the proper functions of the tableware. This should not be surprising, for proper function is normative, as we noted above. And that means not only in the sense that a description of the proper function expresses what a thing is supposed to be able to do, but also in the sense that this is what you are *supposed to do with* that thing. In this latter sense, if you use a tableknife to lift food to your mouth (or worse yet, as a screwdriver), then you are *mis*using it. Misuse here is the correlate on the user's side of malfunction on the side of the artefact.

So one important way in which systems of social order are imposed on individuals is through the generalised insistence on behaving towards items of material culture in accordance with their proper functions. Since these proper functions are stable historically and across groups of similar items, this generates norms of behaviour which persist from generation to generation and across large segments of the population. In Foucault's terminology, the proper functions of items of material culture mediate the government of the actions of individuals by others, and thus mediate the establishment, consolidation and preservation of the power relationships which constitute the social system.

System function, on the other hand, is not normative. It is a matter of what capacities and dispositions a thing has as a matter of fact. Consequently, it is a matter of what you *can* do with it, as opposed to what you are *supposed* to do with it. As we noted in the first section, this means that the concept of system function accommodates the analysis of individual performances of things – even unique or idiosyncratic performances. All that is required is a system context and a thing with a functional role in that context, regardless of whether that thing or anything remotely like it has ever performed that role before. On the user's side, this means that system function accommodates the analysis of the actions of individuals, who may use the material culture at their disposal in very creative or idiosyncratic ways. This is of course especially true in the case of idiosyncratic ongoing system functions, like my using the cord of my radio as an antenna. But even standardised ongoing system functions, like the widespread practice of standing on chairs, represents the activity of individuals transiently and opportunistically reassigning things to functions other than their proper ones. Indeed, system functions of artefacts typically involve a deliberate disregard of the norms of proper usage by individuals. Using spoons as musical instruments or a tableknife as a screwdriver flouts the norm that these artefacts are properly for use with food, as well as the more specific norms regulating that use in each case.

As we noted at the end of the last section, the establishment of a proper function always begins with a system function – a successful performance of a thing in a functional role. Such performances are transmuted into proper functions if that type of thing comes to be reproduced for the sake of the performance in question. The example we discussed earlier was that of pipecleaners, which have come to have proper functions in the activities of crafts hobbyists in addition to their original proper function. Here we can glimpse another aspect of the interaction of the individual with the social order, namely, the creation of social order – here in the form of a proper function and its associated socially sanctioned behaviour – by the actions of individuals in using and reproducing material culture.

Because proper function is a normative group-centred concept, it is linked to the established social order in so far as it operates through material culture. System function, on the other hand, is a non-normative, individual-centred conception of function, and therefore is linked to the activity of individual agents, and in particular to their innovative activity *vis-à vis* material culture. Thus the study of system functions, proper functions, and their interrelationships in material culture has the potential to shed considerable light on the larger question of the relationship between the individual and the social order. One way it does this is by offering a concrete exemplification of how the activities of individuals result in the creation of social order. And perhaps even more importantly, it exhibits the ubiquity of individual activity which either nonchalantly disregards the reigning order, or defies it outright.

This brings us to the second proposal I want to make here – that the distinction between proper function and system function provides a way of understanding and usefully elaborating Foucault's rather abstract claim that the exercise of power necessarily carries with it the permanent possibility of resistance to that exercise. This is Foucault's way of providing for the permanent possibility – indeed, the inevitability – of social change. In other words, if Foucault is right about this, no social system is ever truly static. Furthermore, the source of change he proposes is internal to the system itself, and not an external force impinging on a system in static equilibrium. And the resistance Foucault is talking about is explicitly characterised by him as the resistance of individuals to local exercises of power (Foucault 1982: 211). Thus for Foucault the individual is inherently an instigator of social change in virtue of being inherently a possible locus of resistance to the established order. But two questions immediately spring to mind here. First, is this conception of power really plausible? And second, how does this local resistance result in social change?

The distinction between system function and proper function establishes the plausibility of Foucault's conception of power at a very basic and concrete level. Proper function, as we discovered, is how established power relationships are mediated through material culture. But any item of material culture with a proper function has a whole range of capacities and dispositions. First, unless it is malfunctional, it has whatever capacities and dispositions are required to subserve the proper function. For example, a tableknife has to be thin, rigid, and long enough to provide some leverage. In addition to these it has other capacities and dispositions not required for its proper function. Stainless steel tableknives are heavy. This is not required for their proper functions, since plastic tableknives, which are comparatively speaking very light, also have those proper functions. Similarly, spoons have acoustic dispositions which have no relevance to any of their proper functions. This range of capacities and dispositions offers a range of opportunities for individuals to use things in ways which do not accord with their proper functions. Either set of capacities and dispositions may be co-opted for other purposes in this way. For example, it is because a tableknife is thin, rigid, and long enough to provide leverage that it makes a good system functional screwdriver. On the other hand, it is the heaviness of tableknives which makes them effective as paperweights, and the acoustic properties of spoons which makes them effective as musical instruments. In short, a thing with a proper function is an aggregation of opportunities to use it for something else. Thus the exercise of power through material culture does carry with it the possibility of resistance in the form of opportunities for system functional uses of proper functional items.

But how does this small-scale resistance and inventiveness at the level of commonplace items of material culture constitute, or result in, changes in the social system? In many cases, of course, it does not result in any significant change. The perturbations to the social order from the practice of standing on chairs, or from someone like myself using my radio cord as an antenna, are negligible. In such cases, although an item from one system has been temporarily or permanently reassigned to another system, this reassignment, however inventive it may be in isolation, has no significant effect on the new system context. If all system functional uses of things were like this, then system function would not be of much help in the explanation of social change. But sometimes system functional uses of things do result in significant changes. Here is an example. Les Paul was not the first person to electrify a guitar, but he was one of the first, and he is acknowledged as one of the inventors of the solid body electric. Here is how he began.

> Les first amplified a guitar when he was 12, working to entertain the customers at a local hamburger stand who had complained that they couldn't hear him. So he jabbed a record player pickup into his acoustic guitar, slid a telephone mouthpiece under the strings, and wired up both to his parents' radio which doubled as an amplifier.
>
> (Bacon and Day 1992: 58)

A nicer concatenation of system functional co-optations of proper functional items can hardly be imagined. Paul went on to build a prototype solid body electric guitar, which he took to the Gibson guitar company, hoping to get them to produce and market it. This they at last reluctantly agreed to do, probably in part because they had learned that Leo Fender had formed a company to produce a solid body electric guitar he had just designed. Fender did bring out the Fender Broadcaster in 1950, and it was commercially successful. The Gibson Les Paul came out a couple of years later, and was equally successful. (A version is still made today, in fact.)

Now the solid body electric guitar is important, because without it rock music as we know it would not have been possible. And rock music is important for our present purposes because it does involve a number of significant changes in previously existing cultural systems. I will focus here on change in the musical aesthetic system. The original impetus for electrifying guitars was to make them louder, as the passage above about Les Paul indicates. In this respect, electrification merely provides a better way of amplifying sound than the hollow bodies of acoustic guitars do. But the substitution of one amplifying device for another was not without consequences. An electrically amplified guitar – especially one with a solid body – sounds distinctly different from an acoustic guitar. Even more importantly, the electrification makes possible a whole range of sounds acoustic guitars cannot produce at all, like distortion and feedback. In addition, electrification has spawned a collection of electrical devices which can be attached between the guitar and the amplifier (e.g., the 'wah-wah' pedal), and which allow the player to alter the sound in still further ways. All of these opportunities for producing new sounds with the guitar have been thoroughly exploited in rock music and related genres. The result is that much of the music in our culture now sounds quite different than it did fifty years ago. Moreover, standard playing techniques for the guitar have undergone corresponding significant alterations in this same time period. And these large-scale changes are in part the remote result of Les Paul's youthful experiment with some proper functional parts of a radio, a telephone and a record player.

Two general remarks may be made here with regard to the way this local act of resistance was eventually parlayed into widespread changes in musical culture. First, the changes are clearly not all due to Les Paul, or even to Les Paul and Leo Fender, but are the additive result of many individuals contributing innovations of various sorts over a long period of time. The guitar design team at Gibson had as much to do with why the Gibson Les Paul is the way it is as Les Paul did, for instance. Second, this case illustrates an important mechanism by which initially small changes are transmuted into bigger ones. Things which in one respect may be functional equivalents, like the different means of amplification employed by electric and acoustic guitars, are almost never equivalent in any other respect. Partly this is a matter of having different ranges of capacities and dispositions which subserve the allegedly equivalent function, and partly it is a matter of having different capacities and dispositions in excess of the ones which subserve the function. What this means is that although the functionally equivalent mechanisms do the same thing in one respect, in other respects they can and do do quite different things. So they offer quite different opportunities for co-optation for system functional uses. In addition, the differences sometimes require adjustments to be made in other areas of the system into which the mechanism is inserted. So an initial small change may set off a chain reaction which results in large changes to the system in the long run.[15]

In this application, the distinction between system function and proper function provides a way of conceptualising and investigating the relationship between the individual and the social order. This is an important theoretical problem for the philosopher and the archaeologist alike. So the distinction between system function and proper function promises to be theoretically illuminating, as well as productive in the context of specific research projects like Schiffer *et al.*'s study of reuse.

Conclusion

Recent philosophical research on function has resulted in a number of different conceptions of this phenomenon. Two of the most robust of these are Ruth Millikan's theory of proper function and Robert Cummins' conception of system function. I have argued that rather than being rival accounts of function, these are accounts of two distinct types of function, both of which are required for an understanding of function in material culture. Specifically, proper function is required for an understanding of function as a normative phenomenon – as a matter of what artefacts are supposed to do – while system function is required for an understanding of function as a matter of what artefacts do in fact do in the way of useful performance. That these two types of function are distinct and significant is amply demonstrated through examples drawn from modern material culture. But this distinction is not a 'merely' philosophical one. It can be employed to further the study of material culture in archaeology both at the level of studies of concrete cultural phenomena, such as Schiffer *et al.*'s Reuse Project, and at the level of more abstract concerns, such as Hodder's theoretically motivated call for more attention to the role of the individual in studies of social structure.

Acknowledgements

I owe significant improvements in the final version of this paper to suggestions from Paul Graves-Brown and Michael Schiffer. Any mistakes or infelicities which remain are nobody's fault but mine.

NOTES

1 There are other possible conceptual frameworks for studying material culture which do not advert to function at all. For example, Schiffer and Skibo (1997) present a theoretical framework for analysing artefact variability. They point out that in this explanatory context, the concept of function is a hindrance rather than a help, so they do not include it in their theoretical vocabulary. However, this does not abrogate the importance of function for other explanatory purposes.

2 See Preston (1998) for a more detailed philosophical account and defence of this theory of function.

3 Cummins does not consider cases of this latter sort, precisely because the current capacity does explain location. In other words, he accepts the ambiguity between existence and location inherent in the term 'there' as Wright uses it, and considers only cases where *neither* existence *nor* location can be explained in terms of current utility. In so doing, he misses an important aspect of functionality in material culture, as we shall see.

4 This is function *sensu* Radcliffe-Brown (1952). I owe this reference to Michael Schiffer.

5 Spoons are used as clappers in the indigenous folk music traditions of the US, central Europe and South Vietnam, according to the *New Grove Dictionary of Musical Instruments*. In the US they are usually played by street musicians or folk musicians. The technique, as I understand it, is to hold two spoons back to back in one hand, usually with a finger between the handles, and then strike them against some other part of the body, such as the knee or the opposite hand. A well-known contemporary exponent is Artis the Spoonman, whose most readily available recent work is probably the track 'Spoonman' from Soundgarden's 1994 recording, *Superunknown*. If this outstanding examplar of Seattle grunge rock is not in your music collection, you can probably borrow it from one of your undergraduate students. You can find Artis himself on the World Wide Web at www.olympus.net/personal/artis.

6 It should be noted that she did not propose it *in order to* deal with this problem, since she was not at first aware of the work of either Cummins or Wright. But she later contrasted her notion of proper function with both of their conceptions of function on precisely these grounds. See especially Chapter 1 of Millikan (1993).

7 Unfortunately this advocacy in Millikan (1989) is counteracted by an implicit rejection of system function in some of her more prominent work. See especially Chapter 2 in Millikan (1993), and the discussion of this inconsistency on Millikan's part in Preston (1998).

8 Schiffer notes that this classification was first proposed in Rathje and Schiffer (1982), who in turn were inspired by the related analysis in Binford (1962).

9 Alternatively, the system itself may come into or go out of existence. The spoons may be returned to the kitchen because the band disbands, for instance, but the effect is the same in terms of the loss of the system technofunction. Also note that the spoons retain their proper culinary technofunction throughout the process of gaining or losing the system technofunction.

10 Twist-ties are called different things in different places. They are short lengths of wire encased in paper or plastic, the proper function of which is to keep plastic bags closed. And in case anyone is worried about the practicality of the arrangement described, the cabinet in question is the one in which I keep my good china, so I rarely need to open it.

11 I now know of several other people whose cats are enthusiastic about twist-ties, but all of us seem to have discovered this independently.

12 This may be more the case with regard to the modern material culture of the industrial West than it is in other material cultures. A friend of mine who grew up in India once mentioned to me that the aspect of US culture she found most fascinating was the plethora of special-purpose gadgets available for the most trivial of daily tasks. Thus in other cultures where there are fewer things with proper functions, co-optation may be more often forced than chosen. This would not detract from the importance of the phenomenon, of course, but it might make it more visible to the observer.

13 A fourth category where the form is new but the function is not is logically possible. It would contain cases where alterations are made to the form of a thing in order to restore or enhance its function. This phenomenon is commonplace in the form of sharpening, mending, rebuilding and other kinds of repair which return something to a usable condition. This category would also include cases of customising; for example, when a garment is altered to fit a wearer. Schiffer (1987: 29) calls this fourth category *maintenance*, and explicitly distinguishes it from recycling, on the grounds that the change in form it involves is always minor and in the service of retaining the original function. In short, he does not consider maintenance as a form of reuse at all, but as an aspect of primary use. In one sense this seems right, since maintenance also includes washing, polishing, dusting, and so on – processes which do cause changes in form, especially when frequently repeated over long periods of time, but which intuitively seem to fall on the side of use rather than reuse. Unfortunately, Schiffer is not consistent in this judgement. On the very next page he says:

> Beverage containers are frequently *recycled*, but the modification is simply the addition of new contents. In such cases, the use does not change, and so other lines of evidence must be employed to infer that the process occurred.
>
> (Schiffer 1987: 30; the emphasis is mine)

The beverage containers were, one hopes, also washed before being refilled; but in any case, the process described is one of maintenance (use) not recycling (reuse) according to Schiffer's own definitions. On the other hand, I have questions about the classification of repair processes as use rather than reuse. In most cases repair is necessary, i.e., the alternative course of action is to throw the thing away and get a new one. But since alternatives to discard are precisely the sort of activities Schiffer characterises generally as reuse (1987: 27–28), repair would seem to fall more naturally under the heading of reuse rather than use. In short, while the reuse categories proposed are a brilliant start, more work is clearly needed on the articulation between use and reuse in particular.

14 This suggestion for future research is made explicitly by Schiffer (1976: 39).

15 Schiffer (1992: 77ff.) discusses this phenomenon in more detail.

References

Bacon, Tony and Paul Day 1992 *The Ultimate Guitar Book*. New York: Alfred A. Knopf.

Binford, Lewis R. 1989 *Debating Archaeology*. San Diego: Academic Press, Inc.

—— 1962 'Archaeology as anthropology'. *American Antiquity* 28: 217–225.

Chippindale, Christopher 1992 'Grammars of archaeological design: a generative and geometrical approach to the form of artifacts'. In Jean-Claude Gardin and Christopher Peebles (eds) *Representations in Archaeology* Indianapolis: Indiana University Press.

Cummins, Robert 1975 'Functional explanation'. *The Journal of Philosophy* 72: 741–764.

Foucault, Michel 1982 'The subject and power'. In Hubert L. Dreyfus and Paul Rabinow (eds) *Michel Foucault: Beyond Structuralism and Hermeneutics*. Chicago: University of Chicago Press.

Gould, Richard A. 1980 *Living Archaeology*. Cambridge, UK: Cambridge University Press.

Gould, Stephen Jay 1980 *The Panda's Thumb: More Reflections in Natural History*. New York: Norton.

Habermas, Jürgen 1987 *The Philosophical Discourse of Modernity: Twelve Lectures* (translated by Frederick Lawrence). Cambridge, MA: The MIT Press.

Hodder, Ian 1992 *Theory and Practice in Archaeology*. London and New York: Routledge.

—— 1983 *The Present Past: An Introduction to Anthropology for Archaeologists*. New York: Pica Press.

Millikan, Ruth Garrett 1993 *White Queen Psychology and Other Essays for Alice*. London and Cambridge, MA: The MIT Press.

—— 1989 'An ambiguity in the notion "Function"'. *Biology and Philosophy* 4: 176–181.

—— 1984 *Language, Thought, and Other Biological Categories*. London and Cambridge, MA: The MIT Press.

New Grove Dictionary of Musical Instruments ed. Stanley Sadie. London: MacMillan Press, Ltd., 1984.

Preston, Beth 1998 'Why is a wing like a spoon?: A pluralist theory of function'. 95:215–254 *The Journal of Philosophy*

Radcliffe-Brown, A.R. 1952 *Structure and Function in Primitive Society*. New York: The Free Press.

Rathje, William L. and Michael B. Schiffer 1982 *Archaeology*. New York: Harcourt Brace Jovanovich.

Salmon, Merrilee 1982 *Philosophy and Archaeology*. New York and London: Academic Press.

Schiffer, Michael B. 1995 *Behavioral Archaeology: First Principles*. Salt Lake City: University of Utah Press.

—— 1992 *Technological Perspectives on Behavioral Change*. Tucson and London: The University of Arizona Press.

—— 1987 *Formation Processes of the Archaeological Record*. Albuquerque: University of New Mexico Press.

—— 1976 *Behavioral Archaeology*. New York: Academic Press.

Schiffer, Michael B., Theodore E. Downing and Michael McCarthy 1981 'Waste not, want not: an ethnoarchaeological study of reuse in Tucson, Arizona'. In Richard A. Gould and Michael B. Schiffer (eds) *Modern Material Culture: The Archaeology of Us*. New York: Academic Press, Inc.

Schiffer, Michael B. and James M. Skibo 1997 'The explanation of artifact variability'. *American Antiquity* 62(1): 27–50.

Wright, Larry 1973 *Functions. Philosophical Review* 82: 139–168.

49

3

MAKING CULTURE AND
WEAVING THE WORLD

Tim Ingold

Artefacts and organisms

In his book, *Chance and Necessity* (1972), the distinguished biochemist Jacques
Monod sets out to determine the distinctiveness of living things by means of
a contrast with that other class of things – apparently also endowed with
properties of form and function – commonly known as artefacts. Monod
invites us to imagine ourselves as the intelligent inhabitants of another planet,
who are concerned to find out whether there is any evidence of artefact-
producing activity back on Earth. We plan to send a spacecraft to Earth,
equipped with a computer programmed to distinguish, on the basis of a range
of input data, between objects that are artefacts and objects that are not. How
should this program be written?

Perhaps the machine should be instructed to search for regularities of
form, such as the various kinds of symmetry or the rhythmic repetition of
structural elements. Since these are quite general properties of matter at the
molecular level, it would have to concentrate on the macroscopic features of
the objects it encountered. Even then, however, the things it could potentially
register as 'artefacts' might include the Giant's Causeway, a butterfly's wings,
almost every kind of sea-shell, the beehive, the head of a sunflower, and a host
of other objects that – with the possible exception of the hive – we would
not normally think of as artificial at all. On the other hand, the machine
would discount the crumpled linen of a bed from which you have just risen
after an uneasy night's sleep, and might even place the bed-making that you
do at home every morning in the same category of artefact production as the
bed-making that goes on in the furniture factory!

Maybe the problem arises because in programming our computer to attend
only to the formal, structural properties of objects we have ignored the most
salient feature of artefacts: that they have been designed for a purpose.
Suppose, then, that we make up for this deficiency by instructing the machine
to attend to the performance of things, that is to their capacity to function in
particular ways to which they might seem peculiarly adapted rather than
contingently apt (see Preston Chapter 2). A naturally occurring stone of suit-

able size and shape may, in the absence of anything better, be serviceable for hammering nails into wood, but the carpenter's hammer has been specifically designed for the job, and as such would qualify as an artefact whereas the stone would not. As Monod (1972: 20) points out, however, the property of functional design is not unique to artefacts but is also shared by all living things. Parallels in this regard between human engineering and organic adaptation are legion: the wings of planes and birds, the helical arrangement of fibres in rope and of muscles in fish, the combination of arch and suspension in bridge construction and in the skeleton of the brontosaurus.[1] Our computer, registering these parallels as equivalents, would totally fail to discriminate between artefacts and life-forms.

There is only one solution to the problem, Monod concludes. That is to instruct the computer to look not just at the finished objects, but at the processes wherein they come into being: their genesis and construction. It would then note at once that of objects endowed with form and function, there is one class for which these properties result from the application to their constituent materials of forces *exterior* to the objects themselves, and another class whose properties owe nothing to the action of external forces, and everything to 'morphogenetic' interactions that are *internal* to the objects in question. The first class, then, comprises artefacts, whereas the second comprises living organisms (Monod 1972: 21). The former are 'made' by some agency that lies outside them, the latter just 'grow', entirely of their own accord.

Now let us suppose that we have successfully programmed our computer to attend to formal regularity, functional performance and morphogenesis. Amidst much popular anticipation and excitement, the craft with the computer on board is about to be despatched to Earth. Before taking up the story of what it finds there, let me pause to consider precisely what is implied about artefacts by their characterisation as things that are made rather than things that grow.

Making and growing

First of all, a distinction is assumed between form and substance, that is between the design specifications of the object and the raw materials of which it is composed. In the case of living things, it is supposed that the information specifying the design of an organism is carried in the materials of heredity, the genes, and thus that every new life-cycle is inaugurated with the injection of this specification into a physical medium. But with artefacts, this relation between form and substance is inverted. Form is applied from without, rather than unfurled from within. The very distinction between a within and a without of things, however, implies the existence of a *surface*, where solid substance meets the space of action of those forces that impinge upon it. Thus the world of substance – of brute matter – must present itself to the maker of artefacts as a surface to be transformed.

51

In commonsense, practical terms, this is not too hard to imagine. Many of our most familiar artefacts are (or were, before the days of synthetic materials) made of more or less solid stuff such as stone, metal, wood or clay. The very usefulness of these objects depends on their being relatively resistant to deformation. We ourselves, however, inhabit a gaseous medium – air – which, offering no such resistance, not only allows complete freedom of movement, but also transmits both light and sound. Quite apart from the obvious fact that we need air to breathe, and thus simply to stay alive, the possibilities of movement and perception (visual and aural) that air affords are crucial for any artefact-producing activity. There is, then, a pretty clear distinction between the gaseous medium that surrounds us and the solid objects that clutter our environment; moreover the patterns of reflected light off the surfaces of these objects enable us to see them for what they are (Gibson 1979: 16–22).

These practical considerations, however, all too easily become confused in our thinking with speculations of a more metaphysical kind. To show why this is so, let me return to the case of the beehive whose status as an artefact – as I hinted at above – is somewhat equivocal. Surely, hives don't grow. In so far as it results from the application of exterior force to raw material, the hive would appear to be as much 'bee-made' as the human house is 'man-made'. Or is it? Musing on this question, Karl Marx famously came to the conclusion that 'what from the very first distinguishes the most incompetent architect from the best of bees, is that the architect has built a cell in his head before he constructs it in wax'. In other words, the criterion by which the house is truly artificial – and by comparison the beehive only figuratively so – is that it issues from a representation or 'mental model', which has been fashioned in the imagination of the practitioner prior to its execution in the material. We may assume that bees, by contrast, lack the powers of imagination, and have no more conception of their hives than they do of their own bodies, both of which are formed under genetic control (Ingold 1983, cf. Marx 1930: 169–170)

Here, the exteriority of the forces that shape artefacts is understood in quite another sense, in terms not of the physical separation of gaseous medium and solid substance but of the *meta*physical separation of mind and nature (see Williams and Costall, Chapter 5). Unlike the forms of animals and plants, established through the evolutionary mechanism of natural selection and installed genetically at the heart of the organisms themselves (in the nucleus of every cell), the forms of artefacts are supposed to have their source within the human mind, as preconceived, intellectual solutions to particular design problems. And whereas organic growth is envisaged as a process that goes on *within* nature, and that serves to reveal its inbuilt architecture, in the making of artefacts the mind is understood to place its ideal forms upon nature. If making thus means the imposition of conceptual form on inert matter, then the surface of the artefact comes to represent much more than an interface between solid substance and gaseous medium; rather it becomes the very surface of the material world of nature as it confronts the creative human mind.

This is precisely the kind of view that lies at the back of the minds of anthropologists and archaeologists when they speak of artefacts as items of so-called 'material culture'. The last thing they mean to suggest, in resorting to this phrase, is that in the manufactured object the domains of culture and materiality somehow overlap or intermingle. For nothing about their substantive composition *per se* qualifies artefacts for inclusion within culture. The materials from which they are made – wood, stone, clay or whatever – are in any case generally available in nature. Even with objects manufactured from synthetic materials for which no naturally occurring counterparts exist, their status as items of material culture is in no way conditional upon their 'unnatural' composition. A child's toy made of plastic is no more cultural, on that account, than its wooden equivalent. It is the form of the artefact, not its substance, that is attributed to culture. This is why, in the extensive archaeological and anthropological literature on material culture, so little attention is paid to actual materials and their properties. The emphasis is almost entirely on issues of meaning and form – that is, on culture as *opposed* to materiality. Understood as a realm of discourse, meaning and value inhabiting the collective consciousness, culture is conceived to hover over the material world but not to permeate it. In this view, in short, culture and materials *do not mix*; rather, culture wraps itself around the universe of material things, shaping and transforming their outward surfaces without ever penetrating their interiority. Thus the particular surface of every artefact participates in the impenetrable surface of materiality itself as it is enveloped by the cultural imagination (see Figure 3.1).

On encountering a basket

The spacecraft, having been launched from its home planet, has now arrived on Earth. The machine incorporating our sophisticated artefact-detection program rolls out onto the ground, and its computer sets to work to process the data on the first object it encounters. It is at once thrown into utter confusion. Not that it has too much difficulty with its investigations of form and function: the object is round, with a flat bottom and raised, sloping sides, rather like an upside-down truncated cone; moreover it is hollow and open at the top, which allows it to function as a container and carrying device. The problem arises when it comes to the dynamics of construction. Equipped with a time-reversal facility, our machine is able to clock back to an earlier period and to another locale, where it watches the object gradually taking shape. It wants to know whether it has grown of its own accord, or whether it has been made in the fashion of a true artefact. Let us take a look at what is actually going on.

A human being is at work here, surrounded by a quantity of fibrous

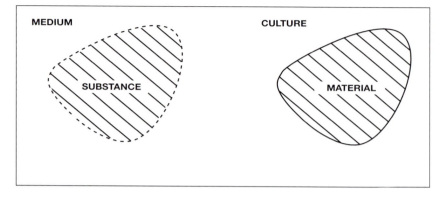

Figure 3.1 The surface of the artefact as a physical interface between solid substance and gaseous medium (left), and as an instance of the metaphysical interface between culture and the material world (right)

material, evidently derived from the stems or leaves of certain plants. Taking a bundle of fibres, placed lengthwise alongside one another to form a kind of rope of about one centimetre in diameter, she deftly begins to turn it between her fingers to produce a flat coil, at the same time using somewhat broader fibres to wrap transversely around successive turns of the coil so as to keep it compact and prevent it from unravelling. After a while, the wrapped coil becomes recognisable as the base of the object. Then, as the work proceeds – evenly, rhythmically and repetitively – the turns of the coil are drawn tighter, so that each rises partly upon the base of its predecessor, thus forming the sides. The machine is, of course, observing the construction of a coiled basket (on this technique, see Hodges 1964: 131–132). I have the finished thing beside me as I write: it is the waste-paper basket in my study (see Figure 3.2).

What is it about this mundane object that causes so much confusion? Why does its construction not seem to conform with our normal expectations of what is involved in making things? I think the reasons are threefold. The first has to do with the topology of *surface*, the second with the application of *force* and the third with the generation of *form*. In all these respects, as I shall argue, basketry appears to confound the distinction between making and growing. Of course the construction of baskets is normally described as a process of weaving. Our computer program was confounded because it tried to comprehend weaving as a modality of making. Thwarted in the attempt, it had to fall back on the default hypothesis that the basket had simply grown under its own internal dynamic, a result that seemed equally implausible. In what follows, I would like to suggest that we think of making, in reverse, as a modality of weaving. This switch of emphasis could, I believe, open up a new perspective not just on basketry in particular, but on our relationships with all the different kinds of objects in our surroundings. But it would also have the

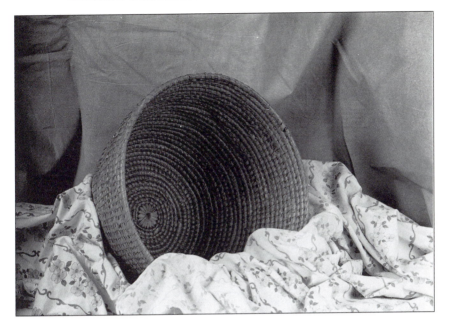

Figure 3.2   My waste–paper basket and crumpled bed–linen

effect of softening the distinction between artefacts and living things which, as it turns out, are not so very different after all.

Surface, force and the generation of form

We have seen that making, in what for convenience I shall henceforth call the 'standard view', implies the prior presence of a surface to be transformed. Thus the flint knapper chips away at the surface of stone, the carpenter carves and chisels the surface of wood, the blacksmith hammers on the surface of molten metal, and the potter applies manual pressure to the surface of clay. But once it has been cut and prepared for weaving, the basketmaker does nothing to the surface of her fibrous material. In the process of weaving, the surface of the basket is not so much transformed as built up. Moreover, there is no simple or straightforward correspondence between the surface of the basket and the surfaces of its constituent fibres. For example, the two outer surfaces of the transverse wrapping fibres are alternately 'outside' and 'inside' so far as the surface of the basket is concerned (see Figure 3.3). Indeed it is in the nature of weaving, as a technique, that it produces a peculiar kind of surface that does not, strictly speaking, have an inside and an outside at all.

In the special case of coiled basketry, there is a limited parallel with the

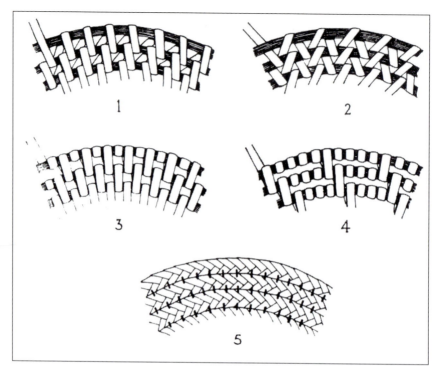

Figure 3.3 Patterns of wrapping in coiled basketry: (1) plain; (2) figure of eight
 ('Navajo'); (3) long and short ('lazy squaw'); (4) Peruvian coil; (5) sewn coil.

Source: From Hodges (1964: 131)

technique of coil-building in pottery. Here the clay is first rolled out into
long, thin, worm-like strips, rather analogous to the fibrous 'ropes' of the
basketry coil. These strips are then wound around and around to form the
base and sides of the vessel. In this case too, a surface is built up. In the
process, however, the original surfaces of the coiled strips congeal into a single
mass, and the final smoothing leaves no trace of the original mode of
construction. But there is another difference, equally critical, which brings me
to the issue of force. The potter may have to contend with the force of gravity
(his material, being both heavy and pliable, is inclined to sag). But the clay
does not exert any independent force. This is not the case with basketry,
however, which involves the bending and interweaving of fibres that may
exert a considerable resistance of their own. Indeed the basket holds together,
and assumes a rigid form, precisely because of its tensile structure.[2] In short,
the form of the basket is the resultant of a play of forces, both internal and
external to the material that makes it up. One could say that the form unfolds

within a kind of force field, in which the weaver is caught up in a reciprocal and quite muscular dialogue with the material.

This observation leads me to the final question concerning the generation of form. According to the standard view, the form pre-exists in the maker's mind, and is simply impressed upon the material. Now I do not deny that the basketmaker may begin work with a pretty clear idea of the form she wishes to create. The actual, concrete form of the basket, however, does not issue from the idea. It rather comes into being through the gradual unfolding of that field of forces set up through the active and sensuous engagement of practitioner and material. This field is neither internal to the material nor internal to the practitioner (hence external to the material); rather, it cuts across the emergent interface between them. Effectively, the form of the basket emerges through a pattern of *skilled movement*, and it is the rhythmic repetition of that movement that gives rise to the regularity of form. This point was made long ago by Franz Boas, in his classic work on *Primitive Art*.

> The basketmaker who manufactures a coiled basket, handles the fibres composing the coil in such a way that the greatest evenness of coil diameter results. ... In making her stitches the automatic control of the left hand that lays down the coil, and of the right that pulls the binding stitches over the coil brings it about that the distances between the stitches and the strength of the pull are absolutely even so that the surface will be smooth and evenly rounded and that the stitches show a perfectly regular pattern.
>
> (Boas 1955 [1927]: 20)

Spirals in nature and art

Boas illustrates the point with a drawing, which I reproduce here (Figure 3.4a). Opposite, I have placed another drawing, this time taken from the work of the great biologist D'Arcy Wentworth Thompson, *On Growth and Form* (Figure 3.4b). It depicts the shell of a certain kind of gastropod. Although both the coiled basket and the shell have a characteristic spiral form, they are spirals of different kinds: the first is an equable spiral, the second logarithmic (that is, the radius of each successive whorl increases arithmetically in the one instance, and geometrically in the other). The equable spiral, as D'Arcy Thompson explains, is characteristic of artificial forms that have been produced by mechanically bending, coiling or rolling up a given length of material, whereas the logarithmic spiral is commonly produced in nature as a result of growth by deposition, where the material is cumulatively laid down at one end whilst maintaining an overall constancy of proportion (Thompson 1961 [1917]: 178–179). Either way, however, the form appears to emerge with a certain logical inevitability from the process itself, of rolling up in the former case and laying down in the latter.

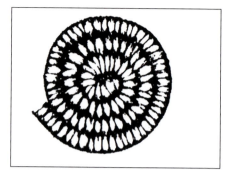

Figure 3.4a   Coiled basketry.

Source: From Boas (1955 [1927]: 20)

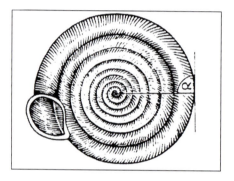

Figure 3.4b   Gastropod shell. The angle α is known as the 'spiral angle', which in this case is large

Source: From Thompson (1961 [1917]: 192)

Now it is very often assumed, in the study of both organisms and artefacts, that to ask about the form of things is, in itself, to pose a question about *design*, as though the design contained a complete specification that has only to be 'written out' in the material. This assumption is central to the standard view which, as we have already seen, distinguishes between living and artificial things on the criterion of the interiority or exteriority of the design specification governing their production without questioning the premise that the resultant forms are indeed specified independently and in advance of the processes of growth or manufacture wherein they are realised. Thus it is supposed that the basic architecture of the organism is already established, as a genetic 'blueprint', from the very moment of conception; likewise the artefact is supposed to pre-exist, fully represented as a 'virtual object' in the mind, even before a finger has been lifted in its construction. In both cases the actualisation of the form is reduced to a simple matter of mechanical transcription: all the *creative* work has already been done in advance, whether by natural selection or human reason.[3]

How then, starting from this premise, might we set about accounting for the formation of spirals in nature and in art, in the shell of the gastropod and the coil of the basket? The account would likely run along the following lines: the form of the shell is internally specified in the gastropod's genetic inheritance, and revealed in its growth; the form of the basket is externally specified in the mind of the weaver, as part of a received cultural heritage, and revealed in its manufacture. Now natural selection, according to Darwinian orthodoxy, designs organisms to be adapted to their particular conditions of life, and as many scholars have suggested, a somewhat analogous process of blind variation and selective retention, operating in the arena of cultural ideas, could do likewise in designing artefacts that are well suited to their purpose. The fact that we come across spirals in the growth of living things (as in gastropods) as well as in the making of artefacts (as in basketry) may be purely fortuitous, or it may be the outcome of some kind of adaptive convergence – of natural selection and the human intellect, operating quite independently, arriving at parallel solutions to what might be, in essence, a rather similar problem of engineering design. If, to be more precise, the solution calls for a spiral of the equable type, or alternatively of the logarithmic type, then this is what we will find in the resultant forms, regardless of whether the design itself is encoded genetically or culturally. Hence by this account, the distinction between equable and logarithmic spirals would not, in itself, be relevant as an index of the organic or artefactual status of the objects concerned.

The limits of design

According to the standard view, as outlined above, form is fully explicable in terms of the design that gives rise to it. Once you have accounted for the genesis of the design you have, to all intents and purposes, explained the form. Or have you? Would it be possible, even in theory, for any design to specify the form of an organism or artefact *completely*? In his fascinating study of the design principles embodied in the construction of living organisms and manufactured artefacts, originally written as a textbook for students of engineering, Michael French speculates on the question of just how much information would be needed to specify every aspect of the form of an organism (1988: 266–267). His conclusion is that the amount would be unimaginably large, far beyond what could be coded in the DNA of any known life-form. Nor is the situation any different with artefacts. True, even the greatest achievements of human engineering are no match for the most commonplace of organisms: thus the steam locomotive, as French wryly observes, 'is simplicity itself compared with the intricacies of the buttercup' (1988: 1). But then, no human design could approach the DNA of the genome in its informational content. Once again, a complete specification would apparently lie beyond the realms of possibility. In short, the forms of both organisms and artefacts seem to be significantly underdetermined by their underlying blueprints. That being the case, French suggests, we may have to recognise that a great many features of organisms and artefacts are merely accidental, due to chance, revealing not the designs themselves but their limitations.

Though intended to shore up the argument from design against the objection that no specification can be exhaustive, this appeal to chance is a *reductio ad absurdum* that does more to highlight the poverty of the argument itself. To show why, let me turn to another example of spiral formation: the vortex of bathwater as it runs out of the plug-hole. Is the form of the vortex a matter of chance? It is certainly not dictated by the specifications of any design. You can determine whether the spiral runs clockwise or anticlockwise by setting up a current through the water with your hand; beyond that, however, the spiral appears to form of its own accord. But its formation is anything but an accident. It can, in fact, be explained in terms of well-established principles of fluid dynamics.

The example of the vortex is not my own; it is taken from the work of the biologist Brian Goodwin (1982), who uses it to say something very important about the generation of spiral forms in living organisms. In a certain species of snail, the majority of individuals have shells with a right-handed, logarithmic spiral, but in some the spiral is left-handed. It has been shown that the direction of the spiral is controlled by the products of a particular gene, just as the direction of the spiral vortex in bathwater is controlled by the intentional movement of your hand. But – and this is the crucial point – the *form* of the shell is no more the product of a genetic programme than is the form of the vortex the product of a design in your mind. There is, in short, no 'design' for the spiral of the gastropod shell. Rather, the form arises through a process of growth within what is known technically as the 'morphogenetic field' – that is, the total system of relations set up by virtue of the presence of the developing organism in its environment. And the role of genes in the morphogenetic process is not to specify the form, even incompletely, but to set the parameters – such as handedness and spiral angle (see Figure 3.4b) – within which it unfolds (Goodwin 1982: 111).

On the growth of artefacts

Returning from the growth of organisms to the manufacture of artefacts, a parallel argument applies. Just as organic form is generated in the unfolding of the morphogenetic field, so the form of the artefact evolves within what I have called a field of forces. Both kinds of field cut across the developing interface between the object (organism or artefact) and an environment which, in the case of the artefact, critically includes its 'maker'. Where the organism engages its environment in the process of ontogenetic development, the artefact engages its maker in a pattern of skilled activity. These are truly creative engagements, in the sense that they actually *give rise* to the real-world artefactual and organic forms that we encounter, rather than serving – as the standard view would claim – to transcribe pre-existent form onto raw material. Moreover as a moment's reflection on the example of the vortex in bathwater will show, the properties of materials are directly implicated in the form-generating process. It is therefore no longer possible to sustain the distinction between form and substance that, as we have seen, is so central to the standard view of making things. Finally, the templates, measures and rules of thumb of the artisan or craftsman no more add up to a design for the artefacts he produces than do genes constitute a blueprint for the organism. Like genes, they set the parameters of the process but do not prefigure the form.[4]

All these points apply to the making of a coiled basket. Thus the equable form of the spiral base of the basket does not follow the dictates of any design; it is not imposed upon the material but arises through the work itself. Indeed the developing form acts as its own template, since each turn of the spiral is made by laying the longitudinal fibres along the edge formed by the preceding one. Now D'Arcy Thompson was of course right to point out that there is a difference between *bending* material into shape, as in basketry, and an organism's *growing* into it, as with the shell of the gastropod, and that this can lead to forms with contrasting mathematical properties. Nevertheless, if the unfolding of the morphogenetic field is described as a process of growth, would it not be fair to suggest that there is a sense in which artefacts, whose forms likewise evolve within a field of forces, 'grow' too – albeit according to different principles?

We could describe that growth as a process of *autopoiesis*, that is, the self-transformation over time of the system of relations within which an organism or artefact comes into being. Since the artisan is involved in the same system as the material with which he works, so his activity does not transform that system but is – like the growth of plants and animals – part and parcel of the system's transformation of itself. Through this autopoietic process, the temporal rhythms of life are gradually built into the structural properties of things – or as Boas put it, with regard to artefacts:

> The rhythm of time appears here translated into space. In the flaking, adzing, hammering, in the regular turning and pressing required in the making of coiled pottery, in weaving, regularity of form and rhythmic repetition of the same movement are necessarily connected.
>
> (Boas 1955 [1927]: 40)

The artefact, in short, is the crystallisation of activity within a relational field, its regularities of form embodying the regularities of movement that gave rise to it.

I would like to conclude this comparison of the coiled basket and the gastropod shell by commenting on the reasons for the remarkable durability of their respective forms. According to the standard view, since form emanates from design, the persistence of form can only be explained in terms of the stability of the underlying design specifications. In the case of the organism these specifications are genetic, in the case of the artefact they are cultural. The constancy of form is thus a function of the fidelity with which genetic or cultural information is copied from one generation to the next, combined with the effects of natural selection – or its analogue in the realm of cultural ideas – in weeding out less well adapted variants.

The argument I have proposed here, however, is just the opposite. If forms are the outcomes of dynamic, morphogenetic processes, then their stability can be understood in terms of the generative principles embedded in the material conditions of their production. For the shell the principle is one of invariant proportion; for the basket it is the principle that every increment of longitudinal extension is coupled to what has gone before by transverse attachment. Whereas the first principle, through simple iteration, will always and everywhere generate a logarithmic spiral, the second will just as reliably generate an equable one. It is these generative principles, and not the fidelity of genetic or cultural copying, that underwrite the constancy of the respective forms, and explain their persistence over immense spans of both historical and evolutionary time.

Baskets and textiles

Let me return to the computerised artefact-detection machine of our earlier 'thought experiment'. It is, we may imagine, still roaming around in search of evidence. Having first had the misfortune to encounter my waste-paper basket, the next thing it runs into is my unmade bed. What is it to make of the bed-linen? The basket, at least, had a clearly recognisable form; the linen appears to have no form at all (see Figure 3.2). Of course, if the machine could only straighten out the sheets, it would immediately notice their perfect rectangular outline. But it is not programmed to do this: for if it was, if it carried an instruction to straighten out whatever it encountered, then it would naturally discover artefacts everywhere – of its own creation!

Now the sheets on my bed are instances of what we normally call textiles. The word 'textile' comes from Latin *textilis*, meaning a woven fabric, and *texere*, meaning to weave. If a textile is anything woven, and given that this applies just as well to baskets as to bed-linen, should not basketry be regarded as a *sub-division* of textiles? One answer might be that it really doesn't matter. Confronted with an object that is evidently the result of some kind of weaving process, it makes no difference whether we call it a basket or not: what matters are the properties of the object itself, and the significance it holds for those who made and use it. But if the distinction is as arbitrary and inconsequential as all that, how come that it is so deeply rooted in our thinking? For some reason, we find that to conceive of a basket as a kind of textile is somehow strange; it seems to turn our conventional understandings upside down. Why?[5]

A clue to the answer lies in our common habit of referring to woven cloth as 'material'. It would seem that in the case of textiles, the weaving process has not in itself produced a form, but only the raw substance for acts of form-making that have still to come. These acts, as in garment-making, may involve cutting out and stitching, stretching on a frame, overprinting, or other techniques, all of which involve the impression or inscription of form upon stuff that has already been woven. In basketry, by contrast, the weaving itself yields a rigid, three-dimensional form. Attempting to assimilate basketry within our overall conception of artefact-making, we are inclined to imagine that this form is somehow superimposed upon raw substance which, in this case, is identified with the original fibrous material. In short, basketry and textiles have been split apart in our thinking by the opposition between form and substance which, as we have seen, lies at the heart of the standard view of what it means to make things. Whereas weaving a basket is conceived as a kind of making, with textiles the making is understood to be secondary to, and to follow on from, the weaving. In both cases, however, the emphasis is placed squarely on the *products* – on baskets as solid forms, on cloth as material substance – at the expense of the *process* itself. There is evidence for this in the fact that in everyday usage, the notion of 'textile' is no longer anchored to weaving at all but is freely extended to any fabrics – including knitted, felted, tufted and bonded materials – so long as they can be worked up in further acts of form-making.

If we attend to the process of weaving, however, we do find a significant technical contrast. It is almost certain that, historically, basketry preceded the weaving of cloth, and there is evidence to suggest that the techniques of the latter actually developed from basketry (which, in turn, may have developed from net-making). The basketmaker's toolkit is a very simple one: even today, no more is required than a sharp knife and a heavy rod (known as a 'driving-iron') used for beating down the weave (Hodges 1964: 147). To weave cloth, however, you need one other piece of apparatus, namely a loom. This is for the simple reason that the constituent fibres of the weave exert no tensile force in themselves. The function of the loom is to keep the warp threads under tension for as long as the weaving proceeds. Once the weaving is complete and the tension removed, the cloth holds together through nothing more than the friction of its fibres. Unlike the basket, however, it cannot hold to a rigid form, for the basket, as we have seen, keeps its form only thanks to the tension exerted by its elements.

Making as a way of weaving

It is now time to return to my earlier suggestion, that we reverse our normal order of priorities and regard making as a modality of weaving, rather than the other way around. One intriguing observation points us in this direction. Our word 'loom' comes from Middle English *lome*, which originally referred to a tool or utensil of any kind. Does this not suggest that to our predecessors, at least, the surface-building activity of weaving, rather than any of those activities involving the application of force to pre-existing surfaces, somehow epitomised technical processes in general?

The notion of making, of course, defines an activity purely in terms of its capacity to yield a certain object, whereas weaving focuses on the character of the process by which that object comes into existence. To emphasise making is to regard the object as the expression of an idea; to emphasise weaving is to regard it as the embodiment of a rhythmic movement. Therefore to invert making and weaving is also to invert idea and movement, to see the move-ment as truly generative of the object rather than merely revelatory of an object that is already present, in an ideal, conceptual or virtual form, in advance of the process that discloses it. The more that objects are removed from the contexts of life-activity in which they are produced and used – the more they appear as static objects of disinterested contemplation (as in museums and galleries) – the more, too, the process disappears or is hidden behind the product, the finished object. Thus we are inclined to look for the meaning of the object in the idea it expresses rather than in the current of activity to which it properly and originally belongs. It is precisely this contemplative attitude that leads to the redesignation of the ordinary objects of the quotidian environment, such as my waste-paper basket, as items of 'material culture' whose significance lies not so much in their incorporation into a habitual pattern of use as in their symbolic function. In suggesting that the relation between making and weaving be overturned, my purpose is to bring these products of human activity back to life, to restore them to the processes in which they, along with their users, are absorbed.[6]

In what way, then, does weaving epitomise human technical activity? What sense does it make to say that the blacksmith in his forge, or the carpenter at his bench, in transforming the surfaces of metal and wood respectively, is actually weaving? Of course, to adopt this idiom is to interpret the notion of weaving more broadly than is customary. It does, however, help to draw atten-tion to three points which I think are crucial to a proper understanding of technical skills.[7] First, skill is not a property of the individual human body in isolation, but of the whole system of relations constituted by the presence of the artisan in a richly structured environment. This system corresponds to what I described above, in specific reference to weaving, as a field of forces. Second, skill is not just the mechanical application of external force, but – as exemplified in weaving – involves qualities of care, judgement and dexterity (see Pye 1968: 22). This implies that whatever the practitioner does *to* things is grounded in an attentive, perceptual involvement *with* them, or in other words, that he watches and feels as he works. As the Russian neuroscientist Nicholai Bernstein wrote some fifty years ago, the essence of dexterity lies not in bodily movements themselves, but in the 'tuning of the movements to an emergent task', whose surrounding conditions are never precisely the same from one moment to the next (Bernstein 1996: 23). Third, skilled action has a narrative quality, in the sense that every movement, like every line in a story, grows rhythmically out of the one before and lays the groundwork for the next. As in weaving, to recall Boas's point, spatial structure grows out of temporal rhythm.

Weaving by birds and humans

In my preliminary discussion of the distinction between things that are made and things that grow, I showed that in the standard view, making takes place at the interface between the cultural imagination and the material world, and therefore that it is an exclusively human achievement. Bees, according to this view, do not literally 'make' their hives, since they have no conception of the task before them. The same could be said of the work of birds in constructing their nests, or of the beaver in building its dam. Unlike the products of human labour, hives, nests and dams are not generally admitted as objects of material culture. Now if weaving is understood as a modality of making, then it, too, must be uniquely human. But if on the other hand – to invert the relation – making is conceived as a modality of weaving, then there is no a priori reason why weaving should be restricted to human beings. More generally, could the qualities of skill outlined above, and which are epitomised in the activity of weaving, be attributed just as readily to the practices of non-human animals?

Perhaps the closest parallel to human weaving in the animal kingdom is furnished by the nest building of male weaverbirds, which has been investigated in a remarkable series of studies by N.E. and E.C. Collias (1984). The nest is made from long strips torn from the leaves of grasses, which are intertwined in a regular lattice formed by passing successive strips over and under, and in a direction orthogonal to, strips already laid. It is held together, and attached to the substrate, by a variety of stitches and fastenings, some of which are illustrated in Figure 3.5. The bird uses its beak rather like a needle in sewing or darning; in this the trickiest part lies in threading the strip it is holding under another, transverse one so that it can then be passed over the next. The strip has to be pushed under, and through, just far enough to enable the bird to let go with its beak in order to shift its hold and pull it up on the other side. If the free end is left too short, the strip may spring back; pushed too far, it could fall to the ground. Mastering this operation calls for a good deal of practice. From an early age, weaverbirds spend much of their time manipulating all kinds of objects with their beaks, and seem to have a particular interest in poking and pulling pieces of grass leaves and similar materials through holes. In females this interest declines after about the tenth week from hatching, whereas in males it continues to increase. Experiments showed that birds deprived of opportunities to practise and suitable materials are subsequently unable to build adequate nests, or even to build at all. Indeed,

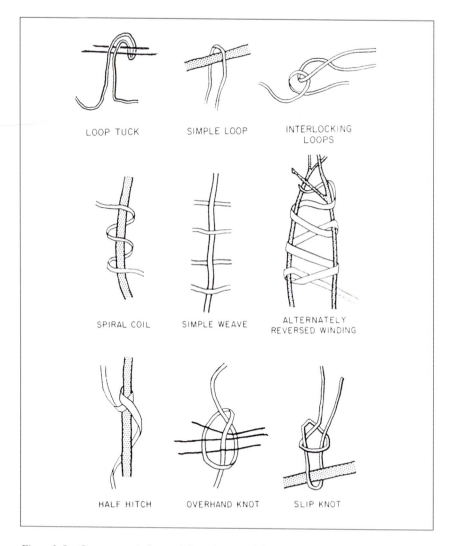

Figure 3.5 Common stitches and fastenings used by weaverbirds in the construction of their nests

Source: From Collias and Collias (1984: 207). Reprinted by permission of Princeton University Press.

fiddling about with potential nest material appears to be just as essential for the bird, in preparing itself for future building, as is the babbling of the human infant in preparing itself for speech (Collias and Collias 1984: 201, 206–207, 212, 215–220).

It is evident from the Collias' account that the abilities of the weaverbird, just like those of the human basketmaker, are developed through an active exploration of the possibilities afforded by the environment, in the choice of materials and structural supports, and of bodily capacities of movement, posture and prehension. Furthermore, what the bird acquires through practice is not a programme of instructions or a set of design specifications to be mechanically applied, but the ability to adjust its movements with exquisite precision in relation to the evolving form of its construction. As Collias and Collias report:

> In watching the numerous attempts of young male weavers to fasten initial strips of nest materials and their gradual improvement in weaving ability, it seemed to us that what every young male weaver has to learn is what in subjective terminology one would call 'judgement.'
>
> (1984: 219)

Finally, the form of the nest results from the iteration of a small number of basic movements, and from the fact that the bird stands throughout on the same spot while it weaves all around – above, below and in front – pushing out the developing shell of the main chamber as far as its beak will reach, and then tilting gradually backwards to complete the antechamber and entrance (ibid. 193, 209–210).

In brief, each of the three qualities of skill which, as I have shown, are exemplified in human weaving, is also clearly in evidence in the nest building of weaverbirds. The conventional notion that the birds' activity is due to instinct whereas humans follow the dictates of culture is clearly inadequate. The form of the nest no more follows the specifications of an innate, genetically transmitted design than does that of the coiled basket, in our earlier example, follow the specifications of an acquired, culturally transmitted one. In all likelihood the human basketmaker has an idea in mind of the final form of the construction whereas the weaverbird almost certainly does not. Yet in both cases, it is the pattern of regular movement, not the idea, that generates the form. And the fluency and dexterity of this movement is a function of skills that are developmentally incorporated into the *modus operandi* of the body – whether avian or human – through practice and experience in an environment. Such skills are fundamentally resistant to codification in the form of representations or programmes, which have then only to be executed in the material. That is why the most sophisticated computer program ever devised, as envisaged in the 'thought experiment' with which I began, could still fail to comprehend the nature of even such a mundane object as a waste-paper basket.

Conclusion

In his study of baskets and basketry among the Yekuana, a native people of southern Venezuela, David Guss observes that the master craftsman in this society, a person accredited with exceptional wisdom, 'not only weaves the world when making a basket, but in everything he does' (1989: 170). Yet this creative process of world-weaving, he suggests, is not limited to the experts. It rather engages all Yekuana people throughout their lives – albeit at a lower level of perfection – in their manufacture of the essential equipment of traditional livelihood, from canoes and graters to houses and baskets. Paradoxically, however, in translating the indigenous term by which such locally produced items are distinguished from commercially manufactured 'stuff' (such as tin cans and plastic buckets) that arrives from outside, Guss renders them as things not woven but made. Moreover the essence of making, in his view, lies in loading the object with metaphorical significance or semiotic content, such that artefacts become a mirror in which people can see reflected the fundamentals of their own culture. The symbolic capacity of artefacts, Guss insists, 'far outweighs their functional value' (1989: 70). Weaving the world, then, turns out to be a matter of 'making culture', of submitting the disorder of nature to the guidelines of traditional design.

Now the idea that in the manufacture of objects like houses, baskets and canoes, people 'weave the world', is entirely in keeping with the argument I have developed in this chapter – namely that making should be regarded as a way of weaving, and not *vice versa*. But the epistemology by which Guss converts these products of world-weaving back into 'things made', instances of the cultural transformation of nature (1989: 161), is one that I reject. It is, as I have shown, an epistemology that takes as given the separation of the cultural imagination from the material world, and thus presupposes the existence, at their interface, of a surface to be transformed. According to what I have called the standard view, the human mind is supposed to inscribe its designs upon this surface through the mechanical application of bodily force – augmented, as appropriate, by technology. I mean to suggest, to the contrary, that the forms of objects are not imposed from above but grow from the mutual involvement of people and materials in an environment. The surface of nature is thus an illusion: we work from within the world, not upon it. There are surfaces of course, but these divide states of matter, not matter from mind. And they emerge within the form-generating process, rather than pre-existing as a condition for it.

The philosopher Martin Heidegger expressed the very same point through an exploration of the notions of building and dwelling. Opposing the modernist convention that dwelling is an activity that goes on within, and is structured by, an environment that is already built, Heidegger argued that we cannot engage in any kind of building activity unless we already dwell within our surroundings. 'Only if we are capable of dwelling', he declared, 'only then can we build' (1971: 160, original emphasis). Now dwelling is to building, in Heidegger's terms, as weaving is to making in mine. Where making (like building) comes to an end with the completion of a work in its final form, weaving (like dwelling) continues for as long as life goes on – punctuated but not terminated by the appearance of the pieces that it successively brings into being.[8] Dwelling in the world, in short, is tantamount to the ongoing, temporal interweaving of our lives with one another and with the manifold constituents of our environment (see Ingold 1995).

The world of our experience is, indeed, continually and endlessly coming into being around us as we weave. If it has a surface, it is like the surface of the basket: it has no 'inside' or 'outside'. Mind is not above, nor nature below; rather, if we ask where mind is, it is in the weave of the surface itself. And it is within this weave that our projects of making, whatever they may be, are formulated and come to fruition. Only if we are capable of weaving, only then can we make.

NOTES

1 These examples are taken from French (1988: 32–36, 117–118, 161), who provides many more. See also Steadman (1979, Chapter 2).

2 To adopt an architectural term, the coherence of the basket is based upon the principle of *tensegrity*, according to which a system can stabilise itself mechanically by distributing and balancing counteracting forces of compression and tension throughout the structure. Significantly, tensegrity structures are common to both artefacts and living organisms, and are encountered in the latter at every level from the cytoskeletal architecture of the cell to the bones, muscles, tendons and ligaments of the whole body (Ingber 1998).

3 This prioritisation of design over execution betrays a ranking of intellectual over physical labour that is one of the characteristic features of Western modernity. It divides the scientist from the technician, the engineer from the operative, the architect from the builder, and the author from the secretary.

4 In a wonderful article on the building of the great cathedral of Chartres, in the thirteenth century, David Turnbull (1993) shows that this most magnificent of human artefacts was preceded by no plan whatsoever. The building took shape gradually, over a considerable period of time, through the labour of many groups of workers with diverse skills, whose activities were loosely co-ordinated by the use of templates, string and constructive geometry.

5 I was moved to reflect on this question by a superb exhibition, mounted in the Righton Gallery of Manchester Metropolitan University in March–April 1996. Entitled *Beyond the Bounds*, the exhibition consisted of works by artists and crafts-people that deliberately set out to explore and challenge the conventional categorical distinction between basketry and textiles. The notes accompanying the exhibition pointed out that baskets and textiles have become so separate in our thinking that we routinely fail to observe the connection between them. Wondering about the reasons for this separation eventually led me to write this paper. I would like to thank Mary Butcher, in particular, for encouraging me to

do so, and participants in the 'Art, architecture and anthropology' seminar at the University of Manchester for their inspiration.

6   I do not intend by this to reinstate the time-worn opposition between practical utility and symbolic meaning. The notion of utility implied by this opposition is an impoverished one that sets up a radical division between the acting subject and the object used, and reduces skilled practice to purely mechanical relations of cause and effect. In speaking of the *absorption* of artefacts into the life-activity of their users my aim is to emphasise, to the contrary, the inseparability of persons and objects in real-life contexts of accustomed (that is, usual) practice. The useful-ness of an object, then, lies not in its possession of utility but in its partaking of the *habituality* of everyday life (Gosden 1994: 11).

7   For a fuller elaboration of these points, see Ingold (1996).

8   Among the Bunu, a Yoruba-speaking people of central Nigeria, this idea is expressed in their weaving of lengths of white cloth:

> Cloths are often removed [from the loom] without cutting, accentuating the endless quality of these pieces. When eventually the unwoven warp is cut in order to use the cloth, the fringes are left, again suggesting conti-nuity rather than the finiteness of cut and hemmed edges.
>
> (Renne 1991: 715)

References

Boas, F. 1955 *Primitive Art*. New York: Dover Publications (original 1927).

Bernstein, N.A. 1996 'On dexterity and its development'. In M.L. Latash and M.T. Turvey (eds) *Dexterity and its Development*. Mahwah, NJ: Lawrence Erlbaum Associ-ates.

Collias, N.E. and E.C. Collias 1984 *Nest Building and Bird Behavior*. Princeton, NJ: Princeton University Press.

French, M.J. 1988 *Invention and Evolution: Design in Nature and Engineering*. Cambridge: Cambridge University Press.

Gibson, J.J. 1979 *The Ecological Approach to Visual Perception*. Boston: Houghton Mifflin.

Goodwin, B.C. 1982 'Biology without Darwinian spectacles'. *Biologist* 29: 108–112.

Gosden, C. 1994 *Social Being and Time*. Oxford: Blackwell.

Guss, D.M. 1989 *To Weave and Sing: Art, Symbol and Narrative in the South American Rain Forest*. Berkeley, CA: University of California Press.

Heidegger, M. 1971 *Poetry, Language, Thought* (trans. A. Hofstadter). New York: Harper and Row.

Hodges, H. 1964 *Artefacts: An Introduction to Early Materials and Technology*. London: John Baker.

Ingber, D.E. 1998 'The architecture of life'. *Scientific American* 278(1): 30–39.

Ingold, T. 1983 'The architect and the bee: reflections on the work of animals and men'. *Man* (N.S.) 18: 1–20.

——— 1995 'Building, dwelling, living: how animals and people make themselves at home in the world'. In M. Strathern (ed.) *Shifting Contexts*. London: Routledge.

——— 1996 'Situating action V: The history and evolution of bodily skills'. *Ecological Psychology* 8: 171–182.

Marx, K. 1930 *Capital*, Vol. I (trans. E. and C. Paul from 4th German Edition of *Das Kapital* 1890). London: Dent.

Monod, J. 1972 *Chance and Necessity* (trans. A. Wainhouse). Glasgow: Collins.

Pye, D. 1968 *The Nature and Art of Workmanship*. Cambridge: Cambridge University Press.

Renne, E.P. 1991 'Water, spirits and plain white cloth'. *Man* (N.S.) 26: 709–722.

Steadman, P. 1979 *The Evolution of Designs: Biological Analogy in Architecture and the Applied Arts*. Cambridge: Cambridge University Press.

Thompson, D.W. 1961 *On Growth and Form*, abridged edition, ed. J. T. Bonner. Cambridge: Cambridge University Press (original 1917).

Turnbull, D. 1993 'The ad hoc collective work of building Gothic cathedrals with templates, string and geometry'. *Science, Technology and Human Values* 18: 315–340.

4

INDIGENOUS THEORIES, SCIENTIFIC THEORIES AND PRODUCT HISTORIES

Michael Brian Schiffer

Introduction

As Rathje (1979) observed in his classic synthesis of modern-material culture studies, archaeologists studying contemporary industrial societies have access not only to artefacts but also to people. Like ethno-archaeologists, students of modern material culture can ask individuals how they make and use artefacts, sample their attitudes about sundry objects, and obtain information on product histories. Thus, the availability of people to talk to is ordinarily regarded as advantageous, particularly since the investigator and her or his informants speak the same language and perhaps share some life-history experiences.

It is also widely recognised that information obtained from living people through conversations, formal interviews and questionnaires can be problematic (Rathje 1979). In a now-famous example, Rathje and his colleagues compared 'front door' and 'back door' data on home beer consumption for a sample of southern Arizona households. They found that the beer consumption reported in interviews was significantly less than that inferred directly from beer containers in garbage (Rathje 1989; Rathje and Murphy 1992). Not surprisingly, behavioural archaeologists have acquired a healthy scepticism toward informant-supplied information (e.g., Jones 1995; Neupert and Longacre 1996; Rathje 1995; Schiffer 1978; Schiffer and Skibo 1987; Wilson 1995).

We maintain that information gleaned from living people should be treated simply as potential evidence that must be source-criticised as thoroughly as any other line of evidence. Just as we have developed principles of formation processes to help explain variability in the historical (Schiffer 1996a, 1996c: Chapter 3) and archaeological records (Schiffer 1996c), so too should we gain an understanding of the processes contributing to the creation of information furnished by informants.

In this chapter, I examine indigenous theories as one cause of the often erroneous information that informants supply. Using, as a case study, my project on the early history of the electric passenger automobile in the United States (Schiffer 1995a, b; Schiffer *et al.* 1994), I discuss the nature and functions of indigenous theories about product histories in industrial, consumer societies. Next, I show that explanations built by many scholars also rest on a foundation of indigenous theories about product histories. Finally, I demonstrate that scientific theories – those from behavioural archaeology in particular – can enable the investigator to construct scientific explanations of product histories that are independent of indigenous theories.

Indigenous theories and the demise of the early electric car

When, in the early 1990s, I first announced my project to unravel the causes of the early electric car's demise, friends and colleagues responded with mild amusement. 'What was the mystery?' many wondered aloud, while offering me explanations for a process that had transpired decades before any of them had been born. At first I was annoyed that people who had not studied early electric cars (i.e., those manufactured before 1920) claimed to know a great deal about them. Soon, however, I recognised an urgent need to identify the sources of this apparent knowledge. The reason was simple: 'commonsense' ideas about early electric cars could be making their way into automobile histories as well as influencing, perhaps insidiously, contemporary discussions about the electric car's future in the United States. As it turns out, I was dealing with a phenomenon of some generality: people in everyday discourse use indigenous theories to invent information that they otherwise could not have (cf. Kellerman *et al.* 1989).

In this section, I bring to light the commonsense ideas about early electric automobiles held by young Americans, drawing upon information supplied by a sample of undergraduate students at the University of Arizona. From this information, I approximate the indigenous theories that help people in consumer societies to generate everyday discourse about product histories.

The data base

Co-teaching a large introductory class in the Fall of 1992, I was in an excellent position to obtain a sizeable sample of responses for documenting the electric-car beliefs of a cross-section of young Americans. This latter population was of special interest to me, because I was curious if they, like my more mature friends and colleagues, also professed to have information about these material-culture processes that had occurred so long ago. Because of severe time constraints, I asked only one principal question: 'What caused the demise of the early electric car – *ca.* 1895–1920 – in the United States?' Students were instructed to answer this question on a piece of paper, and after several minutes the responses were collected.

My working hypothesis was that these students, the vast majority of whom were 18- and 19-year-old freshmen and sophomores, would be mystified by the question. This expectation arose from my appreciation that most history education in the United States, even at the college level, pays scant attention to products and technology; even the obligatory nods to Thomas Edison and Henry Ford are disappearing from secondary-school texts as the latter become more politically correct. Thus, I reasoned that the majority of students, being too young to possess any first-hand information about early electric cars, would have nothing to say. I was wrong.

One hundred and forty-one students – nearly everyone in attendance that day – turned in a piece of paper on which they had written one or more explanatory factors. Only a very few students confessed their ignorance, yet all but one of the latter also offered conjectures about causes. In short, although these students lacked information relevant to the case at hand, they readily furnished a list of one or more factors allegedly responsible for the electric car's early exit from the automobiling world.

The entire list of factors is imposing, with a few predominating, such as the electric car's limited speed and range on one charge of the battery. A few factors are far-fetched, but most responses have the ring of plausibility. Indeed, the factors mentioned by the undergraduate students, who represent every ethnic group and nearly all fields of study at the University of Arizona, differ little from the factors proposed by my friends and colleagues – some of them engineers. Even so, not one student (or colleague) pinpointed the social and behavioural causes that, on the basis of my own research, actually contributed to the electric car's failure to find much of a market (see Schiffer 1995a, b; Schiffer et al. 1994). But more about that below.

Indigenous theories

The intriguing question here is why Americans can offer seemingly plausible explanations for the histories of products that they have never encountered or studied. The answer is that Americans, like people in all other societies, possess indigenous theories (also called 'folk theories,' see Stich 1996: Chapters 2 and 3), among which are theories pertaining to product histories. I suggest that these indigenous theories consist of a general cognitive structure, doubtless seldom expressed explicitly, that people use routinely to invent explanatory factors for the history of specific products (on tacit knowledge, see Reber 1993; cf. Crick 1982).

I further hypothesise that the operative indigenous theory in the present case is actually a set of interrelated, partially overlapping theories which, together, implicate the range of factors that Americans believe can cause products to fail. These theories, I suggest, are differentially held by individuals, and perhaps few people possess a complete set. Even so, the partial theories permit most Americans to offer explanations for any instance of product failure that might crop up in daily discourse.

By seeking to identify higher-order regularities in the students' responses, I have approximated the most salient of these theories as follows.

Vested interest theory

The vested interest theory maintains that socially desirable products can be prevented from reaching the market by the selfish (and often underhand) actions of powerful corporations. It is assumed that corporations act relentlessly to enhance their profits by eliminating or hamstringing competitive products and technologies when possible. Thus, managers who judge that their corporation's profits might be threatened by a new product seek to sabotage it by purchasing and withholding crucial patents, influencing legislation and other public policy, tying up distributors by insisting on exclusive agreements, and so on. As a direct result of these corporate manoeuvres, products that are more consumer- or environment-friendly can be prevented from reaching or succeeding in the marketplace. Typically, oil and gasoline car companies are held responsible for killing the electric car. My own research, however, has revealed not one iota of evidence to finger such vested interests in the case of the electric car (Schiffer 1995b).

Producer constraint theory

The producer constraint theory focuses on factors that influence the activities of manufacturers. To wit, it specifies factors that prevent or hinder manufacturers in their efforts to bring a specific product to market. In the present case, the factors mentioned by the students include insufficient financial backing for electric car companies, greater complexity of components or of manufacture processes, a product not amenable to mass production, and inadequate marketing strategies. Most of the constraints alleged to have affected electric car makers can be shown, upon close inspection, to be without foundation (Schiffer et al. 1994).

Technological constraint theory

The technological constraint theory asserts that products will fail if they depend on technologies having fundamental limitations. Explanations based on this theory point out, for example, that storage batteries (which supply the on-board power for electric cars) have a low energy density (i.e., power per pound), or that electric vehicle technology was 'inefficient' compared to that of gasoline-powered cars. Saddled with these inherent limitations, the electric car was therefore an inferior technology, destined to fail, that engineers and

75

entrepreneurs rapidly abandoned. As we shall soon see, a reliance on storage battery technology does not in itself explain the electric car's problems.

Consumerist theory

In this very widely held theory, it is assumed that consumers determine a product's fate. For example, a product priced too high relative to competitive products will find few customers. Often, adherents to consumerist theory believe that a product will not catch on if it has shortcomings in performance characteristics important to the buyer and/or user. Students listed a number of performance deficiencies of the early electric car, such as low top speed, poor acceleration, limited range on one charge of the battery, unattractive appearance, too costly or difficult to maintain, and, ironically, 'hard to start'. Some of these alleged performance deficiencies inaccurately characterise the early electric automobile (see Schiffer 1995a; Schiffer *et al.* 1994).

Societal constraint theory

Societal constraints that can directly or indirectly affect producers, consumers or both are the basis of this theory. It holds that social, cultural or technological factors ordinarily not under the control of producers or consumers can cause a product's failure. Societal factors listed by the students include lack of home electrification at that time, a dearth of maintenance facilities for electric cars, and a culture that would 'not allow electrics'.

These five indigenous theories easily accommodate more than 95 per cent of the causal factors listed by the students, and most of the remainder fit with only slight strains. Does this mean that such theories are 'real' in the sense they form part of the cognitive structure of most Americans? In view of the long-known difficulties of modelling knowledge structures (e.g., Burling 1964; Crick 1982), my claim is in fact a weak one: Americans must possess these theories or ones like them; otherwise, I submit, it would be impossible to account for their responses to my query. Thus, I acknowledge that another investigator could examine the same response data and arrive at different theories or perhaps similar theories at different levels of abstraction, for such are the vagaries of cognitive modelling. Even so, I also maintain that one cannot explain the students' performances at this task without approximating and invoking comparable indigenous theories.

It is these differentially shared theories, I suggest, that bestow the ring of plausibility on commonsense explanations furnished in the absence of accurate information about specific products. People use these theories along with whatever fragments of related substantive information they have accumulated – in this case about cars, electricity, batteries, behaviour of corporate executives, etc. – to invent explanatory factors. Some individuals are doubtless more skilled in these performances than others (on skilled performance, see Keller and Keller 1996), and there is also variation in the ancillary information people possess. Yet, such individual differences do not obviate the generalisation that Americans employ indigenous theories to invent commonsense explanations, regardless of what they know about the specific product being discussed.

Functions and sources of indigenous theories

Why do such indigenous theories exist? I suggest that indigenous theories about product histories will arise in consumer societies (Schiffer and Majewski n.d.), such as the United States. Participation in a consumer society requires that most people, regardless of socio-economic class, age, gender and ethnic group, be able to engage in conversations about the comings and goings of everyday products. Indeed, the ever-changing panorama of products provides inexhaustible topics for discussions among family members, friends and acquaintances, co-workers, even strangers. I also hypothesise that products are the subject of much daily discourse, and that conversations ostensibly about other topics, including people and current events, are linked, explicitly or implicitly, to consumer goods. Indigenous theories, then, help Americans (and, presumably, members of other consumer societies) to create the illusion – through the invention of seemingly relevant explanatory factors – that they understand why some products have succeeded and others have failed. More importantly, indigenous theories enable people to take part in everyday conversations regardless of the accuracy or quantity of information they actually have. In consumer societies, then, indigenous theories about product histories facilitate social interaction.

It is not difficult to propose a mechanism for how people acquire indigenous theories about product histories. Growing up in America, children are bombarded in the home, in school, in magazines and newspapers, and on radio and television by discussions about product successes and failures. As a result of these incessant exposures, children construct their own theories, not unlike the way they create the grammar of a language, to account for the explanatory factors that people invoke when discussing products (this process has been termed 'private construction' (Stich 1996: 150). In this way are reproduced the indigenous theories that help to perpetuate a consumer society.

This informal theory-acquisition mechanism helps us to understand why indigenous theories may be differentially distributed. It can be readily appreciated that different people will be exposed to varied product discussions, at varying skill levels, during their life histories, and thus can construct product-related theories different from those of other individuals. On the other hand, this mechanism also leads us to expect that some theories, the consumerist in particular, will be shared quite widely because the kinds of experiences that contribute to their genesis are rather common. It is precisely these shared indigenous theories that enable engineers and undergraduate anthropology students to identify – i.e., invent – many of the same factors when furnishing explanations for the demise of the early electric automobile.

Indigenous theory: the dark side

If indigenous theories, such as those approximated above, merely permitted people to participate in everyday conversations about product histories, there would be little cause for alarm. I suggest, however, that indigenous theories have a way of insinuating themselves into product histories created by scholars in disciplines across the academy. Indeed, I expect that explanations of product trajectories offered by historians and others will be informed, like everyday discourse, by indigenous theories. This pessimistic prediction is easy enough to test because innumerable scholars have written histories of the automobile, and not a few have offered accounts of the electric car's demise. Perusal of a few reasonably representative works discloses a lack of explicit scientific theory and, as anticipated, the pervasive influence of indigenous theories on these studies' conclusions.

James J. Flink identified a number of factors that worked against the adoption of the electric automobile as an 'all-purpose, practical road vehicle' (Flink 1970: 240). Among the deterrents he named were many user-related performance characteristics, particularly short range, poor hill-climbing ability, high purchase and maintenance costs, all seemingly sired by consumerist theory (ibid.: 240–242). Flink also noted the poorly developed infrastructure for recharging batteries on the road (Flink 1970: 241), which seems to reflect the societal constraint theory. The gasoline automobile is touted as a better all-purpose vehicle, one especially fit for traversing long distances. Thus, in Flink's view, a rational consumer would have shunned the electric car because it could not perform as well as a gasoline car across the entire range of automobiling activities. Yet, his treatment of activities is far from complete, for he fails to discuss urban transport under all weather conditions, an arena where the electric car clearly excelled. Moreover, he provides no evidence to support his many contentions about the electric automobile's alleged performance deficiencies – some of which are patently incorrect (e.g., gasoline cars also had high maintenance costs (Schiffer *et al.* 1994: 110)). Apparently, Flink's indigenous theories have produced little more than a plausible story.

In *The Evolution of Technology*, Basalla identifies the electric car's 'serious faults' as follows:

> It was slow, unable to climb steep hills, and expensive to own and operate. Above all else, it had a limited cruising range. Its heavy lead and acid storage batteries had to be recharged every thirty miles or

so. The electric was not a vehicle in which to tour the countryside or drive to a distant city.

(Basalla 1988: 200)

By identifying purported shortcomings in performance characteristics from the standpoint of the car's purchaser and driver, this explanation clearly instantiates consumerist theory. Given these performance deficiencies, which were only partially shared with gasoline automobiles, the electric car's failure is made to seem understandable, even inevitable. Needless to say, Basalla provides no evidence to buttress his claims, and some of the latter are clearly wrong, such as the electric's range, which in many makes and models had, by 1910, reached 50–100 miles (Anonymous 1911, 1912; Schiffer *et al.* 1994: 117–118; Towle 1911). Because these kinds of unsubstantiated empirical claims, made plausible by indigenous theory, appear in highly regarded, seemingly authoritative histories, other investigators adopt them uncritically, and thus they are perpetuated and embellished.

Rudi Volti pinpointed several factors that supposedly contributed to the electric car's failure to find much of a market, particularly 'limited speed and range' (Volti 1990: 44). These factors, he emphasised (ibid: 46), were decisive, despite the electric car's image problems – an appeal limited mostly to wealthy women – and a poorly developed infrastructure for taking long trips, i.e., an absence of charging stations and battery-exchange depots (ibid.: 45–46). Volti's explanation is attributable mainly to the workings of consumerist theory: the electric car failed because of poor performance, both mechanical and visual. The infrastructural factors he identified are referable to the societal constraint theory. Although Volti's explanation is more complex and nuanced than others (and lacks conspicuously invented empirical claims), it still rests entirely on, and derives its plausibility from, indigenous theories.

In a feminist tract on the early automobile, Virginia Scharff also took a turn at analysing the electric car. Her narrative attributes the electric car's insubstantial market to the vehicle's 'limited power and circumscribed range' (Scharff 1991: 44). 'Limited power' can be interpreted as a technological constraint, if one assumes that she was alluding to fundamental shortcomings in batteries, or it can indicate power available to the driver – a generalised, consumer-related performance characteristic. Scharff also claims that electric cars were 'more expensive to manufacture ... and were too heavy to climb hills or run at high speeds' (38). Manufacturing expenses seem to stem from the manufacturing constraint theory, whereas hill-climbing ability and top speed derive from consumerist theory. Regrettably, by accepting at face value the statements of other historians and inventing others, Scharff has advanced claims about electric car performance that have no empirical basis. Clearly, Scharff's explanation achieves its ring of plausibility solely because writer and readers share implicit indigenous theories.

The electric car's 'inherent short range was the chief reason for its defeat by the gasoline car' is the conclusion of Robert Schallenberg (1982: 252). However, he also called attention to additional consumer-oriented factors that deterred purchasers, especially high purchase cost (ibid.: 253), observing that 'the electric never had its Henry Ford' (ibid.: 253). Unfortunately, it escaped Schallenberg's notice entirely that some manufacturers were offering, in the mid and late teens, relatively inexpensive electric automobiles (e.g., Anonymous 1914, 1917; Kimes and Clarke 1989; Schiffer *et al.* 1994: Chapter 11). Schallenberg's explanation for the electric car's limited appeal rests on little more than a foundation of consumerist theory, augmented by the producer constraint theory (i.e., the high cost of batteries contributed to the electric's price – Schallenberg 1982: 253).

These examples, which could be proliferated endlessly, support my prediction that even scholars seemingly knowledgeable about a specific product's history employ indigenous theories to construct explanations. Readers of these histories – i.e., other Americans enculturated in the same consumer society – share these theories with the author, and this ensures an explanation's apparent plausibility.

Plausibility aside, commonsense explanations can be shown to contain many empirical inaccuracies – in this case, about the early electric car. These mis-statements occur because investigators tacitly take at face value unsubstantiated empirical claims proffered by other scholars and, at times, invent others that accord with their indigenous theories. Indeed, I suggest that indigenous theories are responsible for many of the errors in product histories that, ordinarily, would be attributed to lapses in scholarship. (Another source of inaccuracies – corporate crypto-history – is discussed elsewhere (Schiffer 1991, 1992a: Chapter 6, 1992b).)

How, then, can a scientifically oriented investigator get beyond the commonsense explanations of product histories that are based on indigenous theory? This can be difficult, not only because scientists in consumer societies hold indigenous theories comparable to everyone else, but also because some explanatory factors identified in commonsense explanations might also play a role in scientific explanations. Our task, then, is to use appropriate scientific theories for establishing agreement on the quality, quantity and diversity of relevant evidence that can suffice to warrant any specific explanation – regardless of its source. Not surprisingly, for the case at hand I make use of theories employed by behavioural archaeologists.

Behavioural theories and scientific product histories

Theories from behavioural archaeology force the investigator to seek evidence of concrete interactions in the life histories of people and artefacts (e.g., Schiffer 1995a; Walker *et al.* 1995; Zedeño 1997). For example, in my studies of the competition between Japanese and American companies over portable radios during the late 1950s and early 1960s (Schiffer 1991, 1992a, b),

I discovered that the most important lines of evidence were in the radios themselves: in traces of manufacture processes, in sizes of parts, in diversity of brands and models, and so on. What is more, I concluded that the explanations offered by many political scientists and economists were erroneous, resting on invented factors and corporate crypto-history. Productive behavioural theories inevitably lead to the hard evidence of objects – and, especially, to their multifarious relationships with people – that can liberate scientific explanations from indigenous theories and invented facts.

Life histories of product types

In seeking explanations for the trajectories of artefacts manufactured in the factories of capitalist, industrial societies, behaviouralists have found it useful to think of product types as having life histories. The life history of a product type, such as portable radio or electric car, consists of three processes: *invention*, *commercialisation*, and *adoption* (e.g., Schiffer 1991, 1996b; Schiffer and Majewski n.d.). In the invention process, prototypes are created, usually with the purpose of attracting capital to finance further research and development and, eventually, mass production. The latter factors come together, and factories are established, in the commercialisation process. Adoption, the third process, begins when finished products first appear in the marketplace and are purchased (i.e., adopted) by consumers; it ends when the product is no longer being manufactured. Such life histories apply to products aggregated in various ways, such as all cars produced by one manufacturer, one model of all manufacturers, and all models of all manufacturers. Because the electric car reached the commercialisation process, we need not spend time here on invention (but see Schiffer *et al.* 1994; Wakefield 1994).

The commercialisation process

With this theoretical apparatus in hand, we can furnish empirically rich expectations for the commercialisation process; these should permit us readily to ascertain if technological and producer constraints were responsible for the electric car's demise. If such constraints had actually hobbled the electric car, then the temporal distribution of all commercially manufactured models should exhibit a rather rapid, unimodal rise and fall. Further, we would expect few companies, if any, to have remained for long in the electric car business. When appropriately aggregated, the data in Kimes and Clark (1989), an exhaustive catalogue of US car-makers and models, permit us to construct accurate trajectories of the electric car as a commercial product. (Remarkably, historians of the automobile have ignored this indispensable source of evidence on the commercialisation of the early electric car.)

These data demonstrate, rather conclusively, that neither technological nor producer constraints had major effects on the electric car's trajectory. Indeed, that 127 companies manufactured electric cars for sale in the United States, for almost a half century, in itself suggests that these automobiles enjoyed some success as a commercial product. But there is more. Figure 4.1 plots the number of companies making electric automobiles in each year from 1894 to 1942. Clearly, the electric car's trajectory is not a highly compressed, unimodal rise and fall; rather, it seems to have experienced, during this lengthy period, at least two peaks of commercial interest. The bumps in this curve reveal considerable complexity in commercialisation, which cannot be dealt with here (see Schiffer 1995a; Schiffer *et al.* 1994). To make a long story short, technological constraints (e.g., poorly designed batteries) did affect the earliest part of the electric car's trajectory, which is often the case with new products, but these constraints were rapidly overcome. Technological constraints thereafter played no role. To simplify matters, I confine my discussions below to the 'Classic Age' of electric cars.

Additional light is shed on the commercialisation process by Figure 4.2, which displays all US electric car companies by their first year of production. Figure 4.2 reveals that new companies put out their first models in almost every year from 1894 to 1924. If the electric car had been crippled from start to finish by technological or producer constraints, why would new companies have continued to enter the market in large numbers more than fifteen years after the debut of the first commercial electric car?

Finally, Figure 4.3 presents data on the longevity of the 127 electric car companies, plotted by total years of production. Surprisingly, eight companies

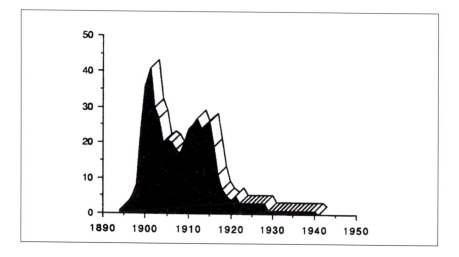

Figure 4.1   The number of companies producing electric passenger automobiles
during the years 1894 to 1942

Source: From Schiffer 1995a

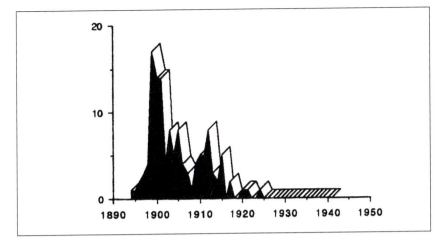

Figure 4.2 The number of companies producing their first electric automobile in a given year

Source: From Schiffer 1995a

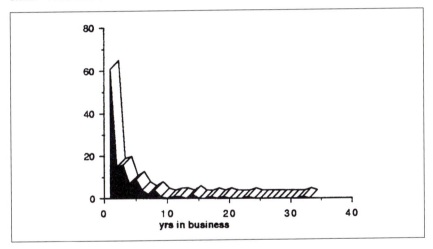

Figure 4.3 The number of companies producing electric automobiles for a given number of years

Source: From Schiffer 1995a

lasted ten or more years, which is hardly the record of an industry struggling throughout its history to surmount technological and producer constraints.

If the electric car's problems did not lie in commercialisation (and certainly not in invention), then behavioural theory requires us to examine the adoption process in detail.

The adoption process

It is in the adoption process where we must seek an explanation for the electric car's demise. What is more, if societal constraints were at work, then their effects should be apparent in adoption.

First we need to examine some large-scale adoption patterns. Regrettably, reliable data on electric car sales are not easy to obtain, but the overarching patterns are clear and uncontroversial (Mom 1997; Schiffer *et al.* 1994; Scott 1966). Bluntly put, electric passenger cars were not bought in large numbers. No more than a few thousand were sold annually until the early teens; sales peaked at about 6,000 in 1913 and 1914, and dropped off rapidly thereafter. In so far as market share is concerned, the picture is equally clear: from a high of 28 per cent in 1900, the electric's share of the passenger car market declined relentlessly to below 1 per cent in 1913. These figures demonstrate that the electric car was a niche product, which failed to reach a mass market. Let us now look more closely at the adoption process, oriented by additional behavioural theory, in order to shed light on consumer-oriented explanations.

Relevant behavioural theory (see, for example, the papers in Spencer-Wood 1987; Schiffer 1995a; Schiffer *et al.* 1994; Schiffer and Majewski n.d.; Schiffer and Skibo 1987, 1997) suggests that different groups of people, who might be engaged in different sets of activities, make purchases on the basis of a product's activity-relevant performance characteristics. Thus, unlike consumerist explanations that often assume a homogeneity of consumers, behavioural theory forces the investigator immediately to confront the considerable behavioural and social heterogeneity of people in industrial societies.

The first step in constructing a scientific explanation of adoption processes is to enumerate potentially relevant groups defined on the basis of socio-demographic criteria, such as rural–urban, social class and gender; these groups serve to frame discussions about the electric car's target and actual markets. In the second step, one specifies each group's automobile-related activities. The third step requires assessment of the performance characteristics of the competing products – e.g., gasoline and electric automobiles – relative to each activity. In this way, the investigator can identify the performance shortcomings, if any, of the electric car *in relation to specific activities of given groups*. Only in these well-defined contexts can we explain, scientifically, the decision to purchase or not purchase an electric car.

Let us now consider the electric car's target market, which can then be compared with its actual market. Using the simple device of a paradigmatic classification (e.g., Dunnell 1971), the investigator organises, and presents economically, summary inferences about both markets. The basic strategy is to employ pertinent evidence for dividing, successively, the members of a society into consumer groups defined on the basis of specific combinations of socio-demographic characteristics (or 'dimensions'). These groups, of course, are believed to have relevance to understanding the adoption of the electric car. Because the adoption process has already transpired, one should be able to identify groups with comparative ease; this contrasts with modern marketing research whose aim is to predict groups that might be relevant to a product's adoption in the future (e.g., Hawkins *et al.* 1992). As stipulated above, I focus here on the 'Classic Age' of electric cars, *ca.* 1909 to 1914 (Schiffer *et al.* 1994: Chapter 10). I have found three dimensions useful for studying Classic Age electric cars: rural–urban, socio-economic class and gender (Figure 4.4).

Much evidence for inferring the target market of the early electric car comes from magazine advertisements. Because ads for electric cars are common in magazines such as *Harpers, Literary Digest* and *Collier's*, there is little doubt that these automobiles were targeted at the urban elite – in which category I include members of the upper and upper-middle classes. Not uncommonly, ads show electric cars taking couples or groups, often in formal attire, to or from elite activities, such as a concert, theatre or a party (Figure 4.5). Some ads also show well-dressed men or women, sometimes alone, using electric cars for transport to leisure activities or for business (Figure 4.6). Other ads depict no people, yet their texts often reveal the same elite orientation, as in: 'The Rauch & Lang Electric never can be "common" – it will always be the car of social prestige, and appeal to those who know that in electrics cheapness is not a matter of price' (*The Literary Digest* 19 October 1912, p. 685).

Analysis of the ads also discloses a pervasive female orientation. To wit, 'among the people shown in and around the electrics throughout the Classic Age, women outnumbered men about three to one. Except in ads for electric roadsters, women were depicted as drivers more often than men' (Schiffer *et al.* 1994: 135). Likewise, pitches based on technical virtuosity, which at that time would have been aimed mainly at men, were muted during the height of the Classic Age.

A product's design also furnishes evidence about the potential market (Schiffer and Skibo 1997). In particular, the electric car's furnishings and accessories underscore the manufacturers' expectations that their cars would be bought by people with 'refined taste'. In the more expensive models, car makers offered luxurious appointments such as richly upholstered seats, reading lights, lady's toilet case, gentlemen's smoking set, flower vase of cut glass and silk curtains. Needless to say, many of these refinements would have been expected to appeal more to women than men.

The ads and other lines of evidence, such as manufacturers' brochures and discussions in trade journals, furnish a reasonably consistent picture: the electric car's target market, during the Classic Age, was urban America's 'horsey set,' especially women (Madison 1912; Smith 1914). However, one surmises from various sources that some manufacturers also expected electric cars eventually to 'trickle down' to a large middle-class market.

Often it is difficult to obtain accurate evidence on a product's actual

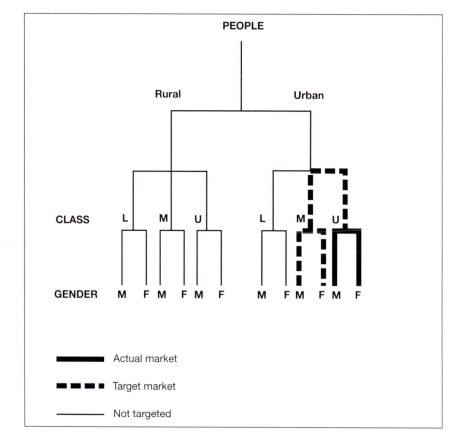

Figure 4.4 A paradigmatic classification, displayed as a tree diagram, representing the target and actual markets of the electric passenger automobile during its

market. Fortunately, all sources – even those written by modern historians (e.g., Scharff 1991) – converge on the conclusion that electric cars were bought, almost exclusively, by America's most wealthy urbanites. Moreover, in these families women often used the cars, especially during the daytime, for running errands and discharging social duties. In a photograph taken in 1914 outside the Detroit Athletic Club, presumably where women were meeting, Georgano (1985) observed that 32 of 35 parked cars were electrics. Telling evidence that women actually drove, perhaps even purchased, electric cars comes from a variety of intriguing ads. In 1912, the Electric Vehicle Association of America inquired of readers, 'Have you noticed that more men are driving Electrics each day?' (*Literary Digest* 13 July 1912, p. 70). An Ad for Motz tyres, addressed to 'Madam', claimed 'No More Tire Troubles on Electric Cars' (*Literary Digest* 2 March 1912). Similarly, in pushing its battery chargers, Lincoln Electric Company ads showed smartly dressed women

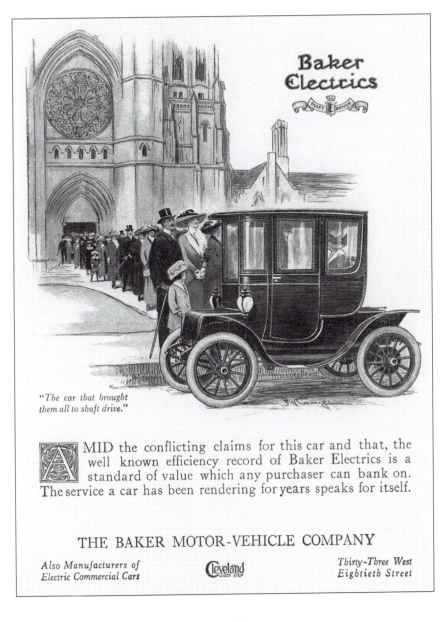

Figure 4.5 Ad for a Baker Electric Automobile

Source: *Life* 18 April 1912

Figure 4.6   Ad for a Detroit Electric, 'Society's Town Car'

Source: *Literary Digest* 20 July 1912

operating the charger's controls (e.g., *Literary Digest* 23 October, p. 928). All lines of relevant evidence leave little doubt that electric automobiles were favoured by women.

Perhaps the most interesting pattern in the adoption process is that many of America's wealthiest families owned both gasoline and electric cars. A case in point was the Henry and Clara Ford family, which had a stable of gasoline cars, including a Rolls Royce, as well as a succession of Detroit Electrics, the latter driven mainly by Clara (Schiffer *et al.* 1994: 168). Thomas and Mina Edison also had 'his' and 'her' automobiles, gasoline and electric (ibid.: 139). Here, then, is an apparent paradox: Ford, who epitomised the triumph of the internal combustion engine, owned electric cars, and Edison, tireless advocate of electric cars and developer of a better battery for them (ibid.), owned gasoline cars. When viewed from a behavioural perspective, however, the paradox disappears. To wit, in America's wealthiest families, different types of automobiles were carrying out different functions. That electric cars were, for several decades, a successful niche product serving wealthy families in ways that gasoline cars could not, is an important empirical pattern to which I return below.

Despite the availability of relatively low-priced electrics, beginning in the mid-teens, there is no evidence that ordinary middle-class Americans were buying them, despite heavy advertising in mass-circulation magazines. Rather, in the teens, gasoline cars – black Model T Fords and dozens of other makes – were finding an enormous, ever-expanding market of middle- and working-class Americans. The numbers are telling: nearly 200,000 Model T Fords were bought in 1913 (Hounshell 1984), compared to a mere 6,000 electrics (Schiffer *et al.* 1994: 146). Despite the electric car's success among members of the urban elite, the vast majority of middle-class families shunned them.

These adoption patterns permit us now to formulate the explanatory question more precisely. Specifically, why did middle-class families almost uniformly choose gasoline over electric cars (even though the price of electricity was dropping and that of gasoline was rising (Schallenberg 1982)? In order to answer this question, we must turn to the performance characteristics of gasoline and electric automobiles relevant to the activities of automobile owners. (In a comprehensive explanation (e.g., Schiffer *et al.* 1994), the investigator also has to consider the availability and employment of other transportation options, such as horse-drawn carriages and trolleys, but to do so here would render the example unnecessarily complex.)

I have pinpointed three major activities in which the automobiles of urbanites participated during the Classic Age: touring, running errands and travelling to social functions (Schiffer 1995a). In touring, the automobile and automobilist embarked on adventures in the countryside, usually on weekends and during longer summer excursions. For many male automobilists, touring, despite its near-constant succession of mishaps, was the *sine qua non* of early automobilism, glamorised in articles in mass-circulation magazines (Sutphen 1901; Johnston 1907). Automobiles were also used for running errands in the daytime, often by women, doctors and salespeople. Finally, automobiles carried people, often dressed in their finest outfits, to social activities, mainly in the evening.

By means of a performance matrix, the investigator can assess the performance characteristics of gasoline and electric automobiles in relation to these three activities (Schiffer 1995a: 31). I have constructed a 'threshold' performance matrix, which simply indicates whether a performance characteristic did(+) or did not(-) surpass a minimal performance level for the activity (for other kinds of performance matrix, see Schiffer and Skibo 1987; Schiffer 1995a).

In so far as the three activities are concerned, the patterns are clearcut (Table 4.1). On the basis of every performance characteristic relevant to touring, electric cars fell considerably short. By the same token, electric cars were decisively superior in the majority of performance characteristics important for the urban activities of running errands and travelling to social functions. These patterns demonstrate that the decision to purchase a car was not that of choosing between functional equivalents. If a family bought one car only, some of its automobile-related activities would be badly compromised, perhaps sacrificed entirely. That is why America's wealthiest families bought both gasoline and electric cars, for they could employ the most appropriate vehicle for any activity, avoiding unhappy performance compromises. Middle-class families during the Classic Age also might have desired to own two cars, to facilitate all automobiling activities, but they simply could not afford to purchase and maintain them. In buying only gasoline cars, middle-class families tilted decisively towards touring, and thus limited the ability of women, especially, to use automobiles for running errands and discharging social duties.

Certainly there is nothing novel about the generalisation that wealthy families can afford more artefacts. What is new is the recognition, grounded in behavioural theory, that wealth makes it possible to avoid the compromises in activity performance caused by the employment of artefacts forced to perform multiple functions. Thus, wealthy families acquire a plethora of products having very narrow functions that enhance the performance of specific activities. This has been stated more formally as the Imelda Marcos hypothesis (Schiffer 1995a: 32–33): in any set of similar social units (e.g., families), those having greater wealth are able to enhance the performance of favoured activities by acquiring additional unifunctional artefacts. (In the present context, 'unifunctional' does not mean literally only one function; rather, the term denotes artefact(s) having a reduced or limited number of functions relative to other artefacts.)

The Imelda Marcos hypothesis helps us to understand how very wealthy families solved the car problem and why that solution was unavailable to the middle class. However, an important question remains: Why did middle-class families privilege touring over urban uses of the automobile? The answer

Table 4.1　A Threshold Performance Matrix for Gasoline and Electric Automobiles, c. 1912. The entries below represent the author's approximation of how these performance characteristics were judged at that time. A plus (+) indicates that the car exceeds the threshold value of that performance characteristic; a minus (–) indicates that the car falls short of the threshold value.

Activity	Performance characteristics	Gasoline	Electric
Touring	Range of 100+ miles	+	–
	Top speed of 40–60 mph	+	–
	Ease of refuelling, recharging	+	–
	Ruggedness	+	–
	Economy of operation and maintenance	–	–
	Repairability in country	+	–
	Can indicate owner's membership in the group 'tourists'	+	–
	Can indicate owner's wealth	+	+
Running errands in town	Range of 50–100 miles	+	+
	Speed of 12–20 mph	+	+
	Ease of starting	–[1]	+
	Ease of driving	–	+
	All-weather capability	–[2]	+[3]
	Reliability	–	+
	Economy of operation and maintenance	–	–
	Ease of refuelling/recharging	+	+[4]
	Can indicate owner's wealth	+	+
	Can indicate owner's social position	+	+
Travelling to social functions in town	Range of 50–100 miles	+	+
	Speed of 12–20 mph	+	+
	Ease of starting	–[1]	+
	Ease of driving	–	+
	All-weather capability	–[2]	+[3]
	Reliability	–	+
	Economy of operation and maintenance	–	–
	Ease of refuelling/recharging	+	+[4]
	Cleanliness of operation	–	+
	Quietness of operation	–	+
	Can indicate owner's membership in the 'horsey set'	–	+
	Can indicate owner's wealth	+	+
	Can indicate owner's affinity for 'high culture'	–	+

Source: (From Schiffer 1995a:31)

Notes:
[1] After 1912, the pricier gasoline cars had an electric starter.
[2] A few expensive gasoline cars, like the Cadillac, had a closed-coach body style, but the touring car exposed the occupants to the elements.
[3] The electric roadster lacked all-weather capability.
[4] In homes without electricity, recharging of batteries could not have been done economically.

implicates the structure of middle-class families (Schiffer 1995: 33; Schiffer *et al*. 1994: 168–169). In the traditional Euro-American patriarchal family, men decided which activities were favoured, and allocated resources accordingly. Thus, middle-class men, captivated by touring, enhanced their own leisure activities by buying gasoline cars. This explanation is adequate only as a first approximation, for obviously it does not go nearly far enough. In future research, we need to construct scientific theories to explain variability in the weightings that families (and communities and nation-states) assign to specific activities. It is weighted activities that, through performance characteristics, crucially set the priorities for allocating resources among competing artefacts and technologies (Schiffer 1995a: 33–34; see also Schiffer and Skibo 1997). (It should be evident that the Imelda Marcos hypothesis, which can be generalised in many ways (e.g., Schiffer 1995a), has implications for building a theory to explain the growth of societal complexity, so long as the latter is defined as the proliferation of functionally differentiated units – e.g., portable artefacts, architecture, social roles and social units.)

The example of the electric car's failure to reach a middle-class market demonstrates that behavioural theories, despite being at a very early stage of development, can be used to advantage by investigators seeking to construct scientific product histories. Behavioural theories require that we obtain and analyse relevant material-culture evidence, whether it comes from collections, collector catalogues, magazine articles and advertisements, product brochures or trade journals (Schiffer 1996a). Such evidence allows the investigator to characterise accurately the principal processes in the life histories of product types – i.e., invention, commercialisation, and adoption. In studies of adoption, consumer-oriented behavioural theory directs attention to ascertaining, again through relevant evidence, a product's target and actual markets in relation to groups defined on the basis of socio-demographic variables. Finally, behavioural theory treating relationships between activities and artefacts requires the investigator to learn about the performance characteristics of artefacts relative to the activities of potential and actual adopters. From these diverse lines of evidence, the investigator is able to construct a scientific explanation independently of indigenous theories.

Discussion and conclusion

The preceding explanation for the adoption patterns of the electric car, grounded in the scientific theories of behavioural archaeology, is unlike any explanation proffered, by layperson or historian, on the basis of indigenous theories. What is more, unlike commonsense explanations buttressed, at best, by anecdotes and invented information, the behavioural explanation is strongly supported by relevant evidence from the historical record. Not surprisingly, the behavioural explanation appears implausible, if not obviously wrong, to the scholars uncritical – perhaps unaware – of their own indigenous theories (e.g., Hugill 1996; Scharff 1995).

Indigenous theories permeate our cognitive processes because they make it possible for people to participate, as skilful performers, in everyday activities. When these activities involve conversations about the causes of product trajectories, such as the demise of the electric car or the beta format VCR or the Edsel, various indigenous theories, such as those approximated above on product histories, come into play. These theories enable people, who usually have no specific information about the product at hand, to appear socially competent. We doubtless possess a large and diverse body of indigenous theories that empower us to perform in the conversations of everyday life in Western societies. Indeed, I expect indigenous theories about political and economic processes to be especially rich and well developed; they should also pervade the literatures of political science and economics.

Clearly, the availability of informants in modern material-culture studies is a mixed blessing. On the one hand, the investigator can secure some kinds of relatively accurate information, such as family composition, household artefact inventories (e.g., Schiffer *et al.* 1981) and recipes for crafts. On the other hand, when informants lack accurate information on a particular subject, indigenous theories help them to fill the void through invention. For the investigator pursuing modern material-culture studies, the boundary between accurate and invented information is not always apparent or clear.

One obvious approach around this problem is to seek informants, of the appropriate age-grade, whose life-history experiences coincided temporally with the processes of interest. One might argue, for example, that older adults today should be able to remember which companies and countries first commercialised particular consumer products. It seems to me, however, that this approach is unrealistic because it assumes that people have accurate information about contemporaneous events, despite being in a highly complex and differentiated society (cf. Schiffer 1978). That is why even middle-aged Americans today erroneously believe that Japanese companies invented the transistor radio; after all, their only direct experience with these products was in listening to the Japanese sets they had received as gifts when teenagers (Schiffer 1991). Evidently, acquiring accurate information about the products and processes of interest requires more than simply locating people of the appropriate age-grade. For, even informants whose activities involved the products of interest can only comment, authoritatively, about the minute set of people–product interactions in which they, themselves, participated.

Although material culture itself, including diverse documents and texts, provides the most relevant and accurate evidence for constructing product histories, we can scarcely expect investigators to forgo the pleasures of interacting with informants. However, investigators must come to appreciate that much – perhaps most – of the 'information' they obtain about product histories, when conducting interviews, administering questionnaires, and just plain gabbing with folks, is invented by people employing indigenous theories. Like other behavioural phenomena, the utterances that indigenous theories help to generate can be studied scientifically. Thus, our aim should be to develop, eventually, a suite of theories for source-analysing the information furnished by informants, not unlike the principles we have laboriously built for studying the formation of the historical and archaeological records. The theory presented above, on why people in consumer societies – Americans especially – hold indigenous theories about product histories, is but one small step in this direction.

Acknowledgments

I thank Maria Nieves Zedeño for furnishing helpful comments on an earlier draft.

References

Anonymous 1911 'Growth of the electric car industry well illustrated in the Chicago show'. *Motor Age* 26 January, pp. 42–46.
—— 1912 'Little known features of modern electrics'. *The Motor World* 8 August, pp. 41–45.
—— 1914 'Detroit concern to market low-priced Columbia Electric: roadster will sell for $784'. *Motor Age* 19 February, p. 26.
—— 1917 'A start towards a million electrics'. *Electric Vehicles* January, p. 1.
Basalla, G. 1988 *The Evolution of Technology*. Cambridge: Cambridge University Press.
Burling, R. 1964 'Cognition and componential analysis: God's truth or hocus-pocus?' *American Anthropologist* 66: 20–28.
Crick, M.R. 1982 'Anthropology of knowledge'. *Annual Review of Anthropology* 11: 287–313.
Dunnell, R.C. 1971 *Systematics in Prehistory*. New York: The Free Press.
Flink, J.J. 1970 *America Adopts the Automobile, 1895–1910*. Cambridge, Massachusetts: MIT Press.
Georgano, G.N. 1985 *Cars, 1886–1930*. New York: Beekman House.
Hawkins, D.I., R.J. Best and K.A. Coney 1992 *Consumer Behavior: Implications for Marketing Strategy. Fifth Edition*. Homewood, Illinois: Irwin.
Hounshell, D.A. 1984 *From the American System to Mass Production, 1800–1932: The Development of Manufacturing Technology in the United States*. Baltimore: Johns Hopkins University Press.
Hugill, P.J. 1996 'Review' of *Taking Charge: The Electric Automobile in America*, by Michael Brian Schiffer. *Technology and Culture* 37: 379–381.
Jones, T.W. 1995 'Archaeology as archaeology'. Ph.D. dissertation, Department of Anthropology, University of Arizona. Ann Arbor, Michigan: University Microfilms.
Johnston, R.H. 1907 'The joys of touring'. *Collier's* 26 October, pp. 9–12.
Keller, C.M. and J.D. Keller 1996 *Cognition and Tool Use: The Blacksmith at Work*. New York: Cambridge University Press.

Kellermann, K., S. Broetzmann, Tae-Seop Lim and Kenji Kitao 1989 'The conversation mop: sciences in the stream of discourse'. *Discourse Processes* 12: 27–61.

Kimes, B.R. and H.A. Clark, Jr 1989 *Standard Catalog of American Cars, 1805–1942* (2nd edn). Iola, Wisconsin: Krause Publications.

Madison, R. 1912 'The lady and the electric'. *Country Life in America* 15 July, pp. 36, 44, 46, 48.

Mom, G. 1997 *Geschiedenis van de Auto van Morgen: Cultuur en Techniek van de Elektrische Auto*. The Netherlands: Kluwer.

Neupert, Mark A. and William A. Longacre 1996 'Informant accuracy in pottery use-life studies: a Kalinga example'. In W.A. Longacre and J.M. Skibo (eds) *Kalinga Ethnoarchaeology: Expanding Archaeological Method and Theory* Washington, D.C.: Smithsonian Institution Press, pp. 71–82.

Rathje, W.L. 1979 'Modern material culture studies'. *Advances in Archaeological Method and Theory* 2: 1–37.

—— 1989 'The three faces of garbage – measurements, perceptions, and behaviors'. *The Journal of Resource Management and Technology* 17(2): 61–65.

—— 1995 'Forever separate realities'. In J.M. Skibo, W.H. Walker and A.E. Nielsen (eds) *Expanding Archaeology*. Salt Lake City: University of Utah Press, pp. 36–43.

Rathje, W.L. and Cullen Murphy 1992 *Rubbish!* New York: HarperCollins.

Reber, A.S. 1993 *Implicit Learning and Tacit Knowledge: An Essay on the Cognitive Unconscious*. Oxford: Oxford University Press.

Schallenberg, R.H. 1982 'Bottled energy: electrical engineering and the evolution of chemical energy storage'. *American Philosophical Society Memoirs*, No. 148.

Scharff, V. 1991 *Taking the Wheel: Women and the Coming of the Motor Age* New York: The Free Press.

—— 1995 'Review of: *Taking Charge: The Electric Automobile in America*, by Michael Brian Schiffer'. *Isis* 86: 351–352.

Schiffer, M.B. 1978 'Methodological issues in ethnoarchaeology'. In Richard A. Gould (ed.) *Explorations in Ethnoarchaeology*. Albuquerque: University of New Mexico Press, pp. 229–247.

—— 1991 *The Portable Radio in American Life*. Tucson: University of Arizona Press.

—— 1992a *Technological Perspectives on Behavioral Change*. Tucson: University of Arizona Press.

—— 1992b 'Archaeology and Behavioral Science: Manifesto for an Imperial Archaeology'. In LuAnn Wandsnider (ed.) *Quandaries and Quests: Visions of Archaeology's Future*. Southern Illinois University, Carbondale, Center for Archaeological Investigations, Occasional Paper 20, pp. 225–238.

—— 1995a 'Social theory and history in behavioral archaeology'. In J.M. Skibo, W.H. Walker, and A.E. Nielsen (eds) *Expanding Archaeology*. University of Utah Press, Salt Lake City, pp. 22–35.

—— 1995b 'The historical context for electric car commercialization'. In NESEA's Sustainable Transportation and S/EV95, *Proceedings*. Greenfield, Massachusetts: Northeast Sustainable Energy Association, pp. 7–18.

—— 1996a 'Formation processes of the archaeological and historical records'. In W.D. Kingery (ed.) *Learning From Things: Method and Theory in Material Culture Studies*. Washington, DC: Smithsonian Institution Press, pp. 73–80.

—— 1996b *Some Relationships Between Behavioral and Evolutionary Archaeologies*. *American Antiquity* 61: 643–662.

—— 1996c *Formation Processes of the Archaeological Record*. Salt Lake City: University of Utah Press.

Schiffer, M.B., T.C. Butts, and K.K. Grimm 1994 *Taking Charge: The Electric Automobile in America*. Washington, DC: Smithsonian Institution Press.

Schiffer, M.B., T.E. Downing and M. McCarthy 1981 'Waste not, want not: an ethnoarchaeological study of reuse in Tucson, Arizona'. In R.A. Gould and M.B. Schiffer (eds) *Modern Material Culture: The Archaeology of Us*. New York: Academic Press, pp. 67–86.

Schiffer, M.B. and T. Majewski (n.d.) 'Modern material-culture studies: toward an archaeology of consumerism'. In T. Majewski and C.E. Orser, Jr (eds) *International Handbook of Historical Archaeology*. New York: Plenum (ms. 1998, in press).

Schiffer, M.B. and J.M. Skibo 1987 'Theory and experiment in the study of technological change'. *Current Anthropology* 28: 595–622.

—— 1997 'The explanation of artifact variability'. *American Antiquity* 62: 27–50.

Scott, R.F. 1966 'Does mourning become the electric?' *Automobile Quarterly* 5: 194–207.

Smith, F.W. 1914 'The electric vehicle of to-day'. *The House Beautiful* April, pp. 56–57.

Spencer-Wood, S. (ed.) 1987 *Consumer Choice in Historical Archaeology*. Plenum, New York.

Stich, P. 1996 *Deconstructing the Mind*. Oxford University Press, New York.

Sutphen, H. 1901 'Touring in automobiles'. *Outing* 38: 197–202.

Towle, H.L. 1911 'Electric vehicles – to-day and tomorrow'. *Collier's* 7 January, pp. 32–34.

Volti, Rudi 1990 'Why internal combustion?' *American Heritage of Invention & Technology* 6(2): 42–47.

Walker, W.H., J.M. Skibo and Axel E. Nielsen 1995 'Introduction: expanding archaeology'. In J.M. Skibo, W.H. Walker and A.E. Nielsen (eds) *Expanding Archaeology*. Salt Lake City: University of Utah Press, pp. 1–12.

Wakefield, E.H. 1994 *History of the Electric Automobile: Battery-Only Powered Cars*. Warrendale, Pennsylvania: Society of Automotive Engineers.

Wilson, D. 1995 'The analysis of domestic refuse in historical archaeology'. In J.M. Skibo, W.H. Walker and A.E. Nielsen (eds) *Expanding Archaeology*. University of Utah Press, Salt Lake City, pp. 126–140.

Zedeño, M.N. 1997 'Landscapes, land use, and the history of territory formation: an example from the puebloan Southwest'. *Journal of Archaeological Method and Theory* 4: 67–103.

5

TAKING THINGS MORE SERIOUSLY

Psychological theories of autism and the material-social divide

Emma Williams and Alan Costall

Psychology appears to have special problems with objects. To the limited extent that psychological theory even touches upon things, they have been regarded as existing primarily in a physical, asocial realm, as distinct from the socio-cultural domain of people. The most familiar treatment of object use in the child development literature is that of the 'neo-Piagetian child' engaged in solitary exploration of the objects in his or her surroundings, actively constructing and testing hypotheses about them through various manipulations. Even so, the child's actions with objects have not been of primary interest in itself to psychologists; instead, the child's activity has been treated as an indirect 'index' of the development of underlying 'cognitive structures'.

In this chapter, we shall take the predominant theoretical approaches to autism as an example or case study of a more general problem psychology has with materiality. Orthodox accounts of autism (e.g., Leslie 1987; Baron-Cohen 1995; Hobson 1993) focus almost exclusively on the difficulties that children with autism have in understanding and relating to other people and largely disregard their relations to things. Although some attention is paid in these theories to certain limited aspects of object use, notably 'pretend play' with objects, these have been of theoretical interest solely to the extent that they provide an 'index' of a supposedly disembodied capacity for symbolism.

Nevertheless, within developmental psychology there does exist an important body of 'socio-cultural' theory and research, largely drawing upon the tradition of Soviet psychology, that challenges any rigid separation of the social and the material in children's developing understanding of their surroundings. In the light of this challenge, it would seem highly unlikely that the problems associated with autism, whatever their underlying 'cause', would be tidily restricted, as current theories seem to suggest, to any particular 'domain' of the child's life. If the child's relations with people are disrupted, then their understanding and use of objects should *also* be impaired – and *vice versa*.

The social context of object use

Our dealings with other people and with objects do not occur in mutual isolation. And this is true not only for adults, but all the more so for infants and young children. Even if children wish to be left alone to discover the meanings of things all by themselves they are seldom left to do so. This is not just a matter of preventing them from investigating dangerous or vulnerable objects such as electric power sockets or delicate china. They are 'introduced' to objects:

> [The] notion of an individual, a child, who is all by itself with the world of objects is a completely artificial abstraction. The individual is not simply thrown into the human world; it is introduced into this world by the people around it; and they guide it in that world.
>
> (Leontiev 1981: 135)

One important aspect of the child's developing sense of the meaning of things is the appreciation that most of the objects they encounter have a single, definite function or, in other words, a 'canonical' (Costall 1997) or 'preferred' affordance (Loveland 1991). Objects can be used in non-standard ways, but this 'misuse' can incur sanctions such as actual damage to the object, social embarrassment, or worse. And, of course, 'mistakes' in the proper use of objects are not confined to children (see Preston Chapter 2). A striking example of 'artefact abuse', recently reported to us by a member of a computer technical support team, concerns a customer's puzzling complaint about the malfunctioning of the 'retractable coffee holder' on his new computer. The 'coffee holder' turned out to be the built-in CD-ROM drive which the user had co-opted in all innocence as a tray for holding his cups of coffee, creating some damage to the equipment and also to his dignity.

Parents and other care-givers play a crucial role in introducing their infants to the shared/conventional meanings of objects by first drawing the child's attention to the object, and then demonstrating how it is used. They also structure the wider setting, to encourage certain actions and discourage or prevent others (Valsiner 1987). For example, in teaching a child to use cutlery, distracting objects (such as toys) may be placed out of reach and sight, and the cutlery placed at an appropriate orientation and distance from the child. In addition to such deliberate interventions, other people's actions on objects also provide a model, not necessarily intentional, for the child to imitate.

Social influence, however, does not simply occur around objects, but through them. Our world has already been shaped by human activity, and is full of things designed by people to be used in specific human activities, by people who share a common body shape, needs and a cultural history. Objects themselves are, as Leontiev (1981: 134) has put, 'a crystallisation of human activities' and hence a 'focus of enduring and cumulative [social] influence'. Artefacts such as a child's toothbrush or potty provide a means by which the child appropriates new action schemes, and in so doing enters into the shared practices of society (Volpert 1985). The very form of objects constrains our possible activities with them, drawing us into common actions. Indeed, objects intended specifically for children are not simply scaled-down versions of the adult article, but are often specially designed to further constrain and guide the infant's activity, such as curved plastic cutlery and trainer cups (Valsiner 1987).

Unfortunately, the fixation with 'mental representations' within modern psychology has not only deflected attention away from the role of other people in the mediation of object use, but also from the psychological significance of objects themselves. This has certainly been the case in much of the recent research on 'pretend play', that is, the child's playful 'misuse' of an object as though it were something else, for example, using a rattle shaped like a dumb-bell as if it were a phone. As we shall see, the standard cognitive accounts of pretend play regard such symbolism as dependent upon a decontextualised cognitive capacity, and largely disregard both the constraining and enabling functions of the object itself. Several recent studies, however, have clearly demonstrated that the object, far from being incidental, is an essential component of the representational act. Children are acutely sensitive to what any specific object could represent, being happy to pretend that a shoe is a boat, for example, but emphatically refusing to treat a comb in the same way (Bugrimenko and Smirnova 1992; Szokolszky 1996).

How children with autism relate to objects

In light of the many ways in which our use of objects is socially embedded, it seems reasonable to suppose that those who experience difficulties in relating to other people (as children with autism certainly do) would also have extensive difficulties in dealing with objects. Yet the recent textbooks on autism, which reflect the current theoretical preoccupation in psychology with internal 'cognitive processes', seem to suggest otherwise. They include little discussion of object use, with the exception of 'pretend play' which they present as a highly specific and circumscribed impairment in the child's dealings with objects (Frith 1989; Happé 1994; Hobson 1993; Baron-Cohen and Howlin 1993; Baron-Cohen 1995).

Puzzled by the discrepancy between the textbook picture of autism and the implications of the socio-cultural approach to human development, we have searched the literature for any studies of autism which might bear, at least indirectly, on the question of object use. As we discovered, there does exist extensive information about how children with autism relate to objects, although this information is scattered, and often appears in publications in which object use is not the focal concern. Once the evidence was collated however, we found that a clear picture emerged. Object use is indeed impaired in many different ways for children with autism and problems are by no means confined to the field of pretend play.

Exploration

The evidence available reveals several unusual features in the early exploration of objects by children with autism, not accounted for by their developmental age: they appear to persist in the early undifferentiated manipulations of objects (waving, banging and mouthing) and show a preference for exploring objects using the proximal senses of touch, taste and smell (Sigman and Ungerer 1984; Freeman *et al.* 1984; Adrien *et al.* 1987; Libby *et al.* 1998); visual inspection of objects frequently takes an unusual form, where objects are twisted close to their eyes (Wing 1969; Hermelin and O'Connor 1970), or just one object or a single part of it is looked at for extended periods of time (Gillberg *et al.* 1990); and objects tend to be used stereotypically such as lining them up in rows or on top of one another (Sigman and Mundy 1987).

The shared use of objects

Children with autism also appear to have particular difficulties both in sharing objects with other people and in learning about object use through copying what other people are doing with them. When encountering objects they seldom engage in social referencing and gestures involving joint attention and their imitation of how other people use objects is mechanical and inflexible (Sigman *et al.* 1992; Smith and Bryson 1994).

The conventional use of objects

In addition, children with autism do not always deal with objects 'appropriately'; they tend to pick out isolated aspects of an object regardless of its functional or conventional use, and fixate on unusual meanings of objects which are tiny or irrelevant and not normally noticed (Lord 1983; Freeman *et al.* 1984), such as the cracks in brickwork (Bosch 1970: 39) or the shape of a jigsaw puzzle rather than its picture (Frith 1989). They also tend to categorise or collect objects on the basis of a peculiar feature, regardless of their normal functions. This difficulty in the conventional use of objects is particularly noticeable in the use of utensils, such as cutlery, where there can sometimes be a delay in acquiring social skills which require a specific 'appropriate' use of objects. Nor do they deal with standard toys in conventional ways; they may, for example, persistently spin the wheels of a toy car, rather than pushing it along the ground (Wulff 1985). Finally, children with autism appear insensitive to the status of objects as property, showing an indifference not only to other people's property, but to many of the objects that rightly belong to them (Bosch 1970; Zabel and Zabel 1982).

In summary, children with autism would seem to be having problems with objects in two interconnected ways. On the one hand, their failure to relate to other people means that they are slow, for example, to understand the proper functions of objects and other conventions surrounding object use, including respect for other people's property. On the other hand, the sense they make of objects and the ways they explore them are often highly idiosyncratic, and this, in turn, further distances them from other people. For objects normally provide an item of 'common interest' (Mead 1934: 46), a focus of joint attention and joint activity, and hence an important basis for the development of communication, including language (Lord 1983; Olley 1983).

Current theoretical models of autism and the material-social divide

Since the initial definition of autism as a distinct clinical entity (Kanner 1943), the theoretical literature has invoked a division between relations to the material world and those to the social world. In his seminal paper Kanner drew a striking contrast between the children's fascination and 'excellent' relations with objects and their apparent disinterest and 'non-existent' relations to people. In fact, Kanner's insistence on such an unqualified contrast is somewhat puzzling given that his own case studies, which formed the basis of his identification of autism as a specific disorder, themselves contain many examples of disruptions in object use: obsessive spinning or other repetitive actions on objects, extreme fear or else fascination with apparently unremarkable objects, the prevalence of oral exploration of objects, and an apparent lack of sense of ownership (ibid.: 218–234).

Kanner's commitment to a division of the material and the social persists in the current predominant models of dysfunction in autism, as does the assumption that object use is largely unimpaired (Leslie 1987; Baron-Cohen 1995; Rogers and Pennington 1991; Hobson 1993). Children with autism are regarded as being relatively successful in their dealings with the 'physical' world of things, but as encountering severe difficulties in the socio-cultural realm of other people.

By far the most influential models of autism have been derived from the 'theory of mind' approach which has dominated developmental psychology over the last decade (Baron-Cohen *et al.* 1985; Leslie 1987). According to this approach, a cognitive capacity for 'meta-representation' comes into play around the middle of the second year. This capacity is supposed to underlie two main psychological functions, pretend play and the understanding of other people's mental states. The concept of meta-representation can perhaps best be explained by relating it to two important issues in representational art (e.g portraiture, sculpture, drama): (1) how does the art object 'represent' its subject? and; (2) the 'presence' in our awareness of the art object as an object (See Polanyi 1970; Costall 1991). For example when we are looking at Leonardo's Mona Lisa, we see the woman depicted and the space of the surrounding landscape, but are also aware of the picture in its own right, as a textured and pigmented surface. The representation is experienced both as a representation and as existing in a 'frame' (literally in the case of the picture) so that what it represents is set apart from its immediate setting, the surrounding wallpaper, etc. (Bateson 1973: 160). Similarly the purpose of the concept of 'meta-representation' within the 'theory of mind' approach is to provide an account of the 'decoupling' of mental representations from 'reality' which they argue occurs both in pretend play and in understanding the mental states of other people. According to the meta-representation account, the capacity to engage in pretend play relies upon two psychological functions: the ability to treat an object as though it were something else (for example, a pen as though it were a rocket), and the appreciation that an object is not really the same as the thing it represents.

Up to this point there is clear agreement with the views developed within the psychology of art. But there is a crucial difference. Theorists working in the psychology of art emphasise that it is the very 'deficiency' of a picture, for example, in not fully replicating what it depicts (i.e its flatness) that ensures that the special status of the representation *as a representation* is manifest to the perceiver. In contrast, the modern cognitive theorists, most notably those adopting the 'theory of mind' approach, radically dematerialise the notion of representation and treat the phenomenon of decoupling as a purely disembodied, conceptual affair. These theorists make no reference to the material properties of the object, even though a pen is conspicuously unlike a rocket in many ways. Instead they insist that pretend play is possible only if the child can engage in higher-level mental representation. Pretend play, they argue, requires not only a first-order representation of the pen as a rocket, but also a second-order representation about this representation (a meta-representation), namely that the representation is not true, the object is not really a rocket.

The main concern, however, of the 'theory of mind' theorists has been to account not for pretend play, but for the child's relations with other people. The capacity for meta-representation, they assert, is essential to any but the most superficial understanding of 'other minds'. After all, what another person may believe, think or say, does not always correspond to reality; they may be mistaken in their beliefs, or else deliberately try to mislead. The child, they argue, thus needs to be able to decouple his or her representation of what the other person believes from the true state of affairs by forming a meta-representation of the first-order representation of the belief.

Baron-Cohen *et al.* (1985) proposed that autism derives from an impairment in the decoupling mechanism necessary for the emergence of meta-representations. In such a 'cerebral' approach, where the exclusive concern is with internal developing cognitive structures, there is little acknowledgement of the specific material conditions of existence. However, the logic of this theoretical position would predict a clear pattern of disruption in dealing with objects, such that those activities requiring the ability to meta-represent would be disrupted, whilst those not underpinned by this cognitive capacity ought to be completely intact. This latter point is clearly illustrated by the approach taken by 'theory of mind' theorists' approach to children's play. The theorists have drawn a rigid distinction between two types of play, 'functional' or 'reality play', on the one hand, and 'pretend play', on the other. Only the latter is supposed to require the ability to meta-represent. Thus Leslie (1987) argued that functional play with real objects or with miniature versions of everyday objects, such as pushing a toy car along the ground or putting a spoon to the mouth of a doll, demonstrates simply a conventional understanding of objects involving only first-order representations. Pretence, on the other hand, is supposed to involve meta-representations and includes using an object in one of the following ways: treating it as if it was something else, attributing properties to it which it does not have, or pretending it is present (i.e. gesturally) when in fact it is not. In the case of autism it is argued that there is a dissociation between the two where the former is intact and the latter absent (Baron-Cohen 1987).

The research evidence, however, defies such a neat demarcation. As mentioned above, there is increasing evidence of a marked difference in the frequency and quality of functional play in children with autism, and corresponding findings that pretend play in many cases is not entirely absent, for even in cases where pretend play does not readily occur spontaneously, there is evidence that it can occur in more structured situations (Sigman and Ungerer 1984; Lewis and Boucher 1988; Whyte and Owens 1989; Libby 1997). Whilst Baron-Cohen (1995) has recently expanded the standard 'theory of mind' model to take into account the observed deficits in autism in joint attention, arguing for the failure of an earlier mechanism required to engage in shared attention, his revised theory still fails to account for observed difficulties in children with autism with entering into the normal conventional uses of objects and problems in functional play.

Other representational theories highlight the failure of different cognitive mechanisms in autism, such as difficulties with 'self–other' representations, leading to problems in imitation (Rogers and Pennington 1991; Barresi and Moore 1996). Whilst deficits in imitation might be expected to predict a wider range of problems with object use than the standard 'theory of mind' approach, such theories postulate a disruption in the autistic child's 'sense of self' in relation to other people, which leaves their relations with objects unaffected.

Hobson's (1993) theory contrasts with all of the above models in that it characterises autism not as arising from a cognitive deficit of some kind but as deriving specifically from a congenital disturbance in the child's ability to relate socially to people. Central to his argument is the triangulation concept of secondary intersubjectivity. This refers to an ability which emerges around the age of nine months (Trevarthen and Hubley 1978) where the child becomes able to link together themselves, objects and other people and so achieve a shared understanding of those objects (or events). According to Hobson, this is the essential starting point for the child to experience that another person's view of an object can differ from their own, and is the precursor of meta-representation. He proposes that the child with autism has problems with making the initial linkage between self, other, and object, and hence has no basis on which to build towards meta-representation. Whilst such a position on the face of it appears to promise an integration of the understanding of people and things, in fact, as the following quote clearly demonstrates, Hobson's emphasis is not on how we achieve a shared understanding of objects in the first place, but on how we come to see things *differently*:

> any object can be construed differently by different people, and any person can apprehend meanings that are person-dependent rather than object specified. Not only may one person find alarming what another finds attractive but also one person may construe something (say a spoon) as a device for feeding, whilst another sees it as an instrument for banging.
>
> (Hobson 1993: 17)

Whilst Hobson's account does acknowledge the necessity of first having a shared view of objects before one can appreciate how people may see and use them differently, how this initial co-ordination comes about is never explained. It is simply assumed as the starting position. In fact Hobson's approach does not represent as radically different an approach from 'theory of mind' as might be expected from its starting premises. Rather its aim is to set up the *preconditions* for a 'theory of mind' to develop and as such it deals only with those problems in object use already identified by 'theory of mind'.

Among recent theorists, Loveland (1991) is alone in emphasising the autistic child's extensive difficulties in dealing with objects. Her paper draws upon Gibson's concept of affordances (Gibson 1979) to develop a theoretical alternative to representationalist and affective accounts of autism. The theory of affordances attempts to put meaning back into the world first by relating meaning to action then by addressing the neglected dualism of agent and world. Gibson proposed that what we primarily attend to in our surroundings are not isolated properties such as shapes and edges but rather 'affordances', the opportunities things offer (afford) for perception and action relative to the specific physical and psychological capacities of a particular organism. For example a chair is 'sit-on-able', a door handle is 'graspable'. The relationship between the organism and their environment is seen as a mutual one, where each develops in relation to the other.

Loveland (1991) identifies three kinds of non-exclusive affordances in the child's environment: the physical, the culturally selected and the social and communicative. She argues that autism involves a specific impairment in the child's ability to detect not only the affordances of other people, but the culturally selected affordances of things. Loveland, in contrast to the other theorists we have considered, does discuss many aspects of object use, including the appropriate use of objects. However, although she certainly discusses the importance of social referencing and joint attention, her account does not fully elaborate upon the developmental interplay between the child's understanding of the culturally selected affordances of objects and of the social and communicative affordances of other people. Furthermore, her account seems to invoke the questionable assumption that, in so far as any autistic child can cope with objects to some degree, this basic level of understanding is *a*social.

The material-social divide

To summarise, we believe that the material-social divide structures all the theoretical approaches to autism we have considered, if in some cases unwittingly. Whilst the standard 'theory of mind' approach proposes an impairment in a specific cognitive mechanism that has consequences for certain relations to objects as well as understanding people's mental states, its consideration of objects has been limited to pretend play. In addition, disruptions in pretend play are simply seen as the manifestation of a particular cognitive incapacity and there is no attempt to link problems in understanding people to disruptions in relating to objects more directly. In more recent developments of this approach, most notably by Baron-Cohen (1995), the assumption of two distinct worlds, the social and the physical, has, if anything become more obvious. Baron-Cohen now invokes a host of cognitive modules, each with its own specific function (e.g. a 'Shared Attention Mechanism' and an 'Eye Direction Detector'), yet the same categorical thinking persists, along with a commitment to a dualism of the social and the asocial. The consequences of autism are assumed to be largely restricted to the child's dealings with other people, and, in particular, divining their 'hidden intentions'. In fact, none of these newly proposed modules which Baron-Cohen claims to be impaired in autism would result directly in disruptions in the child's dealings with things.

Certainly Hobson's (1993) social account of autism starts out in just the right direction. Unfortunately, however, Hobson does not then set out a fresh agenda, but largely confines himself to setting out the preconditions for the development of a 'theory of mind' rather than offering an alternative explanation of autism *per se*. As such, his theory limits itself to an explanation of those problems already identified by proponents of 'theory of mind' and does not explore how the proposed primary difficulties in social intersubjectivity might relate to problems in dealing with objects in the earliest phases of development.

Of all the accounts we have considered, that of Loveland (1991) is the most promising and her work has had an important influence on our own thinking. Loveland addresses several of the difficulties faced by those with autism in their dealings with the material as well as social and communicative problems. She draws an analytical distinction between 'physical', 'cultural' and 'social and communicative' affordances such that the latter two are considered 'social' whilst physical affordances, by implication, would appear to be 'asocial'. Unfortunately, although she insists that these categories are not meant to be mutually exclusive, her account stops short of pursuing their interconnections, and so, by default, leaves the 'social' and 'asocial' disconnected.

'Socialising' affordances

We share with Loveland the view that Gibson's concept of affordances provides a useful framework for considering the problems that children with autism have in relating to their environment. One of the reasons object use has been neglected in current theorising on autism has been the exclusive concern in current theorising on autism with the development of hypothesised 'internal' cognitive structures, leaving no room for any consideration of the child's real world. Gibson's concept of affordances was precisely intended to bridge the gap between activity and its material conditions and hence bring object use back onto the agenda. However, the concept of affordances, as widely understood, seems to underplay the interpenetration between the social and the material. As it stands, his approach can be criticised for presenting an asocial view of perception, to the extent that it has been interpreted, even by sympathetic critics, as only applying to 'simple visually guided behaviour such as that of insects' (Bruce and Green 1990: 390) and not for relations that are culturally specific. Gibson, in his overriding concern to get away from the idea of mediation by internal representations and language and focus instead on the material conditions of action, proved very ambivalent about pursuing the implications of the fact that we develop and live in a socio-cultural milieu (Costall 1995).

In our view a 'socialised' concept of affordances would provide a useful framework within which to account for the picture of widespread disruption in object use evident in children with autism. Our intention, however, is not to formulate an alternative theory so much as to provide a more inclusive description of the child's problems which at the present time none of the predominant theories of autism can explain. In proposing that researchers should take a closer look at the relations of children with autism to objects, we do not mean to play down the social dimension of autism in favour of a material one, but rather to argue against maintaining a rigid material-social divide. If we are to understand the picture of disrupted relations to objects manifest in autism and indeed the use of objects by people in general, both

106

theory and research need to keep the social and material together rather than treating them as if they were separate realms of existence. Objects 'exist' in a social world and are, in turn, an enduring source of social influence, shaping our actions in common ways and serving as a focus of our communications and relations with each other.

Logically it is the case that even if autism is regarded as specifically a deficit in understanding other people, arising from an impairment in a cognitive module, as is posited by the dominant theory considered above, this in itself should lead us to expect correspondingly widespread disruption in the autistic child's use of objects given the extensive socio-cultural research on object use by typically developing children demonstrating that our dealings with objects are mediated by other people. Conversely, if autism involves a disruption in the use and understanding of objects, this should also manifest itself in disturbances in interpersonal relations, given the importance of a shared understanding and use of objects in facilitating interaction.

Conclusion

Our purpose in this chapter has been to present a 'case study' in psychological theory. We have taken the example of autism partly because it relates to our own research interest, but more importantly because it would seem to be the kind of practical human problem that should, if anything, discourage or attentuate the kinds of rigid dualisms which structure modern psychological theory. What we find, however, is that modern theories of autism largely persist in limiting their attention to a highly circumscribed set of psychological 'tasks': pretend play and the understanding of other people's beliefs, despite existing evidence of widespread disruptions in the ways in which children with autism relate to objects.

In our view, the selective focus of modern theories of autism is a reflection of much wider problems in psychology. The most obvious problem is, of course, the dualism of the social and the material. This dualism is not unique to psychology; as Joerges has put it, the natural sciences have abstracted for themselves a 'material world' set apart from human concerns, and the social sciences, in their turn, have constructed 'a world of actors devoid of things' (Joerges 1988: 220). However it is particularly acute within psychology, and for two major reasons. First of all, psychologists have come to trade in a curiously limited conception of the social; the social is largely reduced to the interpersonal, and there is little recognition of the historical or 'institutional' status of objects (see Costall 1997). Second, psychology has become increasingly 'unworldly' in recent years:

[Cognitive psychologists] argue that research should always begin with a theory; not just any theory, but a specific model of the internal processes that underlie the behavior of interest. That mental model is then tested as thoroughly as possible in carefully designed experimental paradigms. When it has been proven false (as it invariably is), a revised model is constructed so that the cycle can begin anew. The aim of the research is not to discover any secret of nature; it is to devise models that fit a certain range of laboratory data better than their competitors do.

(Neisser 1997: 248)

Psychology has thus become introverted in two senses. First of all, researchers devote their time to pursuing artificial problems of their own creation. Second, they are convinced that the real 'object' of their study is not what people actually do and the material conditions of action, but hypothetical and essentially internal structures and processes that supposedly underlie human agency. Yet what people do and the material resources which support this activity should be a serious concern for psychologists. Certainly, the difficulties children with autism have in dealing with and making sense of objects are a significant problem for themselves and their caregivers, not least because their idiosyncratic way of relating to objects sets them apart from other people.

References

Adrien, J.L. Ornitz, E., Barthelemy, D., Sauvage, D. and Lelerd, G. 1987 'The presence or absence of certain behaviours associated with infantile autism in severally retarded autistic and non-autistic retarded children and very young normal children'. *Journal of Autism and Developmental Disorders* 17(3): 407–416.

Atlas, J.A. 1990 'Play in assessment and intervention in childhood psychoses'. *Child Psychiatry in Human Development* 21: 119–133.

Barresi, J. and Moore, C. 1996 'Intentional relations and social understanding'. *Behavioral and Brain Sciences* 19, 107–154.

Baron-Cohen, S. 1987 'Autism and symbolic play'. *British Journal of Developmental Psychology* 5: 139–148.

—— 1995 *Mindblindness: An Essay on Autism and Theory of Mind*. Cambridge, MA: MIT.

Baron-Cohen, S. and Howlin, P. 1993 'The theory of mind deficit in autism: some questions for teaching and diagnosis'. In S. Baron-Cohen, H. Tager-Flusberg, D. Cohen and F. Volkmar (eds) *Understanding Other Minds: Perspectives from Autism*. Oxford: Oxford University Press, pp. 131–152.

Baron-Cohen, S., Leslie, A.M. and Frith, U. 1985 'Does the autistic child have a "theory of mind"?' *Cognition* 21: 37–46.

Bateson, G. 1973 *Steps Towards an Ecology of Mind*. London: Paladin.

Bosch, G. 1970 *Infantile Autism: A Clinical and Phenomenological-Anthropological Investigation Taking Language as the Guide*. New York: Springer.

Bruce, V. and Green, P. 1990 *Visual Perception: Physiology, Psychology and Ecology* (2nd edn). Hove: Lawrence Erlbaum.

Bruner, J. and Feldman, C. 1993 'Theories of mind and the problem of autism'. In S. Baron-Cohen, H. Tager-Flusberg, D. Cohen and F. Volkmar (eds) *Understanding Other Minds: Perspectives from Autism*. Oxford: Oxford University Press, pp. 131–152; 267–291.

Bugrimenko, E.A. and Smirnova, E. O. 1992 'Paradoxes of children's play in Vygotsky's theory'. In G.C. Cupchik and J. Laszlo (eds) *Emerging Visions of the Aesthetic Process*. Cambridge: Cambridge University Press, pp. 286–299.

Costall, A.P. 1991 'Phenomenal reality'. In G. Thines, A.P. Costall and G.E. Butterworth (eds) *Michotte's Experimental Phenomenology of Perception*. Hillsdale, NJ: Erlbaum, pp. 169–172.

—— 1995 'Socialising affordances'. *Theory and Psychology* 5: 467–482.

——1997 'The meaning of things'. *Social Analysis* 41(1): 76–86.

DeMyer, M.K., Mann, N.A., Tilton, J.R. and Loew, L.H. 1967 'Toy-play behaviour and the use of the body by autistic and normal children as reported by mothers'. *Psychological Reports* 21: 973–981.

El'Konin 1966 'Symbolics and its function in the play of children'. *Soviet Education* 8(7): 139–148.

Freeman, B.J., Ritvo, E.R. and Schroth, P.C. 1984 'Behaviour assessment of the syndrome of autism: behaviour observation system'. *Journal of the American Academy of Child Psychology* 23(5): 588–594.

Frith, U. 1989 *Autism: Explaining the Enigma*. Oxford: Basil Blackwell.

Gibson, J.J. 1979 *The Ecological Approach to Visual Perception*. Boston: Houghton-Mifflin.

Gillberg, C., Ehlers, S., Schuamann, H., Jakobsson, G., Dahlgren, S.O., Lindblom, R., Bagenholm, A., Tjuus, T. and Blidner, E. 1990 'Autism under age 3 years: A clinical study of 28 cases referred for autistic symptoms in infancy'. *Journal of Childhood Psychology and Psychiatry* 31(6): 921–934.

Gould, J. 1986 'The Lowe and Costello symbolic play test in socially impaired children'. *Journal of Autism and Developmental Disorders* 16: 199–213.

Happé, F. 1994 *Autism: An Introduction to Psychological Theory*. London: UCL Press.

Hermelin, B. and O'Connor, N. 1970 *Psychological Experiments with Autistic Children*. Oxford: Pergamon Press.

Hobson, R.P. 1993 *Autism and the Development of Mind*. Hillsdale NJ: Lawrence Erlbaum.

Jarrold, C., Boucher, J. and Smith, P.K. 1993 'Symbolic play in autism: a review'. *Journal of Autism and Developmental Disorders* 23: 281–387.

Joerges, B. 1988 'Technology in everyday life: Conceptual queries'. *Journal for the Theory of Social Behaviour* 18: 221–237.

Kanner, L. 1943 'Autistic disturbances of affective contact'. *Nervous Child* 2: 217–250.

Kaufman, B.N. 1977 *Son Rise*. New York: Warner.

Leontiev, A.N. 1981 *Problems of the Development of Mind*. Moscow: Progress Publishers.

Leslie, A. 1987 'Pretence and representation in infancy: origins of "theory of mind"'. *Psychological Review* 94: 84–106.

Lewis, V. and Boucher, J. 1988 'Spontaneous, instructed and elicited play in relatively able autistic children'. *The British Journal of Developmental Psychology* 6: 325–338.

—— 1995 'Generativity in the play of young people with autism'. *Journal of Autism and Developmental Disorders* 25: 105–121.

Libby, S., Powell, S., Messer, D. and Jordan, R. (1997) 'Imitation of pretend play acts by children with autism and Down Syndrome'. *Journal of Autism and Developmental Disorders*, 27: 4, pp. 365–383.

Libby, S., Powell, S., Messer, D. and Jordan, R. (1998) 'Spontaneous pretend play in children with autism: a reappraisal'. *Journal of Autism and Developmental Disorders* 28: 487–497.

Lord, C. 1983 'Autism and the comprehension of language'. In E. Schopler and G.B. Mesibov (eds) *Communication Problems in Autism*. New York: Plenum Press, pp. 257–281.

Loveland, K.A. 1991 'Social affordances and interaction II: Autism and the affordances of the human environment'. *Ecological Psychology* 3: 99–119.

Mead, G.H. 1934 *Mind, Self, and Society from the Standpoints of a Social Behaviorist*. Chicago: University of Chicago Press.

Neisser, U. 1997 'The future of cognitive science: An ecological analysis'. In D.M. Johnson and C.E. Erneling (eds) *The Future of the Cognitive Revolution*. New York: Oxford University Press, pp. 247–260.

Olley, J.G. 1983 'Social aspects of communication in autism'. In E. Schopler and G.B. Mesibov (eds) *Communication Problems in Autism*. New York: Plenum Publishers, pp. 311–328.

Polanyi, M. 1970 'What is a painting?' *British Journal of Aesthetics* 10: 225–236.

Rogers, S.J and Pennington, B.F. 1991 'A theoretical approach to the deficits in infantile autism'. *Development and Psychopathology* 3: 137–162.

Russell, J., Mauthner, N., Sharpe, S. and Tidswell, T. 1991 'The "windows" task as a measure of strategic deception in preschoolers and autistic subjects'. *British Journal of Developmental Psychology* 9: 331–349.

Sigman, M. and Mundy, P. 1987 'Symbolic processes in young autistic children'. In D. Cicchetti and Beeghly (eds) *Symbolic Development in Atypical Children. New Directions for Child Development* No. 36. San Francisco: Jossey-Bass, pp. 31–46.

Sigman, M. and Ungerer, J.A. 1984 'Cognitive and language skills in autistic, retarded, and normal children'. *Developmental Psychology* 20: 293–302.

Sigman, M., Kasari, C., Kwon, J. and Yirmiya, N. 1992 'Responses to the negative emotions of others by autistic, mentally retarded and normal children'. *Child Development* 63: 796–807.

Smith, I.M. and Bryson, S.E. 1994 'Imitation and action in children with autism'. *Psychological Bulletin* 116: 259–273.

Szokolszky, A. 1996 'Using one object as if it were another. The perception and use of affordances in pretend object play'. Unpublished Ph.D. thesis, University of Connecticut.

Trevarthen, C. and Hubley, P. 1978 'Secondary intersubjectivity: confidence, confiding and acts of meaning in the first year'. In A. Lock (ed.) *Action, Gesture and Symbol: The Emergence of Language*. London: Academic Press, pp. 183–229.

Valsiner, J. 1987 *Culture and the Development of Children's Action: A Cultural Historical Theory*. Chichester: Wiley.

Volpert, W. 1985 'Epilogue'. In M. Frese and J. Sabini (eds) *Goal Directed Behavior: The Concept of Action in Psychology*. Hillsdale, NJ: Erlbaum, pp. 357–365.

Whyte, J. and Owens, A. 1989 'Language and symbolic object play: some findings from a study of autistic children'. *The Irish Journal of Psychology* 10: 317–332.

Wing, L. 1969 'The handicaps of autistic children – A comparative study'. *Journal of Child Psychology and Psychiatry* 10: 1–23.

Wulff, S. 1985 'The symbolic and object play of children with autism: a review'. *Journal of Autism and Developmental Disorders* 15(2): 139–148.

Zabel, M.K. and Zabel, R.H. 1982 'Ethological approaches with autistic and other abnormal populations'. *Journal of Autism and Developmental Disorders* 12: 71–83.

6

POMP AND CIRCUMSTANCE

Archaeology, modernity and the corporatisation of death: early social and political Victorian attitudes towards burial practice

George Nash

Introduction: the growth of secularised society

This chapter is concerned with early Victorian attitudes towards burial practice. I have primarily used two early Victorian examples, which, in their own way, exemplify a paradox in the Victorian approach to death. Both Highgate Cemetery (1839) in north London and the Necropolis Railway and Brookwood Cemetery, Surrey (1852) were, in part, introduced to relieve the chronic and insanitary conditions of the churchyards and cemeteries in London. Within this chapter, I wish to explore the way in which attitudes towards bourgeois and commoner burial practice were applied at Highgate and Brookwood cemeteries. Although serving similar needs, both cemeteries appear to represent particular strands within Victorian society. They also reveal a contradiction in terms of how the dead are disposed of and how they were represented in the after-life, especially through the role of iconography and the way the deceased were treated. This chapter will also outline the cultural and secular influences of the day, as well as discussing the social, economic and political constraints which would have controlled and manipulated burial practice during this brief period in Victorian history.

The archaeological record frequently reveals little of how the minds of our ancestors coped with emotions relating to death. As one attempts to comprehend the idiosyncrasies connected to funerary activity from, say, prehistory, or even the early medieval period, the artefact is found to be merely a *thing*, an object potentially devoid of concept or meaning. Relatively speaking, meaning transcends this barrier via assumption and subjectivity. As one looks at modern material culture, *things* become more or less recognisable and develop meaning. However, Shanks and Tilley (1987: 172) suggest that such studies on modern material culture have been largely undertaken using empiricist and functionalist perspectives. This approach has limited the understanding of such articles to disable them merely as objects. One can make an interpretation, an assumption regarding an object; but all that can be made is a primary guess as to its role within society. Even within recent history, the archaeologist and the historian have divorced objects from meaning – we are basically *creatures* of our time (ibid.: 93). The role and meaning of such imagery during the late eighteenth and early nineteenth centuries is slightly more accessible in its relationship between scholar and objectivity.

This notion is further reinforced by Flannery and Marcus (1998: 45) who categorise human intellectual activity under four headings: cosmology, religion, ideology and iconography. Elements of each of these are present throughout most of human history. In attempt to understand what is going on (even during the early Victorian period), a cultural theoretical approach has been incorporated into this chapter. By culture theory, I do not mean social theory. The evidence for this period is very much a straightforward question of assessing the available archaeological and historic data. Using these variables, I have incorporated a 'world view' to the problem of understanding attitude (see Whitley 1998: 1–32). The mechanisms controlling and manipulating such human emotions as grief and mourning are historically recorded and can be more easily understood purely in the knowledge that within our own society similar things go on!

Social change within late-eighteenth- and early-nineteenth-century [British] society is mainly the result of primary and secondary mechanisms of industrialisation, in particular, changes in population dynamics – migration from the countryside to the towns – and the establishment of a rigid class structure. These changes are certainly reflected in the material culture and the literature of the day. Prior to industrialisation, society was dependent upon descending rank. Social structure relied on the patronage of an elite, which, although maintained during the eighteenth century, was somewhat diluted by the mid nineteenth century. By 1815, the term 'middle class' had entered the English language and, with it, a rise in the so-named 'professional and merchant classes'. This new elite resented the feudal regime of the once-powerful clergy and landed gentry (Rose 1985: 276). This resentment is reflected in a change within the burial industry. At about the same time there is a dramatic change in burial practice which includes the establishment of successfully organised cemeteries which are run without the control of the Church of England (Rugg 1998: 44). At this point in time, death had become a visibly commercial institution.

Good mourning: respectability of death

Universally, death creates a period of tension and confusion among the living during which contrary emotions rise to the surface. Should death be celebrated as a joyous release from the trials and tribulations of earthly life, or should this be a time of grieving during which society mourns the loss of one of its own? Should death be feared or should it be embraced? Within late-eighteenth and nineteenth-century Britain there appears to be an element of both. Following death, the deceased won't have become suspended in a 'liminal' state, during which they were neither of this life nor the next. When the body dies, nature begins to stake its claim and the relentless process of bodily decay sets in (Children and Nash 1998: 29). In this condition, the individual is a source of pollution and danger. But this is also a time to reassert what is human.

The enculturation of death may be seen as an attempt to retrieve the deceased from the clutches of nature. The mortuary symbolism of Victorian England concealed the reality of a decomposing corpse, suggesting rather that the deceased was merely sleeping (ibid.: 29). During this period a sophisticated package of mortuary rituals emerged, echoes of which can be traced in the depositional pattern of human remains and the elaborate tomb architecture which characterises this period. In all cases, the status of the deceased was an important factor influencing the treatment of the body. There is little evidence to suggest that all members of early Victorian society are regarded as equal in death. Society refused to allow death to become 'the great leveller'. The status of the deceased was very evident. During the latter part of the seventeenth century, personalised gravestones had become popular and there was a boom in the production of such items amongst the prosperous classes (Tarlow 1998: 42). A pauper would be merely disposed of in an unmarked and makeshift communal grave, while the wealthy (and exclusively male) was assured of a place in posterity (if not necessarily in heaven!) through the sheer monumentality of the mortuary edifice. Monumentality can be clearly witnessed as one ascends Highgate (Cemetery) Hill, where tombs become increasingly monumental, until, at the summit, the dead remain forever visible. The preparation of the body, too, suggests that privilege in life is being carried over into the afterlife. The denial of death reached a high pitch of elaboration by the 1830s. The garish and often overwhelmingly sentimental imagery of the period, which is still evident today in many churchyards, reveals the lengths to which early Victorian society would go in order to conceal the reality of death and decay.

Death extends the *human*, the mundane beyond the daily 'cycles of nature'; it projects the existence of the living into a conscious act into the future, thus establishing a creative discourse (Adam 1997: 518). Moreover, the transition between life and death marks and preserves not just a moment in time when, say, the deceased is part of a melancholy performance – the funeral. The transcendence to death marks a series of 'pasts' and individual characters which, when acted out during life, establishes, not a single person, but a series of characters – a man or woman for all seasons. However, the memory of how one behaved is controlled and manipulated by the living – the dead cannot tell their stories. After death, the living, through memory and story-telling recall a multitude of characters and moods – this can be considered as a transcendence of limited immortality. By limited immortality, I mean the period of time which might constitute two or three generations of one family recalling the memories of the deceased. The only permanent statements of who is buried where, and what he or she stood for, is the gravestone or memorial. The comforting words, gestures and gravestone iconography[1] portray an image that is unreal; the interred is what we want him or her to be and reflects only a tiny segment of reality. The iconic imagery portrayed in most churchyards and cemeteries reflects the (static) transcendence between life and death.

Reflecting this, static icons from the early Victorian period include classical urns, weeping willows, melancholy female figures, upturned torches. Neo-classical in form, all represent the extinguishing of life and are comforting and beneficial icons for the living. The urn appears to be the most popular item in funerary iconography and became part of the conventional funeral and grave furniture during the eighteenth and nineteenth centuries (Llewellyn 1991:99). During antiquity, and especially during the medieval period, the urn served as a repository for ashes and vital organs which were placed within the urn, prior to burial (Pollitt 1986). The remainder of the corpse was placed in a coffin and buried elsewhere (Llewellyn 1991:99). However, funerary icons such as these appear to portray an image that is obsessed with 'the journey' or 'rite of passage' – the body suspended is neither in life nor death. At Highgate and other secularised cemeteries, for example, the iconic imagery portrays no evidence of an afterlife – no heaven, no hell, no ascent or descent. Accepting that *life* displays either a cyclical or linear process (Bourdieu 1977: 154–5), the deceased (and the living) need to know where their final journey ends – if it does at all!

Time for change

Prior to the Industrial Revolution, the church stood at the centre of rural life. Birth, marriage and death were served by the same institution (Hurd 1973: 195). By the time industrialisation had reached its height, population dynamics had shifted people away from rural areas and into the city. The community centre, too, had moved – from the church to the mill and factory. Adult life expectancy was low and infant mortality high (up to 50 per cent). This was not only confined to the lower classes. High mortality rates are recorded across the classes. Victorian values focused upon the family, which was to be united, not only in life, but also in death.

Changes to the social fabric are also reflected in the various cultural movements of the day and had an enduring effect on funerary practice and the design of funerary paraphernalia. By the mid eighteenth century, the baroque movement was replaced by neo-classicism coinciding with the decline of the feudal aristocracy. Also linking within the chronological framework is a fundamental shift in the perception of human consciousness, thereby introducing new approaches of understanding and knowledge as well as placing society into a stratified historical framework. Society could now question and reflect on its own identity and where it stood, especially in death.

The Gothic revival of the mid-nineteenth century can be considered a rejection of the elitist values of the baroque and preceding cultural movements. Although employing many of the artistic temperaments of the baroque, the Gothic movement relied more on the revival of history, in particular, the ornamentation and garnish of the high medieval period. The imagery expressed in, say the architecture appears to be utilised in most walks of society. Certainly, Highgate Cemetery is an early product of the Gothic revival. However, it must be stressed that the architecture at Highgate is not elitist; moreover, the mechanisms in promoting Highgate were considered 'fashionable', which by its nature created a barrier between those who could afford and those who could not. In conjunction with cultural and artistic developments within late-eighteenth-century and early Victorian society, and in parallel to changing relations between the classes, attitudes were also changing towards the treatment of death (Rose 1985: 277). The historical and literary record relating to nineteenth-century burial practice provides an ideal basis for discussing materiality and nineteenth-century attitudes towards modernity.

Health and social security

The problem of overcrowding in London's metropolitan cemeteries had been an ongoing problem, certainly since the reign of Edward VI (c.1547). At this time, Bishop Riley (of London) had questioned the reasoning behind 'harbouring its dead within the walls' (Bowdler 1989). After the Great Fire of 1666, there was a plan to relocate the city burial grounds to sites outside the city walls. Relocation, however, was a problem inasmuch as vital revenue was gained from burial by parishes within the city. Any legislation to remove this was fiercely contested by the (Metropolitan) church authorities. The problem of insanitary burial and, eventually, the imminent risk to public health continued up until the late 1840s. Graveyard overcrowding in London came to a head with the outbreak of a number of epidemics, particularly cholera in 1848–9, which resulted in 15,000 deaths in London. By this time, urban sanitation had become an urgent requirement. In order to relieve some of the overcrowding of London's churchyards, a number of entrepreneurial schemes were set up, including the formation of the London Cemetery Company in 1836. This consortium established the so-called 'Magnificent Seven'[2] – a number of new cemeteries which catered for all pockets, but in particular, the fashionable tastes of the rich and famous (Children and Nash 1998: 25). Highgate Cemetery, one of the 'Magnificent Seven' was partly the result of scandalous insanitary conditions of London's burial grounds.[3] Churchyards within the city catered mainly for the middle and lower classes. The poor could be buried free. Simple coffins were stacked in mass graves up to twenty deep. At Highgate, the rich could afford more grandiose monuments, many of which were built on patronage. Here, immortality was guaranteed. The mill-owner, the factory-owner, the nobility would have his signature indelibly stamped on the largest monument in the most prestigious corner of the cemetery (ibid.: 28). The Highgate Cemetery ethos preached prosperity and status.

Along with graveyard burial, the church vault had, during the eighteenth century, become a fashionable alternative among the rising middle classes. Coffins, many elaborate in design, could be intermittently viewed by the deceased's relatives. At St Pauls, Chadwell (London) and Christ Church, Spitalfields (London) for example, a series of early-nineteenth-century vaults were sold to individual families on a freehold basis (Cox 1998; Reeve and Adams 1993). Each vault would portray family identity and the coffins were draped with symbolic elaboration. For instance, located around the side panels of each coffin, grip-plates, made from stamped cast iron, depicted images such as the weeping willow, an upturned torch or a melancholy female figure, all showing that life had been extinguished. Also manufactured were elaborately pressed tin (coffin) grip plates which subtly portray death in the form of a single human skull held by a melancholy cherub. During this period, the 'mourning' industry prospered further with the production of mourning jewellery which was personalised and included hair crosses,[4] watch-chains, rings and necklaces. An emphasis was placed on the personal. Special items, such as jewellery were usually commissioned as a one-off.

However, contrary to this, and according to Julian Litten (1998), the funeral furnishing trade between the years 1700 and 1850 had little to be proud of. Driven by the politics of the day, the funeral trade was 'entrenched in the middle ground of steadfast conservatism and quasi-respectability'. This retrospective view appears to ignore the direct impact of impending urbanisation; much of the burial industry infrastructure required to sustain a rising mortality was not in place. The need to supply an ever-increasing public demand for the 'most lucrative trade ever invented' (ibid.: 16) by the beginning of the nineteenth century was, indeed, overwhelming.

Ascending Highgate Hill

The siting of Highgate Cemetery, north London, on a prominent hill overlooking what was then the world's most prosperous and largest city represented a corporate image intertwined with the grand and the monumental. Consecrated by the Bishop of London, Highgate Cemetery soon became London's most fashionable necropolis, at the same time as it promoted the fashionable architecture of the day. The buildings were elegantly designed by Stephen Geary and James Bunstone Bunning and the grounds of the cemetery were laid out by David Ramsay.[5]

The entrance to the cemetery consists of a gate house with central entrance, flanked by two Gothic chapels leading to ornamental porticoes. This was the main focus of the façade, outside the main cemetery gates.[6] Passers-by were permitted a glimpse of the exclusive world of the dead within. Set in seventeen acres,[7] the (Western) Cemetery was laid out according to one's pocket. By entering the cemetery, one was penetrating a sacred space; one leaves 'there' and enters 'here' (Ching 1996: 238). The cemetery plan was such that the higher one travelled up Highgate Hill, the higher the status one enjoyed in life. Within the 'Old Ground', or Western Cemetery, individualism appeared to be the main preoccupation of many of the interred. This created an immortality that was both personal and distinctive within grave monument design. The 'signs' of death are all apparent; soldiers with their swords pointing down, a cricketer 'bowled-out', a faithful dog lying beside his master. All these symbols metaphorically indicate life but were used for the after-life. It would appear that the interred were just asleep and not dead. Elsewhere within the upper cemetery, pagan and classical symbols are abundant. The downturned torch, the draped urn and the mythical gods all relate to the need to belong, to create a dynasty, an ancestry. These symbols had been the influence of such furniture designers as Adam, Chippendale and the architects Inigo Jones and Nash – all firmly based within the classical revival movement.

Pagan and near-Eastern influences are clearly visible at the summit of Highgate Cemetery. Here, a series of terraced family vaults embodies a self-contained community for the dead. The façade entrance leads into an Egyptian avenue containing sixteen vaults (Figures 6.1 and 2). Beyond this, a further twenty vaults (or catacombs) form a circular terrace, 'the Circle of Lebanon', around an ancient raised cedar tree.[8] Each vault entrance has projecting door cases with Egyptian pediments with added design to the jamb and head (Gay and Pateman 1992). The architecture is indeed solemn. The cost of each vault would have been around 200 guineas (£220), a small fortune even for an upper-middle-class family.[9] With a capacity of up to fifteen coffins, each vault would have accommodated a 'gloomy dynasty'. The architectural style of the circle portrays a consistent image of near-Eastern decadence and monumentality. Outside the inner circle, past the outer pylons of the northern entrance to the avenue, there is a shift in architectural design; the near-Eastern imagery is replaced by a classical pediment enclosure. The section of the cemetery is further complicated by classical Greek influences. Directly behind the circular vaulting is the Julius Beer[10] mausoleum. Built in 1876, at a cost of about £5,000 and made from (white) Portland limestone, this structure was modelled on one of the ancient wonders of the world – the great Mausoleum of King Mololus at Helicarnassus. Nothing but the best materials were used. The austerity and monumentality of both this structure and the 'Circle of Lebanon' indicates a secularisation of high Victorian society. As we have seen, the Victorians went to enormous lengths to convince themselves that, behind a veil of metaphor and symbolism, their loved ones were merely sleeping. Highgate Cemetery along with others owned by the London Cemetery Company represent the characteristic individualism of Victorian society. This is certainly noticeable in the case of classic revival and near-

Figure 6.1   Highgate Cemetery – entrance to the 'Circle of Lebanon'
Source: English Heritage Photo Library

Eastern monumentality. More importantly, there appears to be an underlying tension with the emotion and the justification of expression for the dead. This is represented by the way architectural forms, such as vaulting and mausoleums, are viewed and approached; the architecture of the dead is enclosing itself onto the living.[11]

The 'social' organisation of space between the main burial centres was so designed as to utilise a series of strategic pathways which eventually lead to the summit of Highgate Hill. The location of each sacred space is directly serviced by an established path. This would eventually terminate at the Beer mausoleum; what Ching regards as a *termination of space* (1996: 264–266). In order to reach the final destination, each pathway must pass through a number of sacred spaces, creating a series of patterns based on rest and movement, through time and space, within the cemetery ground plan.

Termination at the London Necropolis[12] Company Terminus

By the 1850s, burial practice had become more commercialised, resulting in a utilitarian approach; death appeared to embrace the class divide. This is made obvious with a number of bizarre entrepreneurial schemes which were

Figure 6.2 Within the 'Circle of Lebanon' – a self-contained city of the dead
Source: English Heritage Photo Library

Figure 6.3 Termination at the London Necropolis Company Terminus

Source: From the J.M. Clarke Collection

installed to relieve the chronic overcrowding of London's graveyards. One such venture – the London Necropolis Company Terminus[13] – created an interesting paradox with traditional cemeteries and graveyards, both in Victorian London and the provinces, and challenged the status of the deceased individual (see Figure 6.3).

To relieve the threat of insanitary burial practice within the city, the government of the day introduced the Metropolitan Interments Act of 1850. This piece of legislation halted further burials in London churchyards. At about the same time, there were a number of schemes to locate burial grounds outside the city. However, a problem existed of how safely and hygienically to transport corpses from the metropolis to a suitable necropolis.

In 1849, Sir Richard Broun and Robert Sprye proposed a scheme of transporting the dead via the London and Southwest Railway (L&SWR) to a large cemetery site at Woking in Surrey. This service was to be swift and affordable while retaining a certain degree of dignity for relatives and loved ones (Bowdler 1989; Clarke 1992, 1995). Broun's synopsis[14] examined the previous problems of burial within the capital. Over the past thirty years, an estimated 1.5 million corpses had been 'partly inhumed or partly entombed within the metropolis'. Furthermore, the new generation of suburban cemeteries, including Highgate, were quickly being filled. Moreover, they were mainly aimed at an exclusive clientele. Broun also claimed that the poor could not afford the hearse journey to such places, let alone the cost of the plot and the burial. A site either side of the London–Southampton railway line at Woking was proposed as a potential cemetery site (an area thirty times larger than Kensal Green Cemetery). Corpses could be transported to the new cemetery site by railway from central London. Through an Act of Parliament in 1852, and incessant board-room strife, the London Necropolis and National Mausoleum Company was formed.

The first terminus, located at 188 Westminster Road, Lambeth, and designed by architects William Tite and Sir William Cubitt, was completed in 1854 at a cost of £23,000. The deceased were brought to the station entrance via horsedrawn hearse. With discrete dignity, coffins were raised by lift to a 'chapel of rest' which was level with the railway platform. From the chapel, coffins could be easily lifted onto the railway hearse van (Figure 6.4) which would have been pulled by locomotives leased from the L&SWR (Weddell 1979: 581). The cost of transporting a corpse by rail to Brookwood was dependent on the status of the deceased and the pocket of the bereaved. A pauper (3rd class) was charged 2s 6d (12.5p), artisans (2nd class) 5s (25p) and others £1. Attendants and mourners could travel just as cheaply. The low fares for both the living and the dead was a marketing ploy to encourage greater use of the service (Clarke 1995: 104). After the funeral service, mourners could return to Waterloo or Clapham, via the same train, using the same ticket.

The Brookwood Cemetery at Woking was to rival Westminster Abbey for the grandeur of its monuments. One such monument, the 'Mausoleum Cathedral', was constructed of iron and glass and was modelled on Michelangelo's design for St Peter's in Venice. As part of the Act of Parliament, an emphasis had been placed on providing a cheap and efficient service out of London by rail. Shareholders of the L&SWR were at first concerned about the commercial viability of transporting corpses along a mainline railway (Clarke 1995). None the less, Broun had suggested that a site near Waterloo Station would be an ideal location for the terminus (121 Westminster Bridge Road).[15] Reasons for location were that the site was far enough away from

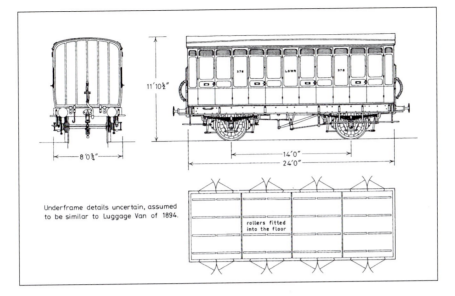

11'10½"

8'0¾"

14'0"
24'0"

Underframe details uncertain, assumed
to be similar to Luggage Van of 1894.

rollers fitted
into the floor

Figure 6.4   Plan and section of the S.W.R. Hearse Carriage (drawn by G.R. Weddell)

Waterloo Station; the numerous railway arches would act as ideal temporary storage space of corpses and the site had easy access to the River Thames, in case there were requests to transport bodies to the cemetery via the river. On an aesthetic note, the route between the London terminus and Brookwood Cemetery passed through uninterrupted rolling countryside which would have consoled mourners accompanying the deceased[16] to his or her final resting place (Bowdler 1989: 2).

At the cemetery, there were separate stops for denominations other than Church of England (see Figure 6.5). According to Bowdler (1989) this was the only segregation within the cemetery. Here, death was treated as a great leveller. The deceased, irrespective of class or status, were transported by the same hearse van and onto the same train and stopped at the same cemetery station. The Railway Magazine of 1904 remarked that the cemetery's railway station was 'the most peaceful in three corners of the kingdom – this station of the dead. Here, even the quiet, subdued puffing of the engine seems almost sympathetic with the sorrow of its living freight'. Arguably though, the way in which the deceased were buried and commemorated still relied on one's pocket.

The cemetery was laid out as a garden cemetery on the Loudonesque principle[17] and was reported as being 'the most beautiful in the world' (see Figure 6.6). The cost-effective layout of each plot allowed for ambitious planting regimes to take place – creating a Garden of Eden for the dead. The monumentality which expressed the rigid class structure at the cemeteries run

Figure 6.5   The Non-Conformist Chapel at Brookwood Cemetery
Source: From the Barry Devonshire Collection

by the London Cemetery Company, in particular Highgate, was in one respect also present at Brookwood. However, for a few extra shillings, all classes could be catered for by Necropolis. The journey from Westminster Bridge Road to the final resting place allowed pauper and banker alike to travel that same route.

The architecture of the cemetery also reflected an ambiguous attempt to disguise class; a very different approach to the ostentatious designs of Highgate and the other 'Magnificent Seven' cemeteries. The two cemetery stations, North Station and South Station, were located on a branch-line off the main London and South Western Railway, opposite the Brookwood Station (see Figure 6.7).

Each station served particular areas of the cemetery. The North Station served the non-conformist area, while the South Station served the Anglican area (Clarke 1995: 37). Both stations were designed by Sydney Smike, architect for the London Necropolis Company, and, according to Clarke (ibid.: 37), were originally built as temporary measures – probably for something more grandiose. The designs for both stations appear standardised and similar to most railway station architecture of the time. The outer wall covering consisted of vertical whitewashed wooden weather-boards which were slatted

Figure 6.6 Plan of the London Necropolis Brookwood Cemetery

Source: Courtesy of the Brookwood Cemetery Society

Figure 6.7 The Last Stop (for the dead). Brookwood Cemetery Station (*c.* 1900)
Source: From the Barry Devonshire Collection

against a substantial timber frame. Both stations placed an emphasis more on the living with a refreshments area and mourners' waiting rooms enclosing an open central space where mourners could congregate, mingle and reminisce. There were five waiting rooms either side of a quadrangle which could accommodate more than one funeral at a time. The design and layout of the Brookwood stations is in complete contrast to the mourners' reception rooms within the Anglican Chapel at the Western Cemetery at Highgate. Every feature of the mortuary chapels and the inner courtyards reflect melancholy images of (Gothic) foreboding. For example, the battlemented parapets, traceried lancet windows, octagonal and gabled buttresses all reflect a sense of despondency. The visitor and mourner alike are visually reminded that Highgate is a place where the *dead* are actually dead. Highgate Hill, the dark undergrowth, exotic trees and architectural imagery cast a shadowy gloom across the entire cemetery. At Brookwood, quite the reverse prevails. Here, *life springs eternal!* The architecture of the stations, chapels and cemetery reminds the visitor that they are in a garden, a cemetery where the dead are merely asleep and have become an organic part of the garden (see Figure 6.8). In contrasting the two cemeteries, one could use Unwin's architectural remarks that 'the admission of light accentuates the place, and allows it to be a garden rather than a forest' (1997: 28).

To summarise …

Within this chapter, I have attempted to draw distinctions between two different burial practices that are occurring alongside each other during the

Figure 6.8   Main entrance to the Garden of Eden – Brookwood Cemetery (Postcard
            c. 1920)

Source: From the Barry Devonshire Collection

early part of the reign of Queen Victoria. The underlying socio-political
structure governing both types of burial are the same. Furthermore, the clientele using both cemeteries is identical. However, the Highgate 'experience'
develops some twelve years prior to the Necropolis enterprise. This relatively
short period of time saw dramatic changes in Victorian society, in particular,
the emergence of a rigid and prosperous middle class. The class structure
appears to be not only governed by a strong socio–economic base, but a political will based on factions of Liberalism and Conservatism. It could be argued
that the Necropolis Railway, although considered an ingenious
entrepreneurial enterprise, was also a radical attempt to liberalise the way in
which the dead should be treated. The burial[18] vaults at St Pauls, Chadwell
and Christ Church, Spitalfields and later the high status burials at Highgate
appear to mark a hiatus in status burial practice at a time when the Industrial
Revolution had altered the demography of most towns and cities of Britain.
Within the metropolis, parishes and boroughs once considered exclusive to
the rich were, by the mid nineteenth century, being colonised by the vast
influx of people from the provincial towns and countryside. One of the few
bastions of status to survive these changes was the way in which the very rich
and the rising middle classes could bury their dead. As with the ghettoisation
of the parishes and boroughs between rich and poor, the churchyard and
cemetery also displayed similar prejudices.

For the individual, the emergence of a merchant 'middle' class came with the need to assert one's status. In life, as well as in death, the trappings and paraphernalia are clear to see. However, within early Victorian society, there is a paradox in burial tradition. At the great metropolitan cemeteries, including Highgate, there is a greater emphasis on the monumentality of the individual, and, throughout the Victorian period, this ethos prevails. At the same time, and across the River Thames, at Woking, the London Necropolis Company was providing an 'express' service which not only had wide appeal across the classes but the meaning of grandiose death was not an issue. Although the dead were mourned and respected, the Necropolis excursion catered more for the needs of the living.[19] Furthermore, the funeral package offered by the company transcended the classes. This service was based on pocket and commercial appeal. Trains for mourners and the deceased, although governed by 1st, 2nd and 3rd class fare, travelled along the same railway line using the same hearse vans. This fact alone suggests that, for a brief part of the 'journey', death had become a 'great leveller', especially in a period when class divisions were so strong.

NOTES

1 The term 'iconography' according to Flannery and Marcus (1998: 43) can either refer to the iconography of art or its subsequent analysis. For the sake of this chapter, I use the term to discuss iconography as an art form.
2 The 'Magnificent Seven' included Kensal Green (1833 – 77 acres), Norwood (1838), Abney Park (1840 – 32 acres), Brompton (1840 – 39 acres), Nunhead (1840 – 52 acres), Tower Hamlets (1841 – 33 acres) and Highgate (1839) (Holmes 1896).
3 This went against the Christian ethos that in death, the body was redeemed and purified prior to resurrection (Cox 1996: 106).
4 Only samples were taken from the cadaver. Hair jewellery was usually made of hair from the living (Litten 1985: 9–13).
5 The design of ornamental gardens within the Western Cemetery were regarded as having created 'the most magical place in London' (Gay and Pateman 1992).
6 The Western Cemetery has several buildings which are designated Grade II Listed; the former Mortuary Chapel, the Anglican Chapel, the Dissenters' Chapel and the Terrace Catacombs.
7 Due to the demand for burial space and the frequency of burial, the London Cemetery Company acquired twenty acres to the east side of Swain's Lane – opened in 1854 and referred to as the Eastern Cemetery. No burials occurred here until the 1860s (Holmes 1896, Gay and Patemen 1992). The layout of the Eastern Cemetery is far more formal and mundane, probably due to financial considerations rather than desirability and innovation.
8 The cedar tree predates the cemetery by at least 150 years (English Heritage and FOHC).
9 It is true to say that Highgate Cemetery did cater for all pockets. Many of the graves are unmarked and unostentatious. These however, are all located within the Eastern Cemetery.
10 Julius Beer, newspaper baron, owner of *The Observer*. His daughter owned *The Sunday Times*.

11 Sir John Betjeman referred to Highgate Cemetery as a 'Victorian Valhalla'.
12 Necropolis – 'city of the dead'.
13 I am indebted to Roger Bowdler and Cathy Boughton (English Heritage), John Clarke (author of *The Brookwood Necropolis Railway* The Oakwood Press) and Barry Devonshire and Frank Law (The Brookwood Cemetery Society) for permission to use text and illustrations within this chapter.
14 Extracts from Broun's *Extramural Sepulture*. Synopsis of the London Necropolis and National Mausoleum at Woking of 1851: 'It is considered within the London Bills of Mortality … there are about 200 golgothas of one description and another, the area of the whole not exceeding 218 acres. Within these numerous and loathsome decomposing troughs, for centuries past in the heart of the capital of a great Christian nation, the most depraved system of sepulture has existed that has ever disgraced the annals of civilisation. Within have been partly inhumed, partly entombed, within the metropolis.'
15 The original location for the LNC terminus was in York Street, Lower Marsh, with an entrance at 188 Westminster Bridge Road (Bowdler 1989: 2).
16 The deceased would have been placed in separate, specially constructed carriages (hearse vans) which were constructed of twelve coffin cells. The size of each was important in order to accommodate coffin dimensions of different religions (Clarke 1995: 90–91).
17 J.C. Loudon (architect) was, along with John Paxton (architect of the Great Exhibition Crystal Palace of 1851), responsible for the design and promotion of garden greenhouses using glass and iron girder structural principles during the early/mid nineteenth century (Frampton 1992).
18 The vaulting at both churches were not originally considered for burial. At Christ Church, Spitalfields burial within the vaults commenced between 1729 and 1859. Of the 68,000 intramural burials between these dates at Spitalfields, only 950 or so were *exclusively* placed within the vaults (Cox 1996: 5).
19 The promotion of the Necropolis service advocates more of the architectural detail of the palatial and sumptuous interior of the Westminster Bridge Road Terminus than the needs of the deceased (Anon 1904).

References

Adam, B. 1997 'Perceptions of time'. In T. Ingold (ed.) *Companion Encyclopaedia of Anthropology: Humanity, Culture and Social Life*. London: Routledge.

Anon. 1904 *The Head Offices and Railway Station of the London Necropolis Co.*

Bourdieu, P. 1977 *Outline of a Theory of Practice*. Cambridge: Cambridge University Press.

Bowdler, R. 1989 'London Necropolis Company Terminus, 121 Westminster Bridge Road, London Borough of Lambeth'. Internal notes – English Heritage Report. London.

Children, G. and Nash, G.H. 1998 'Smoking, exposing and disposing the ancestors: the emotion of death, mortality and grief (Pt. 1)' *3rd Stone*. Extracts from issue 27.

Ching, F.D.K. 1996 *Architecture: Form, Space and Order*. New York: Van Norstrand Reinhold.

Clarke, J.M. 1992 *An Introduction to Brookwood Cemetery*. Necropolis Publications, Publ. by The Brookwood Cemetery Society.

—— 1995 *The Brookwood Necropolis Railway*. London: The Oakwood Press. 143: 1–51.

Cox, M. 1996 *Life and Death in Spitalfields 1700 to 1850*. Council for British Archaeology.

—— (ed.) 1998 *Grave Concerns: Death and Burial in England 1700–1850*. CBA Research Report 113. Council for British Archaeology.

—— 1998 'Eschatology, burial practice and continuity: a retrospection from Christ Church, Spitalfields'. In M.Cox (ed.) *Grave Concerns: Death and Burial in England 1700–1850*. CBA Research Report 113. Council for British Archaeology.

Flannery, K.V. and Marcus, J. 1998 'Cognitive archaeology'. In D.Whitley (ed.) *Reader in Archaeological Theory: Post-Processual and Cognitive Approaches*. London: Routledge, pp. 35–48.

Frampton, K. 1992 *Modern Architecture: A Critical History*. London: Thames and Hudson, pp. 33–36.

Gay, J. and Pateman, J. 1992 *In Highgate Cemetery*. London: Friends of Highgate Cemetery.

Hurd, G. 1973 *Human Societies*. London: Routledge and Kegan Paul.

Holmes, B. 1896 *The London Burial Grounds: Notes on Their History from the Earliest Times to the Present Day*. The Gresham Press.

Litten, J.W.S. 1985 'Post medieval burial vaults: their construction and contents'. *Bulletin CBA Churches Comm.* 23: 9–17.

—— 1998 'The English funeral 1700–1850'. In M.Cox (ed.) *Grave Concerns: Death and Burial in England 1700–1850*. CBA Research Report 113. Council for British Archaeology.

Llewellyn, N. 1991 *The Art of Death*. London: Victoria and Albert Museum Press.

Pollitt, J.J. 1986 *Art in the Hellenistic Age*. Cambridge: Cambridge University Press.

Reeve, J. and Adams, M. 1993 *The Spitalfields Project Volume 1 – The Archaeology – Across the Styx*. London: CBA Volume No. 85.

Rose, M.E. 1985 'Society: the emergence of urban Britain'. In C. Haigh (ed.) *The Cambridge Historical Encyclopaedia of Great Britain and Ireland*. Cambridge: Cambridge University Press, pp. 276–81.

Rugg, J. 1998 'A new burial form and its meanings: cemetery establishment in the first half of the 19th century'. In M. Cox (ed.) *Grave Concerns: Death and Burial in England 1700–1850*. CBA Research Report 113. Council for British Archaeology.

Shanks, M. and Tilley, C. 1987 *Re-Constructing Archaeology: Theory and Practice*. Cambridge: Cambridge University Press.

Tarlow, S. 1998 'Romancing the Stones: the graveyard boom of the late 18th and 19th century'. In M. Cox (ed.) *Grave Concerns: Death and Burial in England 1700–1850*. CBA Research Report 113. Council for British Archaeology.

Unwin, S. 1997 *Analysing Architecture*. London: Routledge.

Weddell, G.R. 1979 'LSWR 24ft Hearse Carriage'. *The Model Railway Constructor* 46: 581–582.

Whitley, D. (ed.) 1998 *Reader in Archaeological Theory: Post-Processual and Cognitive Approaches*. London: Routledge.

7

NEVER MIND THE RELEVANCE?

Popular culture for archaeologists

A.J. Schofield

Snapshots

It is 1975 – twenty-two years ago at the time of writing. Britain is facing a dark future. Unemployment is high; fewer and fewer teenagers now have the opportunity to find employment or an apprenticeship. Unemployment benefit of £18 a week brings these teenagers close to the Government's poverty line. The rate of inflation is constantly 10 per cent or more. Wage strikes rock the country and in 1976 race riots break out. The decline in tax receipts linked to the lack of income of increasing numbers of the population ruins the municipal authorities and their services. Whole districts of cities begin to show signs of decline: the effects of sixties city redevelopment policy mean that stone deserts are created out of decaying architecture. This situation is coincident with right-wing conservatism which becomes Government policy with the election of Margaret Thatcher as Prime Minister in 1979. The headlines in the mass media hammer the word 'crisis' into the public consciousness in larger and larger letters. A call for 'law and order' sweeps across the country. The Sex Pistols, recently formed, release their debut single 'Anarchy in the UK' (after Wicke 1990: 140–141).

★ ★ ★

Mid August 1969 – 'The Woodstock Music and Arts Fair: An Aquarian Exposition'. Max Lerner described Woodstock as 'a turning point in the consciousness generations have of each other and of themselves'. The 450,000 people present fan out across America to tell of an Utopia that in size and spirit has surpassed all countercultural fantasies. Bands who perform find themselves part of history. The following year – 1970, closer to home on the Isle of Wight: 'our Woodstock'. This too is to become a turning point, but few can agree whether this, the third Isle of Wight pop festival, with its pitched battles and moments of collective euphoria, will represent the 'bitter death cry of the pure hippy dream, or the radiant dawn of hip capitalism' (Williams 1995: 2).

★   ★   ★

1962 – The Beatles. They were revolutionaries, said Melly (1973: 26), who, in a Britain immersed in a workers' playtime mentality, wrote the rule book of popular music and determined the course youth culture was to take, both in terms of music, fashion and attitude. Their early recordings, represented on their 'Live at the BBC' issued in 1994, and hailed by the popular press as the most important archaeological discovery since Tutankhamen's tomb, now represent a snapshot of a distant era. As Derek Taylor describes in the sleevenotes: although only thirty years ago, this was a world in which, 'London was six/eight hours from Liverpool, when London was the Big Time and almost still "The Big Smoke". Trains were still steam. There was no take-away save fish and chips. No "Sun". The rudest thing in newsprint was "Reveille". Television was black and white; there were two channels.' This was a time in which The Beatles were woven into the fabric of British life and their music remains its enduring soundtrack (1994: 3).

★   ★   ★

These snapshots illustrate some of the most significant, obvious and best known developments in post-war popular (and specifically youth) culture. Readers will be familiar with some, and may indeed have been participants, whether hanging-out on Chelsea's King's Road in 1975, present at Afton Down in 1970 or at the Cavern in 1962. Or perhaps these are too distant, and a snapshot from the mid 1980s or 1990s would have been more familiar, on Ibiza maybe, or among the crowds at the G-Mex at the height of 'Madchester'. The general point here, however, is the central theme of this chapter: that although popular perceptions are of a heritage embracing the country's infrastructure, industry, religion and military acitivity, and usually confined to the more distant past, professional concerns are being increasingly drawn towards the achievements and cultural values of modern youth culture in all its multifarious forms and manifestations. This chapter explores that issue in four ways:

1   it briefly defines the relationship between high (elite) and popular (mass) culture, and perceptions of what constitutes the heritage (much of this is covered in detail in Lowenthal 1997 and Samuel 1994, so only a short outline is presented);
2   it briefly considers how definitions of heritage influence what we regard as historic;
3   it examines the evidence in England and the United States for a developing professional concern for the heritage of post-war youth culture (as a component of a wider popular culture); and
4   it considers the academic value in conserving and researching remains of our recent past. In short, what can be learnt about both the more distant past, and about ourselves and our future, from studying aspects of twentieth-century youth culture? What sort of an archaeology is it?

Above all, however, this chapter takes a pragmatic view, being more about conservation practice in England and the United States than conservation philosophy more widely. To emphasise that point, questions of value will be addressed not in the abstract, but using the three snapshots presented above as examples of what can be achieved, and the types of material culture available for study. I should stress that, for this second part of the chapter, I have borrowed from published sources (all of which are referenced), undertaking only limited original research.[1]

Introducing popular culture

Strinati (1995) provides a summary of the various theories and interpretations of popular culture, and borrows from Hebdige (1988: 47) when defining it as, 'a set of generally available artefacts, films, records, clothes, TV programmes, modes of transport etc'. Different societies, different groups within those societies, and societies and groups in different historical periods can all have their own popular culture, with their own artefacts and social processes: hence, for a definition of youth culture, it is the specific set of artefacts belonging to that group that is relevant. And music, design and fashion, as well as codes of behaviour and their associated material culture, will characterise and serve to identify each 'styletribe' within the group (Polhemus 1994). Punk is an outstanding example of this (described below), as is ecstasy culture and the rave scene. In this latter case white gloves were worn to reflect LSD-enhanced lights and lasers; dummies were sucked or gnawed-on as the E buzz wobbled the jawbone; and Vicks inhalers were used to clear the lungs so intensifying the 'hit' (Collin and Godfrey 1997: 249). To understand this materiality requires a broad appreciation of drug culture but also of the chemical properties of the drug(s) in question – artefacts in context, as the cliché goes.

As well as being fascinating in its own right, twentieth-century youth culture has received much academic attention in recent times. The journals *Cultural Studies, Youth and Society, Journal of Contemporary Ethnography, Media, Culture and Society* and *Popular Music and Society*, for example, contain analyses of the value and interest of youth culture in its many forms and manifestations. Many books have been written on the subject (eg. Thornton 1996; Collin and Godfrey 1997), while the popular press has chronicled the evolution of styletribes, especially over the last ten years: magazines like *The Face* and *i-D* are of particular relevance here (Benson 1997). The subject is also now becoming a part of the educational curriculum, thereby attracting more attention than ever from theorists and researchers in the humanities and the social sciences (Strinati 1995: xiii). This level of attention reflects the cultural significance of youth culture. Hobsbawm, amongst others, has emphasised this point within a broad social historical context (1995: 325ff). He talks of the extraordinary power of youth in the later twentieth century indicating a profound change in the relations between generations; youth from around the 1950s became an independent social agent, at a time when the traditional groupings of class, region, religion and ethnicity declined in importance, leaving the individual free to pursue life as he or she chose. This is reflected in the number of definable subcultures present during this period, and their increase in variability with time. As Collin has said: after the raves of 1989 propagandised ecstasy to the entire country, house culture began to diversify. 'There would never again be one single defined "scene", but scores of interlocking subgenres, sub-cultures, split along fault lines of class, culture, area, musical preference and drugs of choice' (Collin and Godfrey 1997: 243). This process continues apace at the time of writing.

So youth, and youth culture, when viewed within its broader social context, took on a significance in the post-war years never seen before. And this raises the question of whether the various manifestations of this emerging and increasingly disparate youth culture should be recognised and valued as heritage, whether defined in terms of popular perception or professional concern?

134

Heritage and anti-heritage: definitions, contradictions

First, let us consider briefly the definition of heritage, and specifically its application to the recent past (see Lowenthal (1997) and Samuel (1994: 205–312) for a fuller discussion of these points). Of course, definitions are numerous: UNESCO refers to cultural heritage in terms of its 'outstanding universal value' for instance, while the first national heritage conference in 1983 defined it as, 'that which a past generation has preserved and handed on to the present and which a significant group of the population wishes to hand on to the future'. This reference to the wishes of a 'significant group of the population', is addressed by Robert Hewison (1989: 22) who noted how it is virtually inevitable, with any definition based on a majority view, that museums, ancient monuments and material culture will record the achievements and values of the *dominant classes* – the establishment. However, evidence appears to suggest that conservation practice now recognises a more liberal definition. As Samuel has noted (1994: 205): 'Heritage is a nomadic term, which travels easily, and puts down routes – or bivouacs – in seemingly quite unpromising terrain (such as) Liverpool 8, that erstwhile twilight zone, now peppered with Beatles memorabilia.' It could be said therefore that qualification of the materiality of popular culture as heritage and, as we'll see below, its importance – a central issue in conservation practice and to the principles of sustainability – is now being separated from class, and also from the following distinctions. Commitment to diversity, multiculturalists suggest, should override consensual national heritage (Lowenthal 1997: 83):

High culture	elite culture	art	upper/middle class	establishment
Low culture	mass culture	entertainment	working class	anti-establishment

The perceptions of the youth community itself are interesting here, as they display evidence for an appropriation of historic fabric, formerly part of elite culture, into the context of mass culture; the symbolic crossing of a boundary the heritage establishment appears no longer to recognise. Dance events are now frequently staged in redundant industrial buildings for example, and some of the 'coolest' squats are those in old churches and country houses (La Trobe Bateman personal communication). Art also reflects this crossover. In Berlin in 1989 the Mutoid Waste Company, salvage sculpture artists cum post-apocalypse travellers, built a spectacular Day-Glo painted Stonehenge on the site of Hitler's bunker at Potsdammer Platz out of decommissioned Eastern Bloc tanks; and planted MIG fighters in the ground, the latter resembling bizarre techno-flowers (Collin and Godfrey 1997: 238–239).

Some examples illustrate the acceptance of recent remains as part of our cultural heritage. In England, coal mines are now accepted as part of the heritage. From the time of the National Coal Strike to Michael Heseltine's announcement of massive closures in June 1992, the industry suffered devastating blows. At the time of writing there are just thirty collieries left, with predictions that the number could fall to twelve. In 1985, 133 were open. Some of these coal mines, still in operation three to four years ago in a few cases, are being treated as heritage, are being assessed by English Heritage (the British government's adviser on heritage matters in England), with the most worthwhile cases being afforded statutory protection through 'scheduling'. Chatterley Whitfield is one example, scheduled recently following closure in 1977. Some coal mines are being presented to the public as industrial heritage, as is the case for instance at Snibstone Discovery Park. Similarly, remains of the Cold War, such as Orford Ness – abandoned by the Atomic Weapons Research Establishment in 1971 – and earlier monuments of the Second World War are now widely accepted as heritage sites (Dobinson et al. 1997; Schofield 1999; Samuel 1994: 205). At High Down, a short distance from the Needles on the Isle of Wight, is the test site of the Black Knight rocket, in use between 1956 and 1971. This has strategic significance, as a part of our involvement with developing rocket technology, and is presented as a piece of history by its owners, the National Trust. Another example is modern architecture, now the subject of review as part of English Heritage's post-war listing programme (Cherry 1996) – 'listing' being a statutory designation appropriate for the management of historic buildings which remain in use. In 1996, 154 post-war buildings were listed, ranging from acknowledged masterpieces such as Coventry Cathedral to structures such as the railway stations at Birmingham New Street and Oxford Road, Manchester.

A similar trend can be seen in the United States. In terms of protection, at the end of 1994, 2,035 properties 'listed' on the National Register of Historic Places had achieved their significance over the past fifty years. Of these 464 reflect some aspect of history since 1950, and 77 since 1974 (Shull and Savage 1995: 3). President Clinton's birthplace was listed in 1994, despite the fact he only lived there for four years, because it was 'most significantly and exclusively associated with President Clinton's humble beginnings, the inner strength he learned from his mother, and the dedication to purpose that has sustained him throughout his distinguished political career'. Similarly, the Dealey Plaza Historic District in Dallas was designated a National Historic Landmark in October 1993, as the site of John F. Kennedy's assassination almost thirty years earlier.

These are all subjects whose inclusion as heritage might reasonably be expected to attract public sympathy. But there is evidence to suggest that a more liberal (even radical) definition is gaining credibility, one which openly embraces the material manifestations of youth culture. Put another way, the heritage now appears to include both manifestations of the production and work ethic of the pre-war and war years (machines and factories, heavy industries, and infrastructure), and the conspicuous consumerism of the post-war period; a culture of the masses, of society's working class, and the workers' playtime mentality. As Strinati puts it, people at this time were encouraged to consume, leading to 'a post-modern popular culture which celebrates consumerism, hedonism and style' (1995: 236). In the United States, four specific examples can be cited. First, icons of popular culture are recognised in diverse listings related to the film industry. As the National Register explains, an African work boat now moored in Key Largo, Florida, was as much a star of the 1951 film The African Queen as were Humphrey Bogart and Katherine Hepburn. The nomination explains the development of the film industry and describes how, in the late 1940s the industry responded to the growing competition from the emerging television industry by turning to popular stories such as the novel by C.S. Forester upon which the film was based (Shull and Savage 1995: 9).

Second is the listing on the National Register of Graceland in 1991 (Stager 1995). From 1957 until his death in 1977, Graceland was the home of Elvis Presley, a cultural icon whose first appearance on television frightened and outraged a generation of parents. Stager describes the case:

> To fans and historians of music, it may seem clear that the property should receive recognition for Presley's importance in modern music, but to historians, architectural historians and historic preservationists, the eligibility was not self-evident. Although there are other sites associated with Presley, no one argued strongly that Graceland was not his legacy and the landmark best associated with him. Yet some questioned why this relatively new house and new singer should be recognised as historically significant. The property did not fit within ... guidelines for properties that are not yet fifty years old. ... Do Presley and Graceland have exceptional significance, or shouldn't we wait and give the property recognition in 2027? Conversely, why recognise the house when it is Presley's music that is important.
>
> (Stager 1995: 115)

A further example concerns a nondescript two-storey building in Chicago, designated by the Commission on Chicago Landmarks, due to its use between 1957 and 1967 by Chess Records, one of the principal music labels associated with the development of American blues and rock 'n' roll (Samuelson and Peters 1995). This was accepted for designation, despite subsequent alterations to the building, including its later use as a dance and theatre studio. In fact, it was the music specifically which swung things in favour of acceptance: 'mere mention of the song "Johnny B. Goode", recorded by Chuck Berry at the Chess Studios in 1958, was an immediate touchstone to most of those involved. At one City Council meeting, an alderman ... noted, "Yeah, I always liked that song", and voted for designation' (ibid.: 121).

Finally, there is the case of 'Blanket Hill' on the Kent State University campus, where a student protest against the Vietnam War led to confrontation with the National Guard on 4 May 1970, and the deaths of four students (Luce 1995: 15). In 1977 the University proposed building an addition to a gymnasium on part of the field where the conflict took place. The May 4th Coalition was formed to protect the site from development, as a memorial to the students who were killed and to the national impact of those events on ending the Vietnam War. Not surprisingly, the issue found supporters and opponents. Supporters erected a tent city on the site and camped there for sixty-two days. A nomination for the site's listing was presented to the state review board who took the view that the event was too recent to warrant National Register listing. Although rejected, Blanket Hill has aroused considerable interest and sits firmly within the consciousness of the American people. Having once recommended the site to be a National Historic Landmark, Luce, writing in 1995, reflected that rejection may have been the correct decision, allowing not only academic evaluation of an historic site, but also 'healing, understanding, and time for emotions to be sorted out before official recognition is given' (1995: 19).

In England, the same pattern can be seen, for example in the recent – and eventually successful – attempts to place a commemorative plaque for Jimi Hendrix next to the house displaying one for George Frederick Handel. These plaques are issued by English Heritage for London properties associated with famous people, a condition being that they died over twenty years ago, or were born over 100 years ago. Furthermore: there must be reasonable grounds for believing individuals are considered 'eminent' by their own profession; they shall have made some important positive contribution to human welfare or happiness; and they deserve recognition. Interestingly, the Handel Society objected to this proposal on the basis that Hendrix had not lived in the house long enough to merit such recognition; other objections referred to this as a 'dumbing down' of heritage. However, this view was rejected by English Heritage, and the plaque was placed in September 1997 – the first to a contemporary musician. Others may now be considered for the likes of Keith Moon, Brian Jones and Sid Vicious.

In 1995 the National Trust took on management of 20 Forthlin Road, a 1950s mid-terrace council house in Liverpool, acknowledged as the birthplace of The Beatles: it was here that Paul McCartney grew up and where the group rehearsed and composed their early songs, notably 'Love Me Do'. In the words of the National Trust: 'Everyone will have their own opinion of the music of the Beatles, but there can be no denying that they made one of the greatest 20th century contributions to Western musical culture. Their fame and influence are international and they are an inseparable part of Liverpool's culture and folklore.'

There are also examples of the media 'establishment' adopting a more radical definition of what they choose to present as heritage. The BBC for instance screened an *Arena* documentary celebrating the twentieth anniversary of punk, based on the Jon Savage book, *England's Dreaming* (1991). Although the programme was broadcast, it was only after a few years of wrangling over the content. As Jon Savage explained in *The Guardian* newspaper, the main problem was with the attitude 'many television people have towards pop culture in general and punk in particular' (Savage 1995). Another example was the 'Streetstyle' exhibition, held at the Victoria and Albert Museum between November 1994 and February 1995. This described the variety in Western subcultures from 1940 onwards, emphasising what the organisers presented as 'tribal styles', and the diversification of styletribes between the 1950s and today. Polhemus, who wrote the book to accompany the exhibition, made this point:

> Apart from its astounding variety, streetstyle today is characterised by the extent to which it exists within the shadow of its own past. In one sense this ... simply reflects the obvious fact that it now has a past – with some five decades stacked on top of each other. But at the same time the significance of this history has been magnified by the extent to which popular culture – and with it, of course, youth culture and streetstyle – has moved further and further centre stage as a defining feature of 'Western Society'.
>
> (1994: 130)

It is worth mentioning, finally, that this is a heritage acknowledged as having enormous marketing potential, as evidenced by the pilgimage to what Samuel calls 'new historical shrines' (1994: 90): Jim Morrison's grave at Père Lachaise cemetery for instance has more visitors and flowers than the Mur des Fédérés where the martyred dead of the Paris commune are buried. To exploit this market, the British Tourist Board launched a campaign early in 1998 to sell Britain's rock heritage to foreign visitors: the heritage of 'cool Britannia' it would seem is reaching fever pitch.

But one concern underlies all of the examples here, and the principles identified earlier, and this relates not so much to the qualification of popular culture as heritage, but its significance. There are two issues: first, that in sustainability theory there is the premise that in order to sustain our critical assets, and secure them for the benefit of future generations, the resource must have community support, and community is necessarily broadly defined embracing not only youth and adultescents, but older generations as well. Given that youths of the early 1960s will now be approaching retirement however, and that politicians themselves grew up in the environment described in this chapter (the current Prime Minister himself was in a rock band at university), acceptance as heritage and thus community support does appear to exist (cf. Samuel 1994; Lowenthal 1997 also covers this point). Value is more difficult. Certainly value judgements have been made, as the examples above demonstrate, but thought does need to be given to how judgements might be made in future, particularly where thematic reviews are required. Who can decide what is significant? Heritage managers may be able to decide on earlier periods, such as the significance of Beatles landmarks, but are unlikely to be sufficiently 'in touch' to make judgements on anything more recent. Do we simply rely on popular or professional consensus, through a process of consultation? How much weight do we give to the voices of participants, or must we accept that as participants an ability to view value and significance objectively will not be possible? This is a debate that will no doubt be continued as we enter the new millennium.

In summary then, manifestations of the recent past have, over the last few years, become embedded (albeit gradually) into conservation practice; and perhaps with some reluctance, aspects of popular and youth culture, reflecting the consumer ethic of the post-war years, have been similarly embraced, thus creating what we might term an anti-heritage, a heritage not only for the people but of the people. But beyond the obvious economic and recreational values, implicit within a culture of reflective nostalgia, what acadamic worth can be claimed for a subject and of a period so recent? The three examples which follow use the snapshots referred to at the outset to explore in this context three aspects of material culture: song; physical earthwork remains; and clothing and style.

Exploring youth culture: 1962–75

The stuff that screams are made of[2]: The Beatles and the sixties

> If you want to know about the Sixties, listen to music of The Beatles.
>
> (Aaron Copeland)

In a survey by Peter Wicke, rock music is described as a 'mass medium through which cultural values and meanings circulate, through which social experiences are passed on which reach far beyond the material nature of music' (1990: ix). Furthermore: 'Records and songs are not isolated objects; they are the symptoms of an extensive overall cultural context which owes its existence in equal measure to social and political relations as well as to the particular environment of its listeners' (ibid.: viii). A related point is made by Stokes:

> Amongst the countless ways in which we 'relocate' ourselves, music undoubtedly has a vital role to play. The musical event, from collective dances to the act of putting a cassette or CD into a machine, evokes and organises collective memories and presents experiences of place with an intensity, power and simplicity unmatched by any other social activity.
>
> (1994: 3)

I will explore the relevance of The Beatles here in two ways, both of which relate to these statements. First, the contribution listening to Beatles' records can make to understanding 'being' in the sixties (in other words, the Aaron Copeland quotation). Second, I will look at their music in relation to the sense of place it evokes. Is it true to say, for example, that 'The Liverpool Sound', which arguably began with The Beatles, can allow the construction of a sense of difference and distinctiveness; a sense of Liverpool-ness (as Cohen suggests (1994: 133))?

It is generally accepted as fact that The Beatles were revolutionaries who wrote the rule book of popular music (eg. Melly 1973: 26; Harry 1977: 15, but cf. Harker 1980 for a contrary view); 'everyone who came after merely tinkered with the glossary', as a reviewer once put it. Now, reflecting critically on that period, it is revealing to note how the nature and content of their songs changed, sometimes in a subtle way, through the course of the decade. As Ian MacDonald said, in the introduction to his book *Revolution in the Head* (1994), The Beatles' lives and works in the early days were perfect models of post-Christian 'nowness': 'Entirely lacking the proverbial worldly wisdom of pre-1963 popular music, their early lyrics are careless, streetwise, immediate, sensationalistic – the expression of minds without respect for age or experience, interested only in the thrills, desires and disappointments of the present' (1994: 19). Yet consider Britain in the 1950s and this is no surprise:

> Any domestic film of the period will convey the genteel, class-segregated staidness of British Society at that time. The braying upper class voices on newsreels, the odour of unearned privilege in parliament and the courts, the tired nostalgia for the war. … Behind the wiped polished surface of British culture around 1960 lay a festering mess of sexual ignorance, prejudice, and repression only slightly ameliorated since the 19th century.
>
> (ibid.: 7)

By contrast, by 1966–7, records of the period, led by those of The Beatles, displayed a 'light, joyous optimism with a tangible spiritual aura and a thrillingly fresh informality' (ibid.: 15). This was an age of love and peace, and it is reflected in The Beatles producing what are usually considered to be their finest works ('Revolver' and 'Sgt. Peppers' as albums, and 'Penny Lane' and 'Strawberry Fields Forever' as singles). A year later, 1968, 'the year of the barricades', and John Lennon was writing his 'Revolution 1', only months before the student riots in Paris.

To British youth culture, rock 'n' roll and what came immediately after it, 'promoted a utopia which could encompass the everyday experiences of British working class teenagers with all their longings, desires, hopes, frustrations and leisure needs' (Wicke 1990: 61); consequently it became their cultural symbol, a situation which, according to Wicke, represented an 'external attack on the supposed "classlessnes", an attack which considerably disturbed the social peace of the nation', and which ruling Conservative opinion saw variously as a threat (ibid.: 62) and as evidence of moral decline. In 1964, the *New Statesman*, the opinion leader of the political establishment, described the 'menace of Beatleism' thus:

> Both TV channels now run weekly programmes in which popular records are played to teenagers and judged. While the music is performed, the cameras linger savagely over the faces of the audience. What a bottomless chasm of vacuity they reveal. Huge faces, bloated with cheap confectionery and smeared with chain-store make-up, the open, sagging mouths and glazed eyes, the hands mindlessly drumming in time to the music, the broken stiletto heels, the shoddy stereotyped 'with it' clothes: here, apparently is a collective portrait of a generation enslaved by the commercial machine.
>
> (Johnson 1964: 17)

So the culture which surrounded The Beatles and embraced a nation, is reflected clearly in their music: the structure of the music itself, and especially the lyrics, such as the move away from the 'careless, streetwise, sensationalistic' love songs of the early years, to the broader range brought about by, amongst other things, the emergence of an LSD counterculture in around 1966. Sixties culture changed rapidly and dramatically as the decade progressed, and, as we have seen, those changes are reflected in the sequence of their recordings. Specific themes came and went, most notable of which were those exploring the relationship between Beatleism and the establishment, and between youth and the adult generation, as witnessed in songs like 'She's Leaving Home', specifically about the post-war generation gap.

A related matter concerns how music reflects identity and place, a point of interest in any assessment of regional or local character given the fact that, 'what music can do is put into play a sense of identity that may or may not fit the way we are placed by other social facts' (Frith 1987: 149). Recent aboriginal popular bands, for instance, have used music to express pan-tribal solidarities, reflecting claims to political and geographic space (Magowan 1994). In Liverpool, the construction of a 'Liverpool Sound' is seen as a political strategy, a resource through which relations of power at local, regional, national and international levels can be addressed (Cohen 1994: 117). A similar point has been addressed through studies of popular music in Singapore (Kong 1995, 1996).

From recent surveys (reviewed by Cohen), it can be seen that particular musical styles, instruments, voices and sounds, linked with various places, and with characteristics and stereotypes associated with those places, is fairly common. In one study, for example, about a band from Bristol, it was stated that, 'Bristol's character, particularly its pace, does seem to have influenced the music produced there'. Similarly, a journalist wrote of the Manchester band Joy Division, that they 'captured the alienated, terrible glee of a decayed city'. What defines the Liverpool Sound is a matter of debate: some believe it is melodic and harmonious, suggesting a romantic, emotional music to contrast with the masculine tough edge usually associated with the city. The lack of punk bands coming from Liverpool has often been noted. Some, however, point to a certain attitude in Liverpool which comes through in the music, and could be described as individualistic, blunt, combative. As one musician has said: 'There's more of a Liverpool attitude than a Liverpool sound, but most people smoke loads of pot, so there's a sort of dreamy element to the music' (Cohen 1994: 123).

The wider social and economic context of the music is of interest here. Cohen describes, for example, the extent to which Manchester has been wealthier than Liverpool, and that its population has tended to be better travelled, less isolated and wary and more open-minded. Its music therefore reveals a variety of influences, unlike the 'Liverpool Sound', which displays a paucity of influences, a parochialism and an obsession with the past. Cohen goes on to quote the thoughts of a Liverpool musician:

> Maybe it's the space in Manchester and the size. ... Liverpool was described to me as a big village. ... Maybe that restricts artists from being experimental, because people in Liverpool are more likely to put you down or criticise you for being what they would see as, I suppose, pretentious. And in Manchester, you've got space to ... do things ... and not circulate as much with people on a day-to-day basis. You have that creative space as well as a sort of physical space to arse around or become pretentious or ... creative.
>
> (ibid.)

Such distinctiveness can also be seen at a local scale. One musician for example described the cliques of bands existing in different districts of Merseyside, each of which could be seen as a closed shop resistant to infiltration from outside musicians. A north/south divide can be seen in Liverpool with some depicting the north as more 'introverted' and 'inward looking' due to 'upbringing and social class' (ibid.: 124). It is an interesting point that the parochialism and obsession with the past which have influenced the Liverpool Sound may also generate a greater concern for preserving the materiality of past achievements, while the opposite could be true in Manchester. The popularity of The Beatles heritage trail, and absence of anything similar in Manchester (for example to places associated with The Smiths or Madchester), would certainly suggest that to be the case, although it will be interesting to gauge local opinion on any future proposals for listing the Gallagher brothers' family home.

So the notion of a local sound, like the Liverpool Sound, does reflect the desire to 'symbolically assert difference and a sense of local identity' (ibid.: 129), though this regionality has now declined with the reorganisation of the music industry, and with international demand requiring 'geographical agility' of its artists. Nevertheless regional character still exists, and the extent to which that character continues to define an area's cultural identity and heritage is of considerable interest.

The age of Aquarius: Afton Down and the third Isle of Wight festival

> The great pop festivals of the late 1960s were very much a product of their times – youthful rebellion, music as popular art, a derangement of all the senses – but their underlying search for shared freedom and community had deep cultural roots. They contained within themselves the notions of a religious coming together, of a grown-up boy scouts camp – making do in the open air – of a bohemian escape to a land of free love and illegal substances, of a waking dream, even of medieval pilgrimage.
>
> (Hinton 1990: 3)

Pop festivals, and especially that at Afton Down, attracted considerable attention in the early 1970s, and much was written about their economic implications (Baines 1971), their social context (Gostwick 1971), and design and structure (Levens and Durham 1971). Here I will address two aspects of this: the social framework within which the festival took place; and the physical material remains of such festival sites.

The third Isle of Wight pop festival was held in several fields immediately north of Afton Down (or 'Desolation Hill' as it became known), near Freshwater in August 1970 (Figure 7.1). It, perhaps more than its predecessors or indeed any pop festival since, with the notable exception of Woodstock, caught the public attention, aroused great controversy and remains clearly in the memories of both participants and local residents. With video releases of the festival, featuring notably the last live performance by Jimi Hendrix, and books written (eg. Hinton 1990), it has attained heritage status, as seen in the second snapshot at the start of this chapter.[3] Much of the controversy surrounding the festival was committed to paper, and this provides a valuable archive in documenting public perceptions at the time and the increasing threat of youth felt by the island's adult population. If (or when) another Isle of Wight festival is arranged, a comparison of public concerns over a 25–30 year period would be of interest; attitudes are after all a product of their time.

As an example of public concerns, in 1973 (when a fourth festival was planned), local residents produced a document entitled, 'Some observations on a local problem' in which they listed some of the dangers to which all local

Figure 7.1   Crowd scene at 'The Last Great Event', Afton Down 26–30 August 1970

residents were likely to be subjected: drugs, promiscuous sex, rape, mugging and vandalism, theft, indecency, perversion, public flaunting of bodily functions etc. It went on:

> [The] conclusion drawn from these comments is that on balance it would appear that Pop Festivals create a wholly undesirable situation in every way, in relation to all ages. ... Therefore there is everything to condemn them.

The matter was taken up in Parliament, leading to the introduction of a Private Members Bill giving authorities on the Isle of Wight control over holding similar events in the future. Extracts from some of the speeches make interesting (and surprising) reading: Lord Wynne-Jones for example – 'The stimulus which young people get in that environment is undoubtedly a good and healthy thing, and I doubt that any of us would wish to deprive them of it'; and Lord Shackleton – 'The great message that comes over (at these festivals) is of kindness, the gentleness and the truthfulness of the young.'

The festival site itself is remarkable in a number of ways, not least because it, and the material remains which survive, tell a story chronicling not so much the achievements of the counterculture the festival was established to celebrate, but rather its demise. This was also one of the first great festival sites, where the layout was purpose built to service the various needs of massed youth. Over a period of three to four weeks, a town was built, occupied for a week, and then abandoned and dismantled, never to be reoccupied or used again for any purpose other than farming. During the period of construction, nine diggers were on site piping several miles of ditches, more than 1,000 toilets over deep trenches and 100 taps and stand pipes were prepared. Afton Down itself witnessed ad hoc construction and excavation, with holes being dug for bedding-in tents and for toilet trenches. Although never surveyed, traces on aerial photographs appear to show these features scattered across the Down, as well as showing the hollows where bushes were uprooted for burning. The stage itself was of architectural interest and warranted treatment on the front page of a leading architectural journal of the time.

The local topography is central to understanding the site and the events which occurred there. The site chosen for the festival was immediately north of Afton Down, a steep chalk escarpment, owned by the National Trust, running east–west and creating a natural terrace facing and rising high above the arena. The festival site was defined to respect the Down's conservation value and the boundary of the arena ran along its base. Over a length of three miles, two 3 metre high fences of timber and corrugated iron construction were built, with security guards and dogs patrolling the corridor. Not surprisingly, given the views from the Down, and the feeling amongst much of the hippy community, that free music was a right, a community of 10,000 established itself beyond the perimeter fence on Afton Down. It was this community which attempted (and eventually succeeded) in breaching the perimeter fence, an event for which the festival is renowned (Figure 7.2). There are few instances where precise moments, which can be traced in the material record, define turning points in our cultural history: the breaching of the fence at the foot of Afton Down, an event which will have a distinctive archaeological trace, is one. The 'hippy dream' had promised so much to a generation growing up in a post-war environment of tired nostalgia. Quite suddenly, on a summer's night in 1970, that dream died and the world would never be quite the same again.

The only remains of the festival now surviving as earthworks are a series of linear ditches dug by the National Trust, to prevent onlookers driving onto their property to watch the festival. These are now to be found around an existing and much-used car park with no interpretation or explanation. So we have a contradiction: the only component of the festival site visible to the modern visitor had little to do with the hippy population who attended; these earthen ditches were to control the actions of the largely middle-class, car-owning members of the population, locals and holiday makers, who had a fascination for the events unfolding and recorded on television news broadcasts. Other components are visible, but only from the air. Some aerial photographs show, for example, the location of the stage and the perimeter fence as well as the various backstage compounds for press and performers.

Pop festivals can also contribute to an understanding of discard patterns and rubbish disposal at gatherings of this scale. It is unlikely that, given the nature of the clean-up operation following the festival (Figure 7.3), surface

Figure 7.2 The construction of the perimeter fence (top), and its breaching
(bottom), an event representing the death-cry of the pure hippy dream, or
the radiant dawn of hip capitalism?

Source: (after Williams 1995)

collection would reveal much in the way of artefacts indicative of the events
which had taken place there. This is in fact true of most such festivals.
Following the Glastonbury Festival in 1995, for instance, 470 tonnes of

147

Figure 7.3 Cleaning up after the second Isle of Wight festival, Wootton, 1969

rubbish were collected. Indeed, the post-festival clean-up has become an event in its own right; festival litter pickers have a counterculture all of their own, as was described by Ed Vulliamy in *The Guardian* (1995).

As Lefebvre has said (1991: 207), 'festivals contrasted violently with everyday life but they were never separate from it'. In these terms, few would doubt the cultural significance of Woodstock or Afton Down both to their generation, and to the development of youth and popular culture within its wider social context. Afton Down has its own distinctive archaeological record, and is contemporary with some nearby Cold War sites which are now managed and presented as part of the heritage. Although not as obviously visible or 'monumental', why should Afton Down not also be treated in these terms?

Artefacts of futility: the materiality of punk

I'm with you
You with me
We're going down in history

We're going down
We're going down
We're going down

(Iggy and the Stooges: 'Death Trip' – 1973)

Much could be made of this case study, as the references listed below will testify. However, here the point will be simple and specific, providing a cautionary tale (albeit fairly well known) about what we can learn from the present about material culture in the past (and this repeats some of what Hodder has said previously (1982). It also complements Matthews' recent paper, in which he describes how important it is that we recognise minority groups in reading the past, in order that we, 'understand how societies function as entities and celebrate the importance of individual experience in the past and the present' (1995: 587). The literature here is extremely rich: much research has been conducted on and around the ethos and cultural scene which punk (by its various definitions) embraces, perhaps because of the complexity of the message its symbolism conveyed. The Sex Pistols themselves have been the subject of much of this attention, with summaries of their historical development (Savage 1991), and of their significance, and that of punk generally, to the study of stylistic variation and meaning (Hebdige 1988; Wicke 1990). Punk has also been assessed in terms of its philosophy (O'Hara 1995), lyric content (McDonald 1987), symbolism (Goldthorpe 1992; Levine and Stumpf 1983), social frameworks (Hansen and Hansen 1991; Fox 1987) and behaviour in the context of prevailing middle-class values (Fox 1987; Baron 1989.)[4]

Against the political and social background outlined in the first snapshot at the start of this paper, the Sex Pistols appeared as the embodiment of a general situation. They provided the crisis of the time with a cultural symbol which pushed society's pathological nature to monstrous heights, and gave the decline a vivid and immediate form by translating it into chaos and anarchy (Wicke 1990: 141). Their first single 'Anarchy in the UK' was symptomatic of this. For Malcolm McLaren, the band's manager, the new 'anti-music' represented the carefully prepared conversion of an avant-garde art project. McLaren professed the art philosophy of the 'International Situationists', an (anti-)art concept which grew up in the France of the fifties in relation to Paris Dadaism and which experienced a renaissance in British art schools in the sixties. This elitist anti-art programme – which included also his running, with fashion designer Vivienne Westwood, a boutique called 'Sex' in London's Kings Road – rapidly became a teenage subculture which gradually drew in the whole country (ibid.).

Unemployment often creates social isolation and for the punks this manifested itself in the conscious display of division between 'us' and 'them', expressed both in a form of self-presentation, making the contrast quite obvious and visible (they were literally walking rubbish sculptures), and in a distinct anti-music. The term 'punk' is relevant here. As a descriptive term Wicke (ibid.: 138) notes that its origin lies in the attempts by McLaren amongst others, to create a punk-art out of the eccentric anti-art experiments of the New Wave avant-garde of the New York underground. He goes on:

> In this context punk had the meaning of something like muck, trash, rubbish, even whore ... [anything] generally worthless, banal and trivial was to be the starting point for an artistic practice which takes its materials from the suppressed waste products of bourgeois everyday life, whether the obscene sexual fantasies of pornography, the secret horror images behind the normality of bourgeois respectability, the commercial stereotypes of television culture pushing its way into the furthest corners of ordinary life, or simply the rubbish mountains of a questionable civilisation. Using the most shocking presentation possible of what was worthless, the New York punk artists tried to question a value system whose other side they thus displayed.
>
> (ibid.: 138–139)

In other words, the natural meaning was removed and 'artefacts of futility' created; a reversal of the principle of advertising.

Punk material culture reflects this definition, and the description provided by Hebdige (1988: 106–107) is worth quoting in full:

> Like Duchamp's 'ready mades' – manufactured objects which qualified as art because he chose to call them such – the most remarkable and inappropriate items – a pin, a plastic clothes peg, a television component, a razor blade, a tampon – could be brought within the province of punk (un)fashion. Anything within or without reason could be turned into part of what Vivienne Westwood called 'confrontation dressing' so long as the rupture between 'natural' and constructed context was clearly visible. Objects borrowed from the most sordid of contexts found a place in the punk ensembles: lavatory chains were draped in graceful arcs across chests encased in plastic bin-liners. Safety pins were taken out of their domestic 'utility' context and worn as gruesome ornaments through the cheek, ear or lip. 'Cheap' trashy fabrics (PVC, plastic, lurex, etc.) in vulgar designs (e.g. mock leopard skin) and 'nasty' colours, long discarded by the quality end of the fashion industry as obsolete kitsch, were salvaged by the punks and turned into garments ... which offered self-conscious commentaries on the notions of modernity and taste. Conventional ideas of prettiness were jettisoned along with the traditional feminine lure of cosmetics. ... Hair was obviously dyed, and T-shirts and trousers told the story of their own construction with multiple zips and outside seams clearly displayed. ... The perverse and the abnormal were valued intrinsically. In particular, the illicit

iconography of sexual fetishism was used to predictable effect: rapist masks and rubber wear, leather bodices and fishnet stockings, implausibly pointed stiletto-heeled shoes, the whole paraphernalia of bondage – the belts, straps and chains – were exhumed from the boudoir, closet and the pornographic film and placed on the street where they retained their forbidden connotations.

Behaviour was overtly aggressive. The dance for instance, a violent barging style called the pogo, was described once as, 'an indescribable tangling together, shoving, jostling, pushing and jumping, and behind the whole thing only the incessant repetition of one message: NO FUTURE'. Punks caused outrage through the media, using its attention to maximum effect. The Sex Pistols' now legendary television performance, in which an early evening interview with Bill Grundy in December 1976 turned into a national scandal, is an example of this. The headlines the following day reflect the widely felt disgust: *The Daily Telegraph* – '4-Letter Words Rock TV'; *Daily Express*: 'Fury at filthy TV chat'. As part of this general aura of antisocialism, one can also cite obscenity in fashion (e.g. many T-shirt designs which the overriding majority of people found (and still find) offensive, such as Vivienne Westwood's 'Sid 'n' Nancy' design following the death of Sid Vicious's girlfriend). Bad taste has also been reflected in lyrics (e.g. by the American band Dead Kennedys) and record cover designs (often copied to T-shirts). Finally, the lack of respect punk musicians had for their audience was legendary. For example, at the Sex Pistols' third US gig, Sid Vicious announced to a capacity crowd, 'You cowboys are all faggots', and proceeded to smash his bass over the head of a punter who clambered on stage.

As with ecstasy culture, referred to earlier, punk is an extreme and interesting example which demonstrates how the link between youth culture and its material manifestation can be obscure, abstract even: the cultural activities which developed within what may be termed punk philosophy did so with the prerequisite that the world should be experienced as a heap of worthless junk. It is only with this prerequisite that the logic of their strategy is revealed.

Conclusion

So is all this of relevance to archaeologists, or is it, as was once suggested to me, a case of 'Never Mind the Relevance; Here's the ***** ?' In the first part of the chapter I documented, through a series of examples, how the recent past is becoming gradually embraced into a more liberal definition of heritage, and the fact that that definition includes elements of popular or youth culture whose significance is beginning to be realised by the 'dominant classes' (and presumably as one-time rebels become the dominant classes). In short, heritage is becoming increasingly 'of the people' and less of the elite. In the second part, I looked at the intellectual capacity of popular culture and how that could be incorporated into researching the past, and acting as a critique on modern life. Three separate aspects of modern popular culture were considered: the song in relation to its social context and sense of place; material remains defined in terms of their physical (monumental) manifestation – archaeology in its traditional sense; and the confusion of meanings and symbolism which the supermarket of style can generate. Together these examples contribute to numerous related archaeologies. They represent a social archaeology, portraying the growing divide and mutual antagonism between generations in the years 1960–75, and their relative concern with world events, political, economic and especially social. They also represent an archaeology of protest, against the arms race, the staidness of post-war culture, Vietnam and latterly Thatcherite and Tory values. It is an archaeology of youth, and specifically the youth of a society undergoing rapid and radical cultural change. And it is also the archaeology of a poorly understood aspect of the culture process: the emergence, development and fragmentation, and the manifestation of youth culture.

As we've seen, conservation practice is now embracing sites and buildings, places and areas of the recent past, and it is doing so in the related contexts of sustainability and nostalgia. Sustainability means looking at the environment, open countryside, urban developments and everything in between, holistically; and recognising not only that which all agree is 'important' (our 'critical assets'), but also the ordinary features which create local distinctiveness, and which may have a specific but limited value to certain groups of people (English Heritage 1997: 4); and of course these places can be modern just as easily as they can be ancient, provided their recognition and value have community support (Lowenthal 1997: 21). But alongside this is a nostalgia for the present, a desire to hold onto disappearing worlds, and in this context it is interesting to see how heritage has served to modernise and update that which is considered historical, while at the same time extending its social base (Samuel 1994: 208), a point this chapter has sought specifically to emphasise.

The materiality of our recent past therefore, close though it is, and irrespective of our personal feelings towards it, forms an integral part of our heritage, including, as it does, the rich fabric of twentieth-century popular culture; as Hobsbawm says, a defining feature of Western society. As we move into the twenty-first century, this aspect of the recent past seems increasingly secure: historians and philosophers have stated its cultural significance; the philosophical debate about preserving recent remains appears well advanced; and the frameworks for its management are largely in place. The debate is now about pragmatics, and specifically what we preserve of this rich heritage for the future. The examples given in this chapter are just the start.

Acknowledgements

I am grateful to Paul Graves-Brown for inviting my participation at the original TAG session, to Paul Jeffery for inadvertently suggesting a title for the chapter, and staff at the Isle of Wight Record Office for assistance with collating documents for the Isle of Wight pop festivals. The figures are reproduced by kind permission of the Cultural Services Department of Isle of Wight Council. Brian Hinton, Tony Tutton (National Trust) and David Tomalin (Isle of Wight Council) provided useful information about the Isle of Wight festival, and Susan Osborne gave much needed assistance with references. Keith Halstead (National Trust) provided information on 20 Forthlin Road, and Helen Poplett (English Heritage) on the subject of commemorative plaques. I am grateful to Paul Graves Brown, Emily La Trobe Bateman, and various one-time punks, hippies and mop-tops for commenting on an earlier draft of the chapter. Finally, it should be stressed that the views expressed here are my own and do not necessarily represent those of English Heritage. A summary of some of the points raised in the first half of this chapter has appeared elsewhere, as Schofield (1998).

NOTES

1   As Angela McRobbie said on having to travel to warehouses around London to collect her daughter from the very raves she was writing about: 'I feel a sense of acute anxiety at the thought of writing about youth. It is at once too close and too far away. I am too old' (1993: 406).
2   Taken from the article 'Well Now, Dig This' (Bob Wooler 1961).
3   This is also reflected in the recent conversion of Golden Hill Fort, a Napoleonic fortress close to the festival site, into a nightclub featuring, amongst other things, the Experience Bistro, themed on the Isle of Wight festivals.
4   There is a distinction to be drawn here between the punk movement in mid-1970s Britain, and the later 'hardcore' punk movement, predominantly a North American phenomenon. Although there are references here to both, the subject of my discussion is the former.

References

Baines, L.H. 1971 'What price pop festivals?' *Royal Society of Health, 78th Health Congress Proceedings* 125–130.
Baron, S.W. 1989 'Resistance and its consequences: the street culture of punks'. *Youth and Society* 21: 207–237.
Benson, R. (ed.) 1997 *The Face: Club Writing in The Face 1980–1997*. Boxtree.
Cherry, M. 1996 'Listing twentieth century buildings: the present situation'. In S. MacDonald (ed.) *Modern Matters: Principles and Practice in Conserving Recent Architecture*. English Heritage/Donhead, pp. 5–14.
Cohen, S. 1994 'Identity, place and the "Liverpool Sound"'. In M. Stokes (ed.) *Ethnicity, Identity and Music: The Musical Construction of Place*. Oxford and Providence, USA: Berg, pp. 117–134.
Collin, M. with Godfrey, J. 1997 *Altered State: The Story of Ecstasy Culture and Acid House*. London: Serpent's Tail.
Dobinson, C., Lake, J. and Schofield, A.J. 1997 'Monuments of war: defining England's 20th-century defence heritage'. *Antiquity* 71: 288–299.

English Heritage 1997 *Sustaining the Historic Environment: New Perspectives on the Future*. London: English Heritage.

Fox, K.J. 1987 'Real punks and pretenders: the social organisation of a counterculture'. *Journal of Contemporary Ethnography* 16: 344–370.

Frith, S. 1987 'Towards an aesthetic of popular music'. In R. Leppert and S. McClary (eds) *Music and Society: The Politics of Composition, Performance and Reception*. Cambridge University Press, pp. 133–149.

Goldthorpe, J. 1992 'Intoxicated culture: punk symbolism and punk protest'. *Socialist Review* 22: 35–64.

Gostwick, M. 1971 'Indescribable squalor – or good clean fun'. *Municipal Engineering* 16/4/71: 622–624.

Hansen, C.H. and R.D. 1991 'Constructing personality and social reality through music: individual differences among fans of punk and heavy metal music'. *Journal of Broadcasting and Electronic Media* 35: 335–350.

Harker, D. 1980 'One for the money'. *Politics and Popular Song*. London: Hutchinson.

Harry, B. 1977 *Mersey beat. The Beginnings of the Beatles*. London: Omnibus.

Hebdige, D. 1988 *Subculture: The Meaning of Style*. London: Routledge.

Hewison, R. 1989 'Heritage: an interpretation'. In D. Uzzell (ed.) *Heritage Interpretation: Volume 1 – The Natural and Built Environment*. London and New York: Belhaven Press, pp. 15–23.

Hinton, B. 1990 *Nights in Wight Satin: An Illustrated History of the Isle of Wight Pop Festivals*. Isle of Wight Cultural Services Department.

Hobsbawm, E. 1995 *Age of Extremes: The Short Twentieth Century 1914–1991*. Abacus.

Hodder, I. 1982 *The Present Past*. Batsford.

Johnson, P. 1964 'The menace of Beatleism'. *New Statesman* 28/2/64: 17.

Kong, L. 1995 'Popular music in geographical analysis'. *Progress in Human Geography* 19: 183–198.

—— 1996 'Popular music in Singapore: exploring local cultures, global resources and regional identities'. *Environment and Planning D: Society and Space* 14(3): 273–292.

Lamy, P. and Levin, J. 1985 'Punk and middle class values: a content analysis'. *Youth and Society* 17: 157–170.

Lefevbre, H. 1991 *Critique of Everyday Life: Part 1*. London and New York: Routledge.

Levens, L.K. and Durham, J.E. 1971. 'Pop-music festivals: some medical aspects'. *British Medical Journal* 23/1/71: 218–219.

Levine, H.G. and Stumpf, S.H. 1983 'Statements of fear through cultural symbols: punk rock as a reflective subculture'. *Youth and Society* 14: 417–435.

Lowenthal, D. 1997 *The Heritage Crusade and the Spoils of History*. London: Viking.

Luce, W.R. 1995 'Kent State, white castles and subdivisions: evaluating the recent past'. In D. Slaton and R.A. Shiffer (eds) *Preserving the Recent Past*. Washington DC: Historic Preservation Education Foundation, vol. 2: 15–20.

MacDonald, I. 1994 *Revolution in the Head: The Beatles' Records and the Sixties*. London: Pimlico.

Magowan, F. 1994 ' "The land is our märr (essence), it stays forever": the Yothi-Yindi relationship in Australian Aboriginal traditional and popular musics'. In M. Stokes (ed.) *Ethnicity, Identity and Music: The Musical Construction of Place*. Oxford and Providence, USA: Berg, pp. 135–156.

Matthews, K.J. 1995 'Archaeological data, subcultures and social dynamics'. *Antiquity* 69(264): 586–594.

McDonald, J.R. 1987 'Suicidal rage: an analysis of hardcore punk lyrics'. *Popular Music and Society* 11: 91–102.

McRobbie, A. 1993 'Shut up and dance: youth culture and changing modes of femininity'. *Cultural Studies* 7: 406–426.

Melly, G. 1973 *Revolt into Style*. Harmondsworth: Penguin.

O'Hara, C. 1995 *The Philosophy of Punk: More than Noise*. San Francisco: AK Press.

Polhemus, T. 1994 *Streetstyle: From Sidewalk to Catwalk*. London: Thames and Hudson.

Samuel, R. 1994 *Theatres of Memory. Volume 1: Past and Present in Contemporary Culture*. London: Verso.

Samuelson, T. and Peters, J. 1995 'Landmarks of Chicago blues and gospel: chess records and First Church of Deliverance'. In D. Slaton and R.A. Shiffer (eds) *Preserving the Recent Past*. Historic Preservation Education Foundation: Washington DC, vol. 2: 117–122.

Savage, J. 1991 *England's Dreaming: Sex Pistols and Punk Rock*. London: Faber and Faber.

—— 1995 'Never mind the TV bollocks'. *The Guardian* 11/8/95.

Schofield, J. 1998 'This is the modern world: managing "our" legacy for the 21st century'. *The Archaeologist* 32: 24–25.

—— 1999 'Conserving recent military remains: choices and challenges for the 21st century'. In D. Baker and G. Chitty (eds) *Managing Historic Sites and Buildings: Reconciling Presentation and Preservation*. Routledge and English Heritage, pp. 173–186.

Shull, C.D. and Savage, B.L. 1995 'Trends in recognizing places for significance in the recent past'. In D. Slaton and R.A. Shiffer (eds) *Preserving the Recent Past*. Washington DC: Historic Preservation Education Foundation, vol. 2: 3–13.

Spencer, N. 1995 'Four oiks who shook the world'. *The Observer Review* 6/8/95.

Stager, C. 1995 'Graceland and Sun Studio'. In D. Slaton and R.A. Shiffer (eds) *Preserving the Recent Past*. Washington DC: Historic Preservation Education Foundation, vol. 2: 115.

Stokes, M. 1994 'Introduction: ethnicity, identity and music'. In M. Stokes (ed.) *Ethnicity, Identity and Music: The Musical Construction of Place*. Oxford and Providence, USA: Berg, pp. 1–28.

Strinati, D. 1995 *An Introduction to Theories of Popular Culture*. London: Routledge.

Taylor, D. 1994 *Sleevenotes to The Beatles Live at the BBC*. Apple Corps. Ltd.

Thornton, S. 1996 *Club Cultures*. Polity.

Vulliamy, E. 1995 'After the thrash, the trash'. *The Guardian* 4/7/95.

Wicke, P. 1990 *Rock Music: Culture, Aesthetics and Sociology*. Cambridge University Press.

Williams, R. 1995 'Island of dreams'. *The Guardian* 9/8/95.

Wooler, B. 1961 'Well now – dig this! Mersey beat'. *Merseyside's Own Entertainment Paper* 1(5): 2.

8

ALWAYS CRASHING IN THE SAME CAR

Paul Graves-Brown[1]

For Case, who'd lived for the bodyless exultation of cyberspace,
it was the Fall. In the bars he'd frequented as a cowboy hotshot,
the elite stance involved a certain relaxed contempt for the
flesh. The body was meat. Case fell into the prison of his own
flesh.

(Gibson 1983: 12)

The death of Princess Diana in a car crash could have been scripted by J.G.
Ballard along the lines of his controversial novel *Crash!* (1995 [1973]). The
glamorous celebrity (plus lover) pursued by paparazzi photographers dies
under their very lenses. One might almost fancy that Ballard's anti-hero
Vaughan was driving the mysterious Fiat Uno being sought by French police
(although he would have chosen a much more ostentatious vehicle). In reality,
Diana's death was but one of a long line of celebrity road kills that have
achieved the status of martyrdom – Albert Camus, Jackson Pollock, James
Dean, Jayne Mansfield, Marc Bolan. All died and went to celebrity heaven –
in Pollock's case (according to Bayley 1986), his celebrity virtually originated
with his death in a car. Moreover, the deaths of John F. Kennedy and
Archduke Ferdinand while travelling by car are poles around which much
twentieth-century history has revolved.

Why do celebrity road accidents have such an importance? Why is the
novel *Crash!* and the David Cronenberg film thereof still so controversial?
What is the relationship between the car and the body? These are the questions I shall address in this essay, bearing in mind that the Age of the Car is
already passing and that new technologies are intruding into the equation.

Habitat or skin?

The principal theme I want to pursue is a fundamental paradox of the car
culture – a contradiction which extends, indeed, to all aspects of our society.
For on the one hand the car is, in McLuhan's (1964) words, an extension of

our selves, but on the other, following Barthes (1993 [1972]), it is also a habitat – a kind of mobile domesticity.

Barthes (1993 [1972]), in his seminal essays on Verne's *Nautilus* and the Citröen DS, points out how both vessels are a kind of microcosm – sequestered worlds within worlds carrying round all the necessaries of survival and comfort. Despite the vogue at the time for external references to wings and fins, the Citröen's controls, says Barthes, are more like those of a hi-tech kitchen than those of a jet aircraft. The car is a profoundly domestic space which drivers make homely with idiosyncratic decorations (stickers, Garfields, nodding dogs or furry dice, stereos, and even TVs and drinks cabinets). The car is a mobile personal space that is not to be challenged or invaded. This sequestration has odd consequences for the perception of the world around us – a tendency which I term the *privatisation of experience*[2] and which is reflected in other contemporary technologies (a point to which I shall return). As Lefebvre says:

> motorised traffic enables people and objects to congregate and mix without meeting, thus constituting a striking example of simultaniety without exchange, each element remaining within its own compart-ment, tucked away in its shell; such conditions contribute to the disintegration of city life
>
> (Lefebvre 1971: 101)

On the other hand, and apropos of *Crash!*, the car has also been a venue for new forms of encounter. The fact that it is a closed world of its own means that since the 1920s, the car has been the venue for sexual rendezvous – a place where the young or adulterous could meet, free from the strictures of social disapproval. In its role as a domestic space, the motor vehicle is, as Cronenberg (in Rodley 1996) terms it 'a mobile bedroom'. Curiously though, just as Ballard/Cronenberg have made sex in cars controversial, the actuality is that (in the USA at least) the car as a venue for sexual encounters is becoming a thing of the past: 'changing sexual mores and standards of community and parental acceptance have resulted in living arrangements that make mobile lovemaking largely unnecessary' (Flink 1988: 162).

The car, then, is a home from home. We read more and more lurid tales of paedophiles, muggings and murders, rapes and road rage and so our cars become ever more fortified (viz. the vogue for rugged 4×4s) as we travel from one safe location to another. Modern children, couch potatoes and mouse potatoes, see the world only on TV, the Internet or through the car window when travelling to and from school.

But the paradox lies in the fact that this mobile home from home is also an extension of the body, a form of clothing or perhaps more exactly a second skin or exoskeleton. Human beings are inseparable from the technological; as Mauss (1979) was perhaps the first to realise, our techniques are applied both to the external world and to our bodily selves. This relationship extends back to a time before our ancestors were 'human' in any sense we might understand, indeed the use of technology was a contributory factor in our evolution into humans. Thus technology as an *extension* of ourselves is *part of the self*, technology is (as Baudrillard 1981 says) 'confused with' the body.[3] Such a view is echoed in many recent studies, particularly that by Haraway (1991) and those who have followed her 'Cyborg Manifesto'. But many, if not most, accounts of this kind (1) assume that 'cyborg' existence is a novel phenomenon and (2) tend to err on the side of abstracting the 'org-anic' component into the '*cyb*-ernetic'.

There are two principal attributes of the second skin – symbolic and practical. Clearly, as anyone who has seen car advertising knows, cars are symbols of social status, power, rebellion. In Europe the rather late development of car culture has left us with a model based almost solely on elite status – until mass motorisation in the post Second World War period, cars were the preserve of the wealthy and hence we think in terms of prestige – the Rolls Royce being the archetypal example (Graves-Brown 1996, 1997). In the USA by contrast the car *began* life as a mass product, indeed it was the original mass product, and hence its symbolism is more complex and in many ways intertwined with the 'American Dream' and particularly with the ideology of freedom.[4] Initially aimed at the isolated rural populations of the mid west,[5] the car was soon being sold to urban dwellers for quite other reasons (see Schiffer Chapter 4). Personal transport has never been necessary to the urban dweller even if the urban dweller represented a lucrative market for car makers (Flink 1988; Wolf 1996), and hence social style and symbolism became the primary selling point – a process which reached its apogee with the befinned chromium gas guzzlers of the 1950s and 1960s.

Cars can fulfil many different symbolic roles – the sports car for example is not necessarily an elite symbol, but rather a sign of youthful rebellion, perhaps typified in the USA by the Ford Mustang – a fairly basic 'sedan' made exciting by styling (Flink 1988).[6] Equally, through the second-hand trade, elite cars can take on new social meaning – for example the preference for BMWs observed among British street drug dealers. In other contexts the car can appear homely, friendly, as in the case of the VW Beetle or Citröen 2CV. The allure of speed, colourful design and freedom makes at least some cars sexually attractive. In a world where personal space is increasingly privatised, it follows that it is the vehicle that increasingly represents the self to others. And more, as both Lefebvre and Baudrillard point out, this is a world of symbolism that has its own rules and conventions.

But the car is also and perhaps primarily a practical extension of the self, a second skin which not only symbolises the self but transforms it. By allowing rapid movement, motor vehicles embody a sense of freedom[7] – the open road, getting away, escape. So much so that, as Toffler (1970) has observed, people simply drive around to give themselves the sensation of change – stimulating a sense that things are happening in their lives. Like the railway, cars have transformed social relations through perceptions of space and time, they have changed work patterns and living arrangements (and death arrangements – see Nash Chapter 6).

The secret life of things

However, and without wishing to entangle my argument, there is also a third dimension of the car culture which synthesises aspects of the other two. This is the tendency to attribute agency and intention to inanimate objects, a tendency which philosophers term (appositely) the 'pathetic fallacy'. In as much as it is both an extension of the self and a cocoon for the self, the car, perhaps above all other artefacts, takes on a kind of personhood. As well as an object of status and expression, the car becomes a subject acting in its own right. It is often named (as are ships and other vessels), its form includes some anthropomorphic elements, particularly the front elevation with its facelike lamps and grilles. The car is not just a mode of transport, but a member of the family – an image which is examined in numerous examples through film and literature in the late twentieth century (think, for example, of the predatory *Christine* of the eponymous film). The car can threaten, for its power is analogous to that of the beast, yet as a home from home it can also be perceived as a friend or protector.

This aspect of the car culture, and indeed of our relation to material culture merits a study in its own right – it is, as it were, the ultimate 'fetishism' which can be found in many forms in many societies. But, taking a lead from Ballard, who does not even acknowledge the possible agency of the car, I will set this aspect aside and return to its implications at the end of the essay.

Symbolic wounds

How then can we attempt to reconcile the paradox that the car is both habitat and at the same time part of the person? How indeed can we deal with the broader paradox that as our society becomes increasingly global, the personal self becomes ever more withdrawn? In his analysis of *Crash!* Baudrillard claims that Ballard is representing a new social order, a hyper-reality beyond old moralities. The car accident is no longer an aberration but rather a norm of the new social order, and the physical consequences of this – the symbolic wounds that are the result of the crash and the topic of Ballard's novel – are elements of a new semiotics.

Here it is necessary to take issue with Baudrillard on a number of levels. Not least because the sequestration of the physical self, the disembodiment that seems to increasingly characterise the privatisation of experience, runs counter to his view that the accident is somehow normalised. Indeed Ballard himself, despite Baudrillard's dismissal of this point, does see *Crash!* as a moral tale, as a dire warning. If we set aside his dispassionate style, Ballard actually presents the crash metaphorically as an (albeit perverted) attempt to break through the paradox of modern life – to 'Only Connect' as E.M. Forster wrote in another novel (*Howard's End*) dominated by the motor car.

By breaking down the barriers of the second skin, and at the same time breaking into the cocoon of private space, the car accident is a reminder of mortality – a reminder that 'We are meat, we are potential carcasses' (Francis Bacon quoted in Boyne 1991: 289). This explains the impact of the martyrdom of the famous – by dying in a car crash Princess Diana showed in a profound sense that she (like other famous victims) was one of us – not simply an idealised media image but a real piece of meat. Like that most famous of martyrdoms, the car crashes of the famous reveal at last that they have come down from heaven to live and die among us as human beings.

Contrary to Baudrillard, then, the crash is not a move beyond a moral reality into the hyperreal, but rather a step back from the technological brink into a more human world of embodiment.[8] For clearly Baudrillard's claim is based on the notion that the muddling of the bodily and the technical is somehow a novelty which creates the hyper-real. Rather, the symbolic wounds described by Ballard – the scars and imprints of impact – are exactly paralleled in the traditions of body modification which anthropology has recorded and examined for more than a century (Brain 1979). In the novel, as in all societies including our own, modification of the body is used to mark rites of passage, social status, magical transformation. For the Japanese Yakuza practising 'irezumi' – the art of tattooing – body modification 'removes the vaguely animal element of the human body' (ibid.: 64). In other words it is the technical, including the body technical, which sets people apart, which raises them above mere animality by becoming artefacts in their own right.

This again seems paradoxical – for in a sense body modification sets one apart from nature and animality whilst at the same time being a recognition of the physicality of the self. Like the car, the direct physical modification of the body is supposed both to connect the self to society but at the same time to set one apart both from others (as in the Yakuza case) and from nature (see Soyland 1997). Moreover, of course, body modification symbolises the human sense of control over the nature of the physical world and the body – the tattooed or pierced or scarred person has triumphed over the physical suffering needed to modify and thus subdue the body. Yet, among the dysfunctional individuals described in Ballard's novel it is as if this physical suffering is directed in the opposite towards reminding the self of its corpore-ality and hence of reawakening the deadened self and sexuality.

Pornography

According to Ballard, *Crash!* is a pornographic novel and he goes on to observe that 'pornography is the most political form of fiction, dealing with how we use and exploit each other' (1995:6). To be pornographic, rather than simply erotic, a work must in some way degrade and dehumanise the person. Clearly, then, he evokes a sense in which the technology of the motor car is dehumanising, that rather than setting people above their natures, the technical realm actually takes away and degrades humanity. And in effect this is yet another aspect of the same paradoxical episteme. For, as I have suggested, technology is what makes us human in the first place, even in the absence of a material culture beyond the material of ourselves. But at the same time that same technology acts increasingly to degrade and deprave our humanity.

What drives this process is always the claim to or quest for freedom. As noted above the car is said to free us from the constraints of time and locality – it has acted to free the young from the moral constraints of the home, for example. Yet it is clear that the freedom offered by technology in contemporary society is purchased at a price.

Cars are not alone in privatising the self. In music, for example, we have moved from a world of participation to one of recorded music and ultimately to the personal stereo. Recent technical developments on the Internet (e.g. the MP3 standard) have also made inroads into systems by which music is distributed. Where musical events involve group activities – as in the 1980s and 1990s festival/club/rave scene – they become counter-cultural and subversive. Similarly, from theatre we move through cinema, television to video. And needless to say telecommunications are becoming the ultimate privatisation medium – through telephone, Internet and perhaps ultimately 'teledildonics' (Rheingold 1994) the physicality of experience is made entirely private such that the self and others appear to be abstracted. This may be seen to relate to Elias's (1978, 1982) 'Civilising Process' – the increasing formalisation and finessing of our dealings with ours and other bodies. The ultimate expression of this process is a 'gradual privatisation in the organisation of death' (Shilling 1993) – the hiding of the bodily processes of decay and demise which the car crash graphically forces back into our attention.

As evidenced by the quote from William Gibson at the start of this essay, cyberspace eschews meat (see Robins 1995). The ideology of the Net is a claim to escape the physical into a realm where the self can be reinvented – effectively an extension of the ideology of the car. Flink (1988) has suggested that the era of the car is already over. The Internet may represent the next step on from the car culture – for clearly it offers all that the car culture does and more. Indeed, the decline of the car as a social escape reflects general changes in domestic arrangements. Thus, in the UK, a programme to build 5 million new homes without any appreciable growth in population may represent a more profound retreat from public space. Curiously, though, cyberspace is often represented as being a place of community, a manifestation of McLuhan's 'global village,' which actually counters 'the automobile centric, suburban, fast-food, shopping mall way of life' (Rheingold 1994: 25). Yet like the urban space described by Lefebvre, cyberspace is somewhere (nowhere) with many citizens but no residents – a place where people 'congregate and mix without meeting'.

> There is 'group mind' but no social encounter. There is online communion, but there are no residents in [cyberspace] … What we have is the preservation through simulation of the old forms of solidarity and community. In the end not an alternative society but an alternative to society.
>
> (Robins 1995: 150)

This situation *is* an obscenity – a pornographic (in the sense used above) world more extreme than but similar to that of *Crash!* For clearly the Faustian bargain of technological power, of the hypertrophy of technique which our society has developed, is one where humanity is degraded and depraved. Road rage, a phenomenon which is probably as old as car culture, is a case in point – the seclusion of the self in some sense cancels out normal social rules – as the comedian Ben Elton points out, we would not shout at other pedestrians in the same way we abuse other motorists. This is probably what Baudrillard is getting at, except that the crash is counterfactual to his thesis. Surrounded by technology we are no longer fully social beings, and this is partly because we come to forget our embodiment. But more than this our technology, based on a sense of personal freedom, suggests that it will free us from society altogether – a goal which is no doubt at the root of the Thatcher mantra for the non-existence of society. 'Virtual community … reflects the desire to control exposure and create security and order. It is … driven by the compulsion to neutralise' (Robins 1995: 151).

Risk and control

What unites techniques – both of the body and of material culture, is the balance of risk and control. In his study of modern body piercing, Soyland (1997: 5) observes: 'the process of decoration [is] a kind of personal rite of passage: having the will to overcome the fear, and the physical pain; to assert control over the body'. Similarly, body modification in ethnography is often a matter of control – of asserting power over body/nature. The car culture too, in both its paradoxical aspects concerns control. The car as habitat insulates the driver from the world, whereas the car as skin extends the physical control we have over motion, space, time and location. However, it is clear, the sense of control which technology gives is largely illusory and merely masks the necessary underlying risk inherent in being.

The driver deludes him/herself that on the road he/she is in control of his/her fate, since every driver depends upon everyone else. One may be (or at least think one is) the world's best driver, but the folly of others can never be factored out. This is effectively the bargain that all social beings are born into – that from the first we must depend upon others, to risk the self by placing it in others hands. Such a risk is the basis of erotic encounter. Again, then, the metaphor of *Crash!* is clearly that of risk; the characters explore the erotic potential of the car collision, of fast driving and chasing one another, all as a titillation towards sexuality – as a way to find new meaning in stale and empty urban lives.[9] The central character of the novel, named like the author James Ballard, finds that his sex life with his wife is reanimated and extended through his encounters with the anti-hero Vaughan – indeed their adventures on the crowded intersections and expressways of west London allow him to explore the territory of bisexuality too.

By contrast, the ideology of both car culture and cyberculture seems to deny risk – by becoming disembodied the self is impregnable, and the speculation surrounding the possibility of uploading the self into cyberspace itself betrays a desire for the ultimate risk-free existence – immortality. Ultimately, perhaps, the answer to the paradoxes of technological culture is that their premises are founded on illusions. However we delude ourselves about the protection offered by a technological shell, we are forever at risk because our lives remain in the hands of others. And, moreover, it is not possible for us to be fully human unless we risk ourselves by placing trust in others.

In conclusion: who, or what, is to blame?

Risk is not something which the privatised society encourages, but we should not blame technology for this. Latour (1992; Chapter 1 this volume) has spoken of delegation of responsibility to machines. This is in some sense true in that the sense of security offered by technology rests on delegating the self – the technological skin of the car is delegated the role of protecting the body. And, returning to the point made earlier, this process of delegation is expressed in the attribution of agency to the car, its ambiguous personhood. But the technology itself has no intention or sense of responsibility in this regard – the illusion of the agency of technology masks the fact that we place ourselves in the hands of those who *originated* the machine. We may feel that the material barriers around us isolate us from the risks inherent in the 'other', but in effect we place our trust in others indirectly through the medium of the machine, and in the process we can unwitttingly allow others to deceive us. The common example of blaming machines for human failures (computer error), or indeed the attribution of human error as a means of disguising technological failings (as is alleged in many major accidents) illustrates how our desire to see the technical and material as given and existing in its own right masks its essentially social formation and force.

The final question then comes down to the intentions of those who devise and develop technologies and whom, one might argue, have a vested interest in our sense of isolation. The claims of Cyberpunk, of Haraway and many Net enthusiasts, are for a new order of cyborg life. Baudrillard sees this as a step into hyper-reality. In this chapter I have argued that these claims are false. The car culture, like the Internet, has been but one phase in the relationship between humans as flesh and their material culture – this 'hybrid' state is not new. I could just as well have written about the growth of the railways, the use of the horse as a means of transport or the use of the crossbow in medieval warfare – humans have always lived a hyper-reality defined not just by their bodies but by the things they have woven around themselves. What is perhaps distinct about the technological culture of the twentieth century, especially of the last fifty years, is the progressive use of a fundamentally social product, technology, as a means to neutralise, distance and deny one's social existence, a process in which the producers of technology have been knowingly complicit because privatised experience promotes consumption which in turn boosts profit. In this context the car crash becomes a brutal metaphor for breaking out of a dehumanised cul-de-sac.

NOTES

1 With thanks particularly to Tom Cullis for his help in the search for Baudrillard!
2 Here I want to distance my remarks from Marx's concept of *alienation*. From my limited reading of *Capital*, Marx was particularly thinking of the dispossession of the rural population which led to the creation of an urban proletariat. By contrast, the current retreat from public space is an entirely volitional impulse on the part of what could only be a highly affluent population.
3 Although Baudrillard (1981) sees this as a recent phenomenon of 'hyper-reality'.
4 Although see Schiffer Chapter 4 for the slightly different trajectory of the electric car.
5 Of whom Henry Ford was a member.
6 See, e.g., the recent advertisement by Ford which revived Steve McQueen's Bullitt to sell a successor to the Mustang.
7 This was their original appeal to the farmers of the Midwest.
8 This theme is pursued in Ballard's Later novel *The Concrete Island*.
9 Ballard also explores this theme in *The Concrete Island* and *Highrise*.

References

Ballard, J.G. 1995 [1973] *Crash!* London: Vintage.
Barthes, R. 1993 [1972] *Mythologies*. London: Vintage.
Baudrillard, J. 1981 'Crash' in *Simulation and Simulacra*. University of Michigan Press, pp. 111–119.
Bayley, S. 1986 *Sex, Drink and Fast Cars: The Creation and Consumption of Images*. London: Faber.
Boyne, R. 1991 'The art of the body and the discourse of post modernity'. In M. Featherstone, M. Hepworth and B. Turner (eds) *The Body, Social Process and Cultural Theory*. London: Sage.
Brain, R. 1979 *The Decorated Body*. London: Hutchinson.
Elias, N. 1978 *The Civilising Process*. Oxford: Blackwell.
—— 1982 *State Formation and Civilisation: The Civilising Process vol. 2*. Oxford: Blackwell.

Flink, J.J. 1988 *The Car Culture* (second edition). MIT Press.

Gibson, W. 1983 *Neuromancer*. London: HarperCollins.

Graves-Brown, P.M. 1996 'Road to nowhere'. *Museums Journal* November 25–27.

—— 1997 'From highway to superhighway.' *Social Analysis* 41(1): 64–75.

Haraway, D. 1991 'A cyborg manifesto: Science, technology and socialist-feminism in the late 20th century'. In D. Haraway *Simians Cyborgs and Women: The Reinvention of Nature*. London: Free Association Books.

Latour, B. 1992 'Where are the missing masses? The sociology of a few mundane objects'. In W.E. Bijker and J. Law (eds) *Shaping Technology/Building Society. Studies in Sociotechnical Change*. Boston: MIT, pp. 225–258.

Lefebvre, H. 1971 *Everyday Life in the Modern World*. Harmondsworth: Allen Lane.

Mauss, M. 1979 'Body techniques'. In *Sociology and Psychology: Essays by Marcel Mauss, Part IV*, trans. B. Brewster. London: Routledge and Kegan Paul, pp. 97–123.

McLuhan, M. 1964 *Understanding Media: The Extensions of Man*. McGraw Hill, New York.

Rheingold, H. 1994 *Virtual Community*. MIT Press.

Robins, K. 1995 'Cyberspace and the world we live in'. In *Body and Society* 1(3–4): 135–156.

Rodley, C. 1996 'Crash. David Cronenberg talks about his new film *Crash* based on J.G. Ballard's disturbing novel'. *Sight and Sound* 6: 7–11.

Shilling, C. 1993 *The Body and Scoial Theory*. London: Sage.

Soyland, A.J. 1997 'Speaking the decorated body.' In L. Yardley (ed.) *Material Discourses of Health and Illness*. London: Routledge.

Toffler, A. 1970 *Future Shock*. London: Bodley Head.

Wolf, W. 1996 *Car Mania: A Critical History of Transport*. London: Pluto Press.

INDEX

Adam, B. 114
Adams, M. 117
adoption of products 81, 84–92, 92
Adorno, T. 5
Adrien, J.L. 100
affordances 4, 6, 104–5, 106–7
Akrich, M. 17
anthropology 2
anthropomorphisation 158
Appadurai, A. 5
archaeology 2, 10–11, 22–3, 34–40, 46–7;
    behavioural 80–93
art 2; psychology of 102
association context 34–5
autism 3, 7, 97–108
autopoiesis 61

Bacon, F. 160
Bacon, T. 44
Baines, L.H. 144
Ballard, J.G. 156, 157, 159–63
Baron, S.W. 149
Baron-Cohen, S. 97, 99, 101, 102, 103,
    105
Barresi, J. 103
Barthes, R. 157
Basalla, G. 78–9
baskets and basketry 53–7, 61, 62–3, 68
Bateson, G. 102
Baudrillard, J. 4, 158, 159–60, 163–4
Bayley, S. 156
BBC 138
Beatles 132, 138, 140–2, 143
Beer, J. 118
behavioural archaeology 80–93
Benson, R. 134
Berlin key 10, 12–21

Bernstein, N. 65
Bijker, W.E. 2
Binford, L.R. 23
'Blanket Hill' 137–8
Bloch, M. 2
Boas, F. 57, 61
body modification 159, 161
body, the 1, 2, 3; technology and 156–8,
    159, 161–2
Bosch, G. 100, 101
Boucher, J. 103
Bourdieu, P. 115
Bowdler, R. 116, 122, 123
Boyne, R. 160
Brain, R. 160
Brookwood Cemetery, Surrey 112,
    122–6
Broun, Sir R. 122
Bruce, V. 106
Bryson, S.E. 100
Bugrimenko, E.A. 99
building 68–9
Bunning, J. Bunstone 117
burial practices, Victorian attitudes
    towards 3, 112–29
Burling, R. 76
Butler, J. 1, 3

car crashes 156, 159–60
car culture 6–7, 156–64; see also electric
    cars
Carelman, J. 10
cemeteries 112–29
chairs 29, 30, 32, 33
Chatterley Whitfield 136
Cherry, M. 136
Chess Records 137

children, with autism 97–108
Children, G. 114, 116
Ching, F.D.K. 118, 119
Chippindale, C. 23
Clark, H.A. 80, 81
Clarke, J.M. 122, 124
class structure, Victorian 113, 127
Clinton, B. 136
coal mines 135–6
cognitive science 2, 4
Cohen, S. 141, 142, 143
Cold War 136
Collias, N.E. and Collias, E.C. 65, 66, 67
Collin, M. 134, 135
commercialisation 81–3, 92
communication, relationships of 41
conservation practice 36, 135–40, 152
consumerist theory 76, 78, 79, 80
control 161–2
Copeland, A. 140
Costall, A. 2, 3, 5, 6, 7, 97–108
Cox, M. 117
Crash! (Ballard) 156, 157, 159–60, 162–3
Crick, M.R. 74, 76
Cronenberg, D. 155, 156
Cubitt, Sir W. 122
cultural studies 2
Cummins, R. 25, 26, 28, 46
cutlery 41–2, 44; *see also* spoons
cyberspace 160–1, 162

Day, P. 44
death and burial, Victorian attitudes
    towards 3, 112–29
design 2, 58–9, 62; limits of 59–60
determinism, technological 3
Diana, Princess of Wales 156, 160
Dobinson, C. 136
drug culture 134
Dunnell, R.C. 84
Durham, J.E. 144
dwelling 68–9

ecstasy culture 134
Edison, Thomas and Mina 89
electric cars 73–92
Elias, N. 160
elite culture 135
Elton, B. 161
embodiment 3; *see also* the body
enculturation 3

engineering 2
English Heritage 136, 138, 153

Featherstone, M. 1
feminism 1
Fender, L. 45
film industry 137
Flannery, K.V. 113
Flink, J.J. 78, 156, 157, 160
folk theories *see* indigenous theories
force, application of 54, 56–7
Ford, Henry and Clara 89
form: -function relationship 22–3, 34;
    generation of 54, 56–60, 61; stability
    of 62; and substance 51–3, 61
Forster, E.M. 160
Foucault, M. 40–1, 42, 43, 44
Fox, K.J. 149
Freeman, B.J. 100
French, M. 59–60
Frith, S. 142
Frith, U. 99, 100
functionality 2, 5–6, 22–48, 50–1
funerary practice, Victorian 3, 112–29

gastropod shells 57–9, 60
Gay, J. 118
Geary, S. 117
Georgano, G.N. 86
Gibson, J.J. 4, 52, 104, 106
Gibson, W. 6, 156
Gillberg, C. 100
Godfrey, J. 134, 135
Goldthorpe, J. 149
Goodwin, B. 60
Gostwick, M. 144
Gothic revival 116
Gould, S.J. 23, 25
Graceland 137
Graves-Brown, P. 1–7, 156–63
Green, P. 106
growth: of artefacts 60–2; organic 51, 52
Grundy, B. 151
Guss, D. 68

Habermas, J. 40
Hall, S. 2
Hansen, C.H. and Hansen, R.D. 149
Happé, F. 99
Haraway, D. 158
Harker, D. 141

Harry, B. 141
Hawkins, D.I. 85
heart, the 24, 25, 26, 27
Hebdige, D. 2, 133, 149, 150
Heidegger, M. 4, 68–9
Hendrix, J. 138
heritage 134, 135–40, 151
Hermelin, B. 100
Hewison, R. 135
high culture 135
Highgate Cemetery 112, 114, 116–19, 126, 127, 128
Hinton, B. 144
history 2
Hobsbawm, E. 134, 152
Hobson, R.P. 97, 99, 101, 103–4, 105
Hodder, I. 2, 22, 39–40, 41, 46, 149
Hodges, H. 54, 63
Horkheimer, M. 5
Hounshell, D.A. 89
Howlin, P. 99
Hubley, P. 104
Hugill, P.J. 93
Hurd, G. 115

iconography, funerary 114, 115, 118
identity, and musical culture 142–4
ideofunction 29, 30, 31
illusion 6–7
Imelda Marcos hypothesis 90, 92
imitation 103
indigenous theories 6–7, 72–94; and the early electric car 73–80
industrial heritage 135–6
industrialisation 113, 115
informal theory-acquisition 77–8
Ingold, 1, 2, 3, 4, 5, 50–70
Internet 161–2
intersubjectivity 105; secondary 104
invention 81, 92
Isle of Wight pop festivals 132, 144–7

Joerges, B. 2, 3, 107
Johnson, P. 142
Johnston, R.H. 90
Jones, T.W. 72

Kanner, L. 101
Keller, C.M. and Keller, J.D. 77
Kellerman, K. 73
Kennedy, J.F. 136

Kent State University 137–8
Kimes, B.R. 80, 82
Kong, L. 142

lability, of function 33
lateral cycling 36, 37, 38–9
Latour, B. 2, 5, 6, 10–21, 163
Law, J. 2
Lefebvre, H. 148, 157
Lemmonier, P. 2
Leontiev, A.N. 98, 99
Lerner, M. 132
Leroi-Gourhan, A. 2
Leslie, A. 97, 101, 103
Levens, L.K. 144
Levine, H.G. 149
Lewis, V. 103
Libby, S. 100, 103
listed buildings 136
Litten, L. 117
living organisms 50–1, 52, 61; specification of form in 59–60; spiral formation in 57–9, 60
Llewellyn, N. 115
London Cemetery Company 116, 118, 124
London Necropolis Company 112, 119, 121–6, 127, 128
Longacre, W.A. 72
Lord, C. 100, 101
Loveland, K.A. 98, 104, 105, 106
Lowenthal, D. 133, 135, 139, 152
Luce, W.R. 138

McCartney, P. 138
MacDonald, I. 141
McDonald, J.R. 149
McLaren, M. 149
McLuhan, M. 2, 3, 156–7, 161
Madison, R. 85
Magowan, F. 142
Majewski, T. 77, 81, 84
making 51–7, 60–9; distinguished from growing 51–3; as a way of weaving 64–5
malfunction 26–7, 28
Marcus, J. 113
Marx, K. 7n, 52
Matthews, K.J. 149
Mauss, M. 2, 3, 157
Mead, G.H. 4, 5, 101

meaning 4
Melly, G. 132, 141
Merleau-Ponty, M. 4
meta-representation 101–3, 104
Metropolitan Interments Act (1850) 121
migration, rural–urban 113
Miller, D. 1, 2
Millikan, R. 2, 27–8, 29, 46
misuse 42, 99
Mom, G. 84
Monod, J. 50, 51
Moore, C. 103
morphogenesis 51; *see also* form; living
    organisms
Morrison, J. 139
mortality rates, Victorian 115
Mumford, L. 2
Mundy, P. 100
Murphy, C. 72
musical culture 25–6, 35, 45–6, 132, 137,
    138–9, 140–50, 161
Mutoid Waste Company 135
mutuality 4–5, 7

Nash, G. 3, 5, 6, 112–29
National Trust 136, 138
natural selection 27, 28, 29, 52, 59
Needham, J. 2
Neisser, U. 107–8
Neupert, M.A. 72
nostalgia 152

objective capacity 41
O'Connor, N. 100
O'Hara, C. 149
Olley, J.G. 101
organisms *see* living organisms
Owens, A. 103

Pateman, J. 118
Paul, L. 44–5
Pennington, B.F. 101, 103
performance, functional 24, 25, 27, 28,
    50–1
Peters, J. 137
Pfaffenberger, B. 2, 3
philosophy 2; and conceptions of
    function 23, 24–9
pipecleaners 31
place, and musical culture 142–4

play: functional or reality 103; pretend
    99, 101, 102, 103, 105, 107
Polanyi, M. 102
Polhemus, T. 134, 139
Pollitt, J.J. 115
pop festivals 132, 144–7
popular culture 5, 6, 131–52
pornography 159–61
post-modernism 2, 4
post-processualism 4
post-structuralism 2, 3–4
pottery 56
power relations 2, 5–6, 40–1, 42, 43–4
Presley, E. 137
Preston, B. 4–5, 6, 22–48
pretend play 99, 101, 102, 103, 105, 107
privatisation of the self 156, 158, 160, 163
producer constraint theory 75, 80
product histories 72, 73–94; scientific
    80–93
progress 3, 7n
proper function 27–30, 31–47
psychology: of art 102; and the study of
    autism 97–108
punk 134, 139, 148–51
Pye, D. 2, 65

radios 80–1
Ramsay, D. 117
Rathje, W.L. 2, 72
rave scene 134
Reber, A.S. 74
recycling 36, 37
Reeve, J. 117
Renfrew, C. 4
representation: meta- 101–3, 104; self-
    other 103
resistance 41, 43, 44, 45
reuse 36–9
Rheingold, H. 160
risk 161–2
road rage 161
Robins, K. 160, 161
rocket technology 136
Rodley, C. 156
Rogers, S.J. 101, 103
Rose, M.E. 113, 116
Rugg, J. 113

Salmon, M. 2, 22, 23
Samuel, R. 133, 135, 136, 139, 152

Samuelson, T. 137
Savage, B.L. 137
Savage, J. 138, 139, 149
Scarre, C. 4
Schallenberg, R. 80, 89
Scharff, V. 79, 93
Schiffer, M.B. 2, 5, 6, 7, 22, 29–30, 36, 39,
    41, 46, 72–94
Schofield, A.J. 5, 6, 131–52
Scott, R.F. 84
secondary use 36, 37–8, 39
selection history, biological notion of 27,
    28, 29, 52, 59
self, privatisation of the 156, 158, 160,
    163
self-other representations 103
Sex Pistols 131, 149, 150–1
sexuality 1
Shackleton, Lord 145
Shanks, M. 112
shared use of objects 100
shells, gastropod 57–9, 60
Shilling, C. 161
Shull, C.D. 136, 137
Sigman, M. 100, 103
signification 4
Skibo, J.M. 72, 84, 85, 90, 92
skill 64–5
Smike, S. 124
Smirnova, E.O. 99
Smith, F.W. 85
Smith, I.M. 100
Snibstone Discovery Park 136
social change 39–40, 41, 43–6
social context, of object use 98–9
social order, creation of 43
societal constraint theory 76, 78, 79
sociofunction 29, 30–1
sociology 2
Soyland, A.J. 160, 162
Spencer-Wood, S. 84
spirals, formation of 57–9, 60
spoons 24, 25–6, 27, 31, 34–5, 44
Sprye, R. 122
stability: of form 62; of function 33
Stager, C. 137
Stich, St P. 77
Still, A. 2
Stokes, M. 140
'Streetstyle' exhibition 139
Strinati, D. 133, 134, 136–7
structuralism 40

Stumpf, S.H. 149
subjectification 40
substance, and form 51–3, 61
surfaces, transformation of 51–2, 54, 55–6
sustainability 139, 152
Sutphen, H. 89
swastika 31
symbolism 4, 157
system functions 25–6, 28, 29–47;
    ongoing 32–3
Szokolsky, A. 99

Tarlow, S. 114
tattooing 159
Taylor, D. 132
technofunction 29, 30, 31, 32
technological constraint theory 75–6
technological determinism 3
technology 2, 163; and the body 156–8,
    159, 161–2; rocket 136
tensegrity 69n
textiles 62–3
'theory of mind' model of autism 101–3,
    104, 105
Thomas, J. 4
Thompson, D.W. 57, 61
Thornton, S. 134
Tilley, C. 112
Tite, W. 122
Toffler, A. 158
Towle, H.L. 79
Trevarthen, C. 104

Ucko, P.J. 2
Ungerer, J.A. 100, 103
utility 70n

Valsiner, J. 98, 99
vested interest theory 75
Victorians, burial practices 3, 112–29
Vietnam War 137–8
Volpert, W. 99
Volti, R. 79
vortex formation 60, 61
Vulliamy, E. 148

Wakefield, E.H. 81
Walker, W.H. 80
weaverbirds 65–7
weaving 54, 55–7, 63, 64–8
Weddell, G.R. 122

Westwood, V. 149, 150
Whitley, D. 113
Whyte, J. 103
Wicke, P. 131, 140–1, 149
Williams, E. 3, 5, 6, 7, 97–108
Williams, R. 132
Wilson, D. 72
Wing, L. 100
Winner, L. 2
Wolf, W. 157

Woodstock music festival 132, 144, 148
Wright, L. 24, 25, 26, 28
Wulff, S. 100
Wynne-Jones, Lord 145

youth culture 132–4, 136, 140–50

Zabel, M.K. and Zabel, R.H. 101
Zedeno, M.N. 80